Voltaire

Voltaire

THE UNIVERSAL MAN

DEREK PARKER

SUTTON PUBLISHING

This book was first published in 2005 by
Sutton Publishing Limited · Phoenix Mill
Thrupp · Stroud · Gloucestershire · GL5 2Bu

This paperback edition first published in 2006

British Library Cataloguing in Publication Data
A catalogue record for this book is available from the British Library.

ISBN 0 7509 3441 7

Typeset in 10/12.5pt Goudy.
Typesetting and origination by
Sutton Publishing Limited.
Printed and bound in Great Britain by
J.H. Haynes & Co. Ltd, Sparkford.

Contents

List of Illustrations

Acknowledgements

I am grateful to the London Library, which after forty years' membership courteously re-welcomed me as a visitor; to the British Library; to the State Library of New South Wales, and the Mosman Library. My particular gratitude must go to Roland Glasser, in Paris, who diligently tracked down the illustrations. My editors at Sutton, Jaqueline Mitchell and Clare Jackson, have as usual made many useful suggestions. My wife has also read the book in manuscript, and corrected many misprints.

Derek Parker, Mosman, NSW

Introduction

'He taught us to be free.' The words were inscribed on the catafalque which elevated Voltaire at his apotheosis at the Panthéon in Paris in 1790. And indeed the phrase was justified.

Throughout his lifetime most of the citizens of Europe were subject to restrictions and punishments which would seem to us unbearable, and were tolerated by them only because few of those who observed the laws regarded them as unusual. Though Christianity was already in decline, the Church – almost indivisible from the State – exacted extreme penalties for atheism or unorthodoxy where it was voiced. Men's tongues were torn out for blasphemy; they could be executed for presiding over non-Catholic religious services; if they were Protestants they were debarred from certain occupations and professions and, since they were considered not to have been properly married, their children were regarded as illegitimate. Booksellers could be executed for possessing – much less selling – books which had been banned by the censor. Heterodoxy could bring both men and women to the torture chamber or send them to hard labour in the galleys; at worst they died on the scaffold or the pyre in carefully contrived agony. Anyone who spoke out against the State or criticised, for instance, the unjust system of taxation, attracted almost equally severe punishments, while any physical act against the monarch resulted in a death so terrible that even reading a description of it chills the blood.[1]

Voltaire, towards the end of his life, set down a prescription for reform based on his observation of the society in which he had lived. For the individual, he proposed liberty of the person, the abolition of slavery, and freedom of speech and writing, liberty of conscience, security of property, and the freedom to sell one's labour to the highest bidder. In respect of the social order, he believed, the Church should be subject to the State. Taxation should be in proportion to wealth, and churchmen should pay taxes at the same rate as anyone else: the receipts should not go to the aggrandisement of the nobility, but be used to provide proper water supplies, roads, canals, hospitals, orphanages. Begging should not be allowed, but proper alms-houses should be provided for the old and infirm.

To address what Voltaire believed to be the prevailing profound injustices, he advocated that the police should not be allowed to open private letters placed in the post, and anyone accused of a crime should be considered innocent until proved guilty. No one should be imprisoned without there existing some valid reason to believe they had committed a crime. They should not be tortured or tried in secret. Witnesses should appear in public and be subject to questioning on the defendant's behalf. Local laws should be abolished and a national civil and criminal code established. Civil marriage should be legal, and the law should not concern itself with such matters of personal belief, taste and habit as sacrilege, heresy, superstition, suicide and sodomy.

All this sounds very reasonable and proper to a reader in the twenty-first century. Indeed, failure to implement some of Voltaire's proposals now attracts international condemnation (for instance, of England's and Australia's policy towards illegal immigrants, of America's long imprisonment of supposed terrorists at Guantanamo Bay, and of some countries' treatment of homo-sexuals), and most civilised democratic societies observe most of them as a matter of course.

But in 1770 Voltaire's propositions were little short of revolutionary; and it was to take a revolution to put even the least of them into action. The eventual success of his arguments was, of course, not entirely due to him – nor was it complete or permanent; the effect great men have on the life of a society is not necessarily – indeed, never – that. There have been regimes – from those of Hitler and Stalin in the 1930s to that of Mugabe in the 1990s – as repressive, violent and indecent as that of France in the eighteenth century; but that is not to denigrate the life and work of Voltaire, which in any case were not restricted to arguments for reform, for he was one of the most prolific authors of the modern world.

Introduction

A complete list of his books, plays and poems would consist of well over three hundred and fifty separate items, not counting his innumerable pamphlets and the thousands of letters written to correspondents all over Europe. Apart from all that he found time to involve himself in major campaigns on behalf of particular oppressed families, to busy himself in the theatre, and to socialise – he was by all accounts the best conversationalist of his day (though, alas, no one properly recorded his table talk).

Voltaire was also, in terms of his social connections, a major figure of his time, a man familiar with the great. He had a close if troubled friendship with Frederick the Great, indulged in a long correspondence with Catherine of Russia, and for the first half of his life moved in and around the circles of the royal Court of France. He found his literary skirmishes with Jean-Jacques Rousseau and most of his contemporaries in the European literary world irritating but enjoyable, his arguments with the law and the Church almost entirely infuriating. The latter – and his exhausting, long-term but often successful attempts to protect and help those cowering under the heavy hand of ungenerous and frequently oppressive laws – made him a by-word for decency among the educated people of the Europe of his era. For the last twenty years of his life, travellers engaged on the Grand Tour of Europe felt it as necessary to see Voltaire as to see Mont Blanc or St Peter's in Rome.

He was also popular with ordinary people – though it would be a mistake to think of him as a modern liberal: he was by no means that, much less a socialist. Indeed, he was not even much of a democrat. He was a capitalist, in terms of his times a millionaire, a steadfast elitist who believed in the right of those with talent to rise to the top and enjoy the rewards of their merit. He believed it unnecessary to educate those whom he deemed insufficiently intelligent to profit from education, though craftsmen and artisans should be properly taught. He was friendly enough to servants and 'common people', especially if they were reasonably intelligent, but he hated dullness and stupidity and felt that what such people needed was a good kick up the backside.

He was a royalist: he suspected that the best – or, rather the least

Voltaire

worst – means of ruling a country was through the agency of a good and all-powerful monarch. Though no Christian, there is a sense in which he believed in the divinity which hedges a king, and that belief even survived the disappointment with which he eventually recognised the impoverished morality of his two great heroes, Frederick and Catherine. His hatred of dogmatic religion, despotism and military ambition was complete.

Even today he is sometimes spoken of as a downright atheist. He was, in fact, an agnostic. Temperamentally, he was a believer. There is a story that has him climbing with a friend to the top of a hill to see the sunrise: as the sun came into view, with the attendant display of majestic colour, he fell to his knees: 'O mighty God, I believe'. Instantly, however, he added, 'As to M. the Son and Madame his mother, that is another matter'. It seemed probable to him that there was a 'first cause' of some sort, but the nature of Him, Her or It was something he believed no one could know. He perhaps made up the story, which he often repeated, of the Swiss captain who before a battle prayed: 'O God, if there is one, take pity on my soul, if I have one'. Personally, he believed that any man or organisation – most notably the Christian Church – which believed that they held any kind of communication with the Maker insulted the intelligence.

He occasionally equivocated, for the good of his health; he was never entirely confident that he was sufficiently established to escape the torture chamber and the fire, and occasionally allowed himself to bow, or give a cursory nod, in the direction of the Church. As he pointed out in a letter to his old friend d'Alembert, 'I am very fond of the truth, but not at all of martyrdom', while when his secretary asked him how he would have acted had he lived in Spain under the Inquisition, he replied: 'I would have worn an enormous rosary, gone to mass every day, kissed all the monks' robes, and done my best to set fire to their monasteries'.

As much as any writer who ever lived, he was what he wrote, both in his published work and in his letters. His kindness and generosity to his friends, to the unknown victims of persecution and to the workers on his estates was great. His judgement seems from time to time to have been that of a child: he remained faithful to such hangers-on as Thiériot and La Harpe long after others would have cut them off, and he lived for many years with a woman who was not only not his intellectual equal (though who, after all, was that?) but was coarse and vulgar, and carried on numerous affairs under his nose.

Today he is little read, even in France. Of all his works, only *Candide* remains always in print and is always read with pleasure. A few phrases of his crop up again and again, usually culled from dictionaries of quotations; it is many years since any of his plays have been professionally produced. His poetry is by general consent pretty unreadable, perhaps even in the original French. To call him a 'great writer' then, is, probably a mistake. To call Voltaire a great man is only to do him justice.

1

Princes and Poets

The Earthly Paradise is wherever I am.

The Man of the World (1781)

During the bitterly cold winter of 1705 the Jesuit College of Louis-le-Grand in Paris was not the most comfortable of places for a slightly sickly boy, especially when that boy was ill-disposed to sports or outdoor recreation and the fathers had made a strict rule that all exercise should be taken in the open air unless the weather was so cold that the water froze in the chapel font. François-Marie Arouet easily solved that problem. He collected some large chunks of ice and carried them into the chapel. The frozen font having been duly inspected, the eleven-year-old and his fellow students were soon comfortably ensconced before a roaring fire.

The often-repeated story may be apocryphal, but it is highly characteristic, demonstrating ingenuity, intelligence and if not exactly defiance of authority, a strong tendency to criticise and evade rules if they seemed silly or ill-conceived. It would be no surprise if such a plan had indeed been conceived and executed by the boy who was to grow up to become the best-known man in France, even in Europe, under the name of Voltaire.

François-Marie was born in Paris on 21 November 1694, and at the moment he drew his first breath appeared so weak that he seemed unlikely to live. Nevertheless, once he took hold of life he gripped it tenaciously, and was to survive into his eighties through a lifetime of both hypochondria and genuine illness.

He was the descendant of a family that had first come to prominence in the tanning trade and later prospered in wool production in the ancient province of Poitou. In the early decades of the seventeenth century the head of the family, one François Arouet, took his fortune in his hands, went to Paris, and established a business in the Rue Saint-Denis as a wool and silk merchant. It was an excellent move: the aristocracy craved good silks and worthy woollen stuff. He was soon in a good way of business, and his prosperity was enhanced by his marriage to Marie de Mallepart, whose father was a wealthy draper who ran his own bank.

The couple had seven children, the last, born in 1660, named François. When he was twenty-five he bought – or, rather, his father bought for him – a position as a notary. His legal practice was undistinguished but profitable, and he had no difficulty in acquiring a wife, Marie Marguerite Daumard, with her own claim to notability as the daughter of a clerk to the Paris law courts – a considerably more distinguished position than it sounds. In due course, François rose to become official collector of spice taxes, and was able to claim a coat-of-arms and the right to be considered 'noble'.

His youngest child, François-Marie, grew up in a comfortably established family, the head of which remains almost a cipher: a hard-working man, M. Arouet had little time to devote to a small child, and the son almost never referred to his father, and seems to have had no particular feelings for him. Nor did he often speak of his mother, who died when he was seven, though she was lively and intelligent and ran something of a salon. Her brother was comptroller general of the royal guard, which gave her a slight but significant connection with the court of Louis XIV.

François-Marie was the third surviving child of his parents and had two dominant siblings both of whom, in the absence of a mother and of a father's influence, had a strong effect on his development. His brother Armand was ten years his senior, his sister Marie Marguerite three years younger. The latter, he loved and trusted (she was later to produce a daughter who would become his beloved companion and mistress). His relationship with his brother, however, was bedevilled by the latter's devotion to the beliefs of the Jansenists. The sect was

2

named after the Dutch theologian Cornelius Jansen (1585–1638), who preached predestination – that only God could decide whether a man was worthy of His love, and that no degree of godliness or devotion could save someone upon whom He did not bestow his blessing. Arouet senior subscribed to the belief, but was a moderate adherent – steering his elder son towards the same beliefs, he may not have expected the infection to take as virulently as it did. Armand became a passionate Jansenist – and eventually a Convulsionary – a sub-sect whose members worked themselves up into frenzies, indulging in the luxury of making themselves as uncomfortable as possible (sometimes by self-flagellation and even torture), and happily losing touch with reality in the belief that madness brought them closer to God.

Though not quite so desperately pious as completely to lose his senses, Armand went in for dramatic displays of religious fervour such as rolling on the floor to demonstrate the extent of his self-abnegating humility. Even at a tender age François-Marie thought his brother's behaviour idiotic, and when he was able to comprehend the nature of Armand's belief, found that quite as nonsensical. As he wrote in another context, 'It is in my interest, no doubt, that there is a God, but if, in your system, God only came for so few people, if the small number of the elect is so terrifying, if I can do nothing at all by my own efforts, tell me, please, what interest I have in believing you? How can you have the effrontery to show me an infinite happiness to which hardly one in a million has the right to aspire?'[1] As a child he was incapable of putting his scorn into such words, but felt it none the less strongly, and the brothers disliked – even hated – each other from their earliest acquaintance, while François-Marie's mistrust of religious fervour and sectarianism, deep suspicion of people who knew they were right, and hatred of irrationality were stimulated by the relationship.

For three years after his mother's death the youngest child continued to live at home, first at the house in which he was born, on the left bank of the Seine, and later on the Ile de la Cité, where his father was given an apartment in what is now the Palais de Justice. At the age of ten he was sent to the Jesuits, to one of the best schools in France: Louis-le-Grand has been described as a Jesuit Eton, and was attended by two thousand pupils, many of them the sons of France's most eminent aristocrats. It was fairly late for a boy to begin formal education, but he had already been encouraged to read and write, particularly by his godfather, the abbé de Châteauneuf. He had introduced François-Marie not only to the charming fables of La Fontaine but the more earthy verses of the poet and dramatist Jean-Baptiste Rousseau,[2] and also, according to early biographers, to *La Moïsade*, a poem which argued that religion was a trick conceived to keep the lower orders in check ('opium of the people', in fact).

The Jesuit fathers found the boy a quick and apt pupil and taught him well, though the impression is that they perhaps put up with his sometimes irreverent quips because they admired the quickness of his wit. He was clearly confident of his own powers at an early age: his first confessor, a Fr Martin Pallu, is said to have described him in a written report as consumed with the desire for fame. Even at ten or eleven he began questioning his teachers' statements. Was there really a Hell? Did it not seem unlikely? And what was all this about Heaven? – it sounded to him merely like a great dormitory, one step up from the one in which he slept sometimes uneasily, sometimes soundly, with five other boys.

Frs Porée, Thoulier and Tournemine encouraged and nurtured him, and earned his respect – his view of religion did not prevent him revering them for the excellent teachers they were. He was particularly devoted to Porée – 'nothing will banish from my heart the memory of Fr Porée', he wrote many years later; 'no man could have made learning and the pursuit of truth more congenial. The hours spent under him were delightful; I wish that in Paris, as in Athens, one could sit under such a master at any age.'[3]

Any suggestion that the Jesuit college restricted study to strictly Christian topics is far from the truth; indeed, though the classics were taught (Cicero, Virgil, Horace, Ovid) and the boys were encouraged to make their own translations, the Bible was never discussed. School plays and even ballets were regularly presented and there was little restriction on the direction in which the boys' tastes took them. Where François-Marie was concerned, a skill at turning verses showed itself very quickly. Discovered toying with a snuff-box rather than attending to his teacher, he was instructed to write a set of verses on the incident, and did so with considerable dexterity. He also wrote a poem on behalf of a veteran soldier who wanted to petition the Dauphin for a pension; he turned out fifteen lines of creditable verse, and the petition was successful.

François-Marie made several life-long friends among his fellow pupils – Claude Philippe Fyot de la March, for instance (who became chief justice of the Dijon *parlement*[4]); Charles Augustin Feriol, Comte d'Argental, Pierre Robert Le Cornier de Cideville, the Marquis d'Argenson (who was to become government Minister for Foreign Affairs, and a leading voice against the hereditary nobility), and the Duc de Fronsac, who all appear later in this story, some playing important parts.

Voltaire was to some extent self-taught. There were no formal lessons in mathematics, geometry, geography, or philosophy, but he began from an early age to skirmish with them all. He spent almost as many hours at home as he did at the college, and was fortunate in that from birth he was surrounded by intelligent men and women: among them Nicolas Boileau, the leading literary critic of the day, was a next-door neighbour and friend of his father; and the poet and dramatist Pierre Corneille, whose collected works he was many years later to edit, was a regular visitor. Arouet's work brought him into contact with a mixture of stimulating and often unconventional men and women, many of whom became family friends. These included a particularly notorious client, the philosopher and author Ninon de Lenclos, who had been a close friend of Mme Arouet, and who in old age (she was in her eighty-fifth and last year when she met the ten-year-old François-Marie) expressed her irreligious views with the same vigour as when Molière and Saint-Évremond had attended her celebrated literary salons a generation earlier. So impressed was she by the boy's wit that she left him 2,000 livres in her will with which to start building up his own library. François-Marie was no doubt grateful, though he was physically repelled by the old woman, whose beauty, which had once captivated a long line of distinguished lovers, had since decayed into the sere and yellow.

He was taken to see de Lenclos by his godfather (Châteauneuf was said to have been her last lover) and a neighbour, a canon of the Sainte-Chapelle, Nicolas Gédoyn, who has the honour of being probably the first man fully to recognise the boy's promise. The canon was more than a little unconventional, professing to admire the myths of Greece and Rome as much as, if not more than, the Christian apologists. Indeed, he prompted the child to avoid over-enthusiastic religiosity: he regarded Milton's *Paradise Lost* as 'a barbarous and disgustingly fanatical poem'.[5]

It was the Abbé de Châteauneuf who was responsible for introducing François-Marie to a world of libertinism – libertinism both intellectual and physical. He took him, when the boy was still no more than twelve,[6] to the Temple, a building which had been the headquarters of the French Knights Templar (an organisation not marked for its puritanism) and which was later to become the prison of King Louis XIV and Marie Antoinette. The building was the home of the Knights of St John of Jerusalem, but any supposition that it housed a group of religious contemplatives should be rejected. The men who dined there regularly during the first decade of the eighteenth century recognised no boundaries of taste in either art or morality. Its nominal leader was Lieutenant-General Philippe de Bourbon-Vendôme, who presided from abroad, whence he had been exiled by the King for outrageously immoral behaviour, and the dinners were held under the auspices of two indifferent poets, M. La Fare and the Abbé Chaulieu (who declared that wine and women were the most succulent boons granted to man by a generous Nature).[7] Among the diners were two schoolmates and close friends of François-Marie, the Duc de Sully and the Duc de Fronsac; they were no doubt present largely because of their rank, Jean-François because of his wit, personal charm and friendship with them. The fact that his presence was not only tolerated but welcomed demonstrates that already in his early teens he must have had considerable self-possession and innate sophistication.

The company was clever, artistic, dissolute and sexually adventurous: a prominent member was the Abbé Servien, whose two nephews were his catamites and who was later to collapse and die in bed with a ballet boy from the Opéra. The Abbé Courtin became a close friend, though François-Marie did not share his appetite for enormous quantities of food and drink. The Abbé de Bussy was another acquaintance – when he became Bishop of Luçon, the young poet celebrated the occasion by writing an ode on the death of the Bishop's mistress.

We need not be surprised by the fact that many of the more dissolute members of the Temple should have been abbés. The ecclesiastical title was no bar to unecclesiastical behaviour; it simply meant 'father', and was given to secular clerics, whether or not they were ordained. They often wore the cassock, but frequently failed to behave with the propriety that dress implied. Jean-François, some years later, was to describe them as 'young men notorious for their debauches, and appointed to bishoprics through the intrigues of women, [who] make love in public, find fun in composing tender love-songs, give long and exquisite suppers every night, and then go straight to pray for the light of the Holy Ghost and brazenly call themselves the successors of the Apostles . . .'.[8]

There has never been any suggestion that François-Marie was sexually initiated at the Temple, or that at a tender age he was particularly encouraged to indulge in the sexual and gluttonous excesses of the members of that unofficial gentlemen's club. Given the characters of the men with whom he was mixing, this speaks either of considerable self-control (and as an adult he was no monk, but nor was he unduly promiscuous for his time), or of their forbearance towards a boy who already showed signs of being more fastidious in these matters than many of the others around the table. François-Marie found the company exciting and stimulating for other reasons – they provided a welcome opportunity for an exchange of ideas as iconoclastic and potentially dangerous as any sexual adventuring that went on.

There was open criticism of the King, Louis XIV, who during the last fifteen years of his reign thought himself and his armies invincible, and as a consequence had made decisions which resulted in the virtual political and financial bankruptcy of France. He had accepted on behalf of his grandson sovereignty over Spain, thus violating treaties he had formerly made with Austria, England and

Holland; the War of the Spanish Succession followed, with the disasters for France of Blenheim, Ramilles, Oudenarde and Turin. France's best army was lost, together with Bavaria and the Rhineland, Italy and Flanders. Then had come the famine of 1709, leaving the country starving as well as bankrupt. The atmosphere of barely concealed revolt was highly stimulating for a young dissident, and was expressed even more openly in conversation at the Temple than in the streets of Paris. It was all heady stuff.

François-Marie also valued the company at the Temple for another and more important reason. He already knew that he wished to emulate some of its members in at least one respect: he wanted to be a writer. Indeed, he already considered himself one. His interest in reading and writing was bred in his bones, and had been stimulated by the Jesuits, whose training had sharpened and organised his mind and thought processes. He was fascinated by the world of ideas, and from the outset had a fierce desire to communicate his own views and opinions of the world to others. At first, all authors commanded his immediate respect simply by virtue of their profession – even if, when he got to know them better, that respect was tempered by criticism and sometimes jealousy. The first distinguished writer with whom he came into contact was Jean-Baptiste Rousseau, with whose work he was already familiar, and who appeared at the College on prize day 1710 to present François-Marie with an award for literary merit – an honour which the adolescent boy sincerely appreciated.

Stimulated by his contacts with other writers, he now announced the nature of his future career to his father. François Arouet was distraught. The boy had been intended for the law, and indeed had been taken to the law schools and shown the place where he would study and the men who would be his fellows. That had been a mistake. François-Marie was appalled by the ill-breeding and physical grubbiness of the students and the poverty and bareness of their quarters. Under the aegis of the Ducs de Sully and de Fronsac (who were at least clean) he had come to have a keen respect for personal hygiene and elegant behaviour and had acquired a taste for good food and wine; the food at the Temple was far superior to that on which law students broke their teeth. Moreover, his friends at the Temple clearly thought him a person of talent, and talent too superior to be wasted at the Bar. Why else should the company of an otherwise undistinguished teenager be tolerated by so many older men – and men of taste, ability and rank? On one occasion, at a dinner hosted by the Prince de Conti, he remarked that no one sat around the table who was not either a prince or a poet – and was not rebuked. He was already under a delusion which was to be brought home to him painfully in a few years' time: while he was not impertinent, he assumed that he was accepted as a friend and equal, whereas he was really only an object of condescension.

Arouet senior, Voltaire wrote in his brief memoirs,[9] 'believed him entirely ruined because he kept company with people of fashion, and made verses'.[10] Unhappily for the father, a stroke of luck seemed to support his son's view that a career as a writer could be profitable if not distinguished. A titled woman with pretensions to literature employed the sixteen-year-old to smarten up her nondescript verses, and paid him so well that he was able to go out and buy himself a carriage and horses. Unfortunately, he could only afford hacks and a decrepit buggy; the latter fell to pieces while turning a corner, and the former – placed in his father's stables – rioted and destroyed their stalls.

His peers at the Temple, while they may not have set a good example in other ways, were nevertheless deeply committed to literature and encouraged the boy to set his sights high – to enter, for instance, a competition for an ode to the Blessed Virgin on the occasion of the building by the King of an altar in her honour in Notre Dame. He did not win, and did not take his defeat well: 'Quite a good thing, after all, to honour extreme old age,' he said when he heard that the prize had gone to an aged abbé and amateur poet. But though he never again entered any kind of competition, his determination to live the life of a writer was unaffected. He decided to set about a really ambitious project: a tragedy on the subject of Oedipus.

His friends advised against it. The great Corneille had, after all, written a masterpiece on the subject. He could do better than Corneille, he replied, and went ahead. From that time forward, he was indeed a writer, and a professional one at that. No longer did he play at writing; it was now his life. The act of writing became to him as natural as the presence of water in the mouth. His energy as an author remains almost unparalleled. During the next sixty-eight years, until his death in 1778, he wrote plays, poems, satires, novels, criticism, history, biography, novels, novellas, pamphlets – he would work happily on four or five literary projects at the same time, and simultaneously keep up a dialogue with correspondents all over Europe. Boswell, when he visited him in 1764, was taken into a room entirely full of the copies of letters he had written over the previous few years.

2

Imprisonment and Fame

There are two things for which animals are to be envied: they know nothing of future evils, or of what people say about them.

Letter, 1739

François-Marie Arouet may have thought himself capable, at the age of seventeen, of embarking on a career as a professional writer. His father thought otherwise. A writer, in his view, was a man who was completely useless, usually contrived to live off his relatives, and eventually died of hunger. The signs were that the boy was headed straight for the gutter (his father had not been impressed by the fact that while he was still at school, he had gone to a money-lender to bolster his pocket-money, and ended up owing 500 francs). No, he should study law, whether he wanted to or not. And since the company he was keeping at the Temple was clearly incompatible with that notion, he had better be removed as quickly as possible from the influence of the aristocratic rogues with whom he consorted there. He was dispatched to Caen.

The reason for choosing that city, and any indication of what he was supposed to do there, remain obscure but in any event exile did not have the effect M. Arouet anticipated. François-Marie, still determined to be a writer, ignored his law studies and concentrated on making friends and influencing people. In no time he had presented himself successfully as the amusing young exile from Paris whom every man – and in particular every woman – in town must know. He was soon taken up by a wealthy Catholic noblewoman,

Mme Françoise d'Osseville, shone at her soirées and escorted her to receptions in the town and the surrounding countryside. As a young man he never found it difficult to ingratiate himself with women – indeed, with members of either sex. He was by no means handsome; descriptions of him as an adolescent are all unflattering – a police report describes him, a few years later, as being tall and thin, with the appearance of a satyr, and Rousseau wrote of his '*mauvais physionomie*' – though also of his alert and lively expression. For his part, François-Marie described himself as 'thin, stringy and fleshless, without buttocks'.[1] But he had personal charm and quick wit, an elegant and fastidious appearance, and a talent for wearing fine clothes to good effect, attributes that he had already learned to employ to considerable advantage.

As was so often to happen throughout his life, he soon contrived to foul the nest he had made for himself at Caen. Though he knew Mme d'Osseville to be devout, he could not resist making jokes about religion and composing ribald verses on the subject. He also accepted the favours of other women in the area, and was soon forced by his friend's disapproval and jealousy to say goodbye to the comforts of her house and hearth. Instead, he was befriended by a none too respectable Jesuit priest and schoolmaster, Fr de Couvrigny, who thought him a positive genius. The priest was at least in one respect a more valuable companion than Mme d'Osseville, for not only did he share François-Marie's adventurous intellectual temperament, but he was well-read in most areas of contemporary European literature, and introduced the young man to authors whose work might otherwise have escaped him.

François-Marie's stay in Caen was brief, and for whatever reason his father recalled him to Paris in 1713, when he met for the first time his infant niece Marie-Louise Mignot, his sister Marguerite-Catherine's child, born while he was in Caen. He found her an entrancing baby; much later she was to become one of the most important people in his life. Immediately he began to look around for his old companions, and his father, taking the hint, with equal celerity contacted a friend (the brother of the late Abbé Châteauneuf) who was at present French Ambassador to Holland, and invited him to make use of François-

Marie as best he might, in whatever capacity suggested itself. So, in the autumn of 1713, the Marquis de Châteauneuf acquired a new secretary.

Once more, young Arouet had no difficulty in putting himself about, in particular among the ex-patriot French Huguenots and political refugees who had settled in The Hague. He was delighted to find that a large number of them were barely distinguishable from his old acquaintance at the Temple – quite as delightfully given to extreme social and political views.

One of the most prominent of the ex-patriots was a Mme Du Noyer, no more chaste than she might be, who had left France for England to escape religious persecution (or, perhaps, the violence of her husband; from time to time she claimed both reasons for her exile). She had led a notoriously immoral life in London, and for undisclosed but probably scandalous reasons had moved to The Hague, where she wrote and disseminated scurrilous pamphlets and set up a news-sheet, *La Quintescence*, which purveyed gossip and scandal. François-Marie delighted her by passing on snippets of information, both real and fictitious, about prominent men and women in Paris. He was soon a favourite with her and her two daughters, handsome girls who were so pretty that it was doubted whether they could indeed be the children of so ugly a woman. The youngest was a lively creature called Olympe, known as Pimpette, who was soon head over heels in love with the visitor from Paris.

Mme Du Noyer liked François-Marie well enough and found him useful, but had no intention of agreeing to her daughter's marriage with a penniless young man seemingly without prospects. She had succeeded in marrying off her elder daughter to a wealthy officer, but there had already been one failure with Pimpette: a leading Protestant and Calvinist, Jean Cavalier, had offered for her, but then (some said because of the reputation of her mother) had skipped to England and been seen no more. Though Pimpette and François-Marie were not only clearly in love but indulging that love without unnecessary reticence, Pimpette's mother was determined to have none of it. She turned up at the door of the French Embassy and complained to the Marquis de Châteauneuf that one of his secretaries was outraging morality in a manner no virtuous Huguenot parent could tolerate; he must be dismissed at once.

But now a new factor entered the equation. Mme Du Noyer's husband was a French captain who had remained in his native country, had from time to time tried to persuade his wife to return to him, and now suddenly decided to make a strenuous effort to get possession of his daughter. He wrote to the Ambassador informing him he had promised that if his wife sent his daughter to him, he would convert to Catholicism and force Pimpette to do so too. As a result, his application was backed up by an order from Louis XIV instructing his Ambassador to return the girl to Paris.

The Ambassador immediately told François-Marie that he was dismissed, and must return to Paris within twenty-four hours. No pleas could move him. The lover wrote to his young mistress telling her that there was nothing for it: he must leave The Hague, and she must follow him. If she waited until she was sent off to her father, the chances of their being able to meet in Paris were negligible. When he found that his letter had been intercepted, he ordered his valet to disguise himself as a travelling tradesman, gain access to the girl, and hand her a note telling her to sneak out of her mother's house at midnight, when they would elope together.

> I will leave the house incognito, hire a coach or carriage, we will flee like the wind . . . Nothing can part me from you. Our love is based on virtue – it will last as long as our lives. Order the bootmaker to fetch a carriage – but no, I don't want you to trust him. Be ready at four o'clock, I will wait for you near your street. Goodbye, there is nothing I would not risk for you, you deserve much more.[2]

He sent Pimpette a set of his clothing, in which she dressed herself, escaped, and made her way into the French Embassy, where François-Marie greeted her with enthusiasm and a degree of erotic excitement at her appearance in male dress. However, there was no persuading the Ambassador to ignore the royal command, and the lovers were separated, François-Marie sent back to Paris, Pimpette under close watch in The Hague. Both professed undying love, but neither suffered for long. Pimpette continued for a while to dispatch frenzied letters to Paris, but was then courted and consoled by a rather more handsome lover, and eventually married into the nobility. Meanwhile, François-Marie, ignoring her letters, was once again facing the prospect of becoming a law student. His father, having first threatened him with imprisonment and then with exile to the West Indies, subdued him sufficiently to persuade his son to enter the office of a royal notary called Alain. January 1714 found François-Marie back at his studies – or, rather, sedulously avoiding them – in company with a fellow-clerk, Nicolas-Claude Thiériot.

We know very little about Thiériot except, that is, that he was to batten on Voltaire for the next sixty years. The writer was to lend him money, entrust him with tasks he never performed and go out of his way to procure employment for which Thiériot proved totally unfitted. He was a dishonest, incurably lazy liar. Biographers have speculated about their relationship ever since. What was Thiériot's hold over Voltaire? The answer seems to be very simple: Thiériot was the first young man of his own age with whom Voltaire could talk about his great love, literature, and for that matter the first with whom he could giggle, tell smutty jokes, talk freely about women. Their shared love of poetry was clearly an important factor – Thiériot could and did recite, from memory, for hours. We must presume that he was an agreeable companion, and he must certainly have had a certain charm, a charm not only for Voltaire but also for others. When he tired of his friend's company, he would make for the nearest rich man he could find, and usually managed to settle in comfortably as a permanent toady with a taste for unlimited quantities of champagne. At one time or another he lived in this way off a number of noblemen and women, and for some years was a house guest of the Archbishop of Cambrai.

At all events, Voltaire clearly took to him, and the two young men very quickly made M. Alain's life a misery by their obvious dislike for their studies and their careless neglect of every task he set them. After six months, the notary informed M. Arouet that it was a waste of everyone's time for François-Marie to remain in his chambers.

The young man celebrated his release by publishing two satirical poems, the first an attack on an aged member of the Académie Française who some little time ago had voted against awarding him the prize for his ode, and the second, entitled *L'Anti-Giton*, a verse satire directed against the homosexual Marquis de Courcillon.[3] The poem was not particularly effective, and certainly not obscene, but as far as M. Arouet was concerned it was the last straw, and he prepared to apply for a *lettre de cachet*[4] which would enable him to have his son committed to prison. As so often in François-Marie's life, a rescuer appeared at the last moment – this time an old acquaintance from the Temple, the eighty-year-old M. de Caumartin, Marquis de Saint-Ange, who had been a distinguished member of the Court of the Sun King.

Caumartin invited the young man to his château at Saint-Ange, near Fontainebleau, where he fascinated his guest with reminiscences of life at Court. François-Marie found his interest in French history awakened, and began to make notes for a possible book on the age of Louis XIV (Caumartin was a particular admirer of that monarch, and encouraged his young friend to study his reign and to think of writing an account of it; the result was, eventually, the celebrated long poetic history *La Henriade*, first published in England in 1727). Voltaire paid tribute to his host in a poem: Caumartin had

> *. . . dans sa tête sont écrits*
> *Et tous les faits et tous les dits*
> *Des grands hommes, des beaux esprits . . .*

> [Written in his head
> all the doings and sayings
> of all the great men, the fine wits.]

Now twenty, François-Marie took a new mistress, a 23-year-old actress, Mlle Duclos, who was to join the Comédie Française two years later and become the greatest tragedienne of her generation under the stage name of Adrienne Lecouvreur.[5] She shared his sense of humour, and he dedicated *L'Anti-Giton* to her – in bed they had giggled together at the feminine antics of the Marquis de Courcillon. He was thoroughly in love – but the idyll ended when a nobleman, the Comte d'Uzès, talked his way into her favour. It was a lesson: even the wittiest and most charming of penniless young men must give way to position and money. 'Now,' he sighed, 'every morning La Duclos takes a pinch of senna and cloves, and every evening a portion of the Comte d'Uzés.'

Fortunately, he had something else to occupy his time, his tragedy on the subject of Oedipus which he was trying to get staged. He persuaded a number of people to listen to his readings of it, among them the Duchesse du Maine, an influential woman whose receptions at her Château de Sceaux were well attended by people he thought to be influential in the arts. They listened, criticised, sometimes laughed – and he hung ostentatiously upon their every word as though his auditors were paragons of taste and critical acumen. He did not necessarily believe this, but had already learned the value of flattery. As far as genuine critical attention was concerned, he set greater store by the remarks of his old friends of the Temple.

That group was now more prominent and perhaps more influential than ever, for on 1 September 1715 King Louis XIV had died, and the moral climate had changed, and changed quickly. Towards the end of his long life, the King had grown increasingly pious (prompted by the religiosity of his mistress, Mme de Maintenon, and his increasing reliance on the notably puritanical Fr Tellier, his confessor). His death resulted in an immediate relaxation of social and sexual conventions, and also in a political gavotte led by the Duc d'Orléans, his forty-year-old nephew.

The Dauphin, the King's eldest son, had died in April 1711, followed by his grandson, the new Dauphin, on 18 February 1712, and instantly by a second grandson, the Duc de Bretagne. A third grandson had forfeited the throne by accepting that of Spain, which left as heir a fifth, now five years old and sickly. Louis named the Duc d'Orléans as President of the Council, who would therefore have great power in the event of the death of the monarch. D'Orléans was extremely dissolute. He had been brought up by his homosexual father to be ignorant of the meaning of the word restraint, was a drunkard, kept innumerable mistresses and spent his leisure hours in the company of men who appeared to be chosen for their willingness to spend freely on furnishing their houses with the most beautiful women and the most luxurious means of making love to them. It was commonly said that d'Orléans had an incestuous relationship with his daughter, the Duchesse de Berry, which may or may not have been true – she was almost as debauched as he. He was also said to be a poisoner (of various relatives) and to be interested in black magic. In an attempt to protect his heir from any excesses the Duc might commit after his death, the King had made a will entrusting the child to the care of the Duc du Maine and the Comte de Toulouse, two bastard sons of his own by his mistress Mme de Montespan, and whose birth he legitimised.

The funeral of the man who had until almost the end of his life been regarded as a benevolent royal autocrat, was scarcely what might have been expected. The streets of Paris were cheerfully crowded as though for a fair, lined with tents and booths selling sausages and brioches, wine and cups of chocolate (against the bitter autumn weather). The people sniggered and capered as the funeral cortège, with line upon line of gilded coaches bearing courtiers, cardinals and bishops, trundled past accompanied by squadrons of musketeers and cavalry. Voltaire was among the crowd. While he may have concurred with some of the criticism of the King readily expressed by the company in which he moved, he had harboured a sneaking admiration for Louis and the magisterial way in which he had controlled his State, and for the way in which he had encouraged artists and in particular the architects who had enormously beautified Paris during his long reign.

Immediately upon the King's death, the Regent announced to the *parlement* of Paris that the royal will was invalid. The Duc and the Comte were deprived of their power and found themselves mere bastards again. Meanwhile, d'Orléans presided over a considerable relaxation of public morals, which Voltaire later noted in verse:

> *Voila le temps de l'aimable Régence*
> *Temps fortuné marqué par la licence,*
> *Où le folie, agitant son grelot,*
> *D'un pied léger parcourt toute la France*
> *Où nul mortal daigne être dévot . . .*

> [Voila: the congenial age of the Regency,
> that happy age marked by licence
> when folly, shaking its cap of bells,
> danced light-footed over all France,
> where no-one deigned to be devout.][6]

Indeed, now 'debauchery became a kind of etiquette', as one French historian put it.[7]

It would be a mistake to suppose that because the Regent was dissolute and immoral he was incapable of governing well. One of his first actions was to order the release of all prisoners in the Bastille who had not actually been convicted of a serious crime (some of them, it turned out, had no idea for what reason they had been imprisoned there). He made excellent public appointments, often preferring to high office men who were highly critical of him – promoting to chief of the Council of Finance, for instance, a man who had once actually threatened to assassinate him; he also promoted a number of covert Protestants. Himself an atheist (he had been seen to read Rabelais in church), he winked his eye at a number of publications which during the late King's reign would have landed their authors in prison for blasphemy.

He showed himself friendly, too, to a number of men whose behaviour had alienated the late King. He sent, for instance, for the exiled Philippe de Bourbon-Vendôme, who though riddled with venereal disease openly resumed his leadership of society at the Temple, where François-Marie, now in his twenty-first year, was among the most prominent of regular diners. He was still by no means the most dissolute of the young men at table – the greed and immoderate sexual appetites of the members revolted him, apart from which his weak stomach made it impossible for him to compete with their gluttony at table (he actually warned his friends of the danger of drinking too much brandy). While by no means averse to women – his current mistress was the Marquise de Mimeure – and by his own confession 'excessively dissipated and immersed in all the pleasures common at his time of life',[8] François-Marie was much more sexually restrained than his contemporaries, and certainly than his elders. He once remarked to a friend that as far as he was concerned, 'friendship is a thousand times more precious than love. It seems to me that I am in no degree made for passion. I find something a bit ridiculous in love . . .'.[9]

His acquaintances at the Temple neither belittled nor made fun of him for his physical restraint. Most of them had a serious interest in the arts and were ready to encourage a young writer in need of advice. So they listened to his readings of *Œdipe* and were free with their criticism – and François-Marie was happy to listen to them in turn, and to heed their appraisal. Throughout his life he positively welcomed the criticism of those whose opinions he respected, and returned again and again to his manuscripts to rework them.

He was taking pains to align his social life to his ambition, but had unfortunately miscalculated in allying himself with the group of people who collected around the Duchesse du Maine. She and her husband (the Duc was an illegitimate son of the King by his mistress Mme de Montespan) were in bad odour with the Regent. The Duc had himself expected to be appointed to that position, and was bitterly disappointed by the selection of Philippe d'Orléans; so, naturally, was his wife, and realising that passages from *Œdipe* could be interpreted as unflattering comments on the Regent, she was delighted to take snippets of the piece out of context and spread them about as criticisms of the regime at Versailles. Never able to resist the blandishments of the rich and nobly born, and with a keen sense of mischief which was too often to get him into trouble, François-Marie was easily persuaded to turn out a number of lampoons commenting on the private life of d'Orléans, whose alleged incestuous relationship with his daughter, the Duchesse de Berry, was common currency, but not a phenomenon he necessarily wanted bruited abroad in libellous verses. The verses were fairly obscure, but their meaning was clear, and the result was that, not for the last time, Voltaire attracted the attention of the police.

He swore blind that he was not responsible for the libellous verses – he would not, he claimed, have written lines so crude and badly scanned. His accusers were not convinced, but either because they were not sure of their ground or because of his youth, rather than sending him to the Bastille exiled him to Tulle, a small provincial town miles away in the Massif Central, where the only activity was the making of silk net.

His father was once again aghast, but not so outraged that he could not sympathise with his son's anguish at the prospect of having to live in such a dead-and-alive hole. He interceded with the Regent, and François-Marie was sent to happier exile at Sully, to the château of his friend Maximilien-Henri, Duc de Sully, the nephew and lover of the Abbé Servien. The unmarried duc entertained a wide range of friends and acquaintances, there was a fine library in the house, and the young author could have done some serious work had not the social life been so lively. There was a theatre at the château where amateur and professional actors appeared, and it was at Sully that his life-long infatuation with the theatre was fully nurtured. There was also a pretty young girl on hand with whom to fall in love: Suzanne de Livry, with whom he formed an amorous as well as a theatrical partnership. She decided to become a professional actress, and chose François-Marie as her impresario. They set up house in Paris, in a *ménage à trois* with their mutual friend Lefevre de Genonville. Perhaps because François-Marie could never have been accused of jealousy in his personal relationships, and also because sex was never very important to him, this was one of the happiest times of his youth. Later, he wrote of

> les beaux jours de notre vie,
> Nous nous aimions tous trois. La raison, la folie
> L'amour, l'enchantement des plus tendres erreurs,
> Tous réunissait nos trois coeurs.
>
> Que nous étions heureux! même cette indigence,
> Triste compagne des beaux jours,
> Ne put de notre joie empoisonner le cours.
> Jeunes, gais, satisfaits, sans soins, sans prévoyance,
> Aux douceurs du présent bournant tous nos désirs,
> Quel besoin avions-nous d'une vaine abondance?
> Nous possédions bien mieux, nous avions les plaisirs.[10]

[. . . the lovely days of our life [when]
We loved each other, all three. Reason, folly,
Love, the witchcraft of most tender foolishness,
Bound our three hearts together.

How happy we were then! Even poverty,
The melancholy companion of those ravishing days,
Could not poison the stream of our joy.
Young, gay, happy, without worries, without any plans,
Our desires seated in the pleasures of the present
– what could we want with useless surfeit?
We had something better. We had happiness.]

Restlessness persuaded François-Marie to write to the Regent asking for pardon, accompanying his request with a fulsome set of complimentary verses. Virtual imprisonment at Sully was simply killing him, he said (this was of course a lie: he had been far from imprisoned there, and even further from unhappiness); he must be at liberty to rove – why, he was so restless that he would sometimes sit on ten different chairs in the same room in the same evening! How could such a fidgety creature survive in one place? The Regent, charmed like most people by the exile's wit and humour, was also complimented by the verses, forgave him, and gave him permission to return to Paris, ignorant of the fact that he was already living there. His father suspected that life in the capital would be his son's ruin, and it soon looked as though he was right, for an encounter with a stranger at the inn at which he was living in October 1716 got him into trouble. The man with whom he had a drink, and to whom he made some witty but rash remarks about the Regent, turned out to be a police spy who reported to the Regent that the young writer had claimed that he had been exiled because he had spoken of the Duchesse de Berry as a whore who was pregnant by her father, even naming the house where she was about to be confined.

The Regent was again offended, and on 16 May 1717 the police produced a warrant personally signed by him, and the young man was dispatched to the Bastille. He took the opportunity, however, to revenge himself on the more offensive of the police officers who had arrested him, one Inspector Isabeau. When a search of his rooms revealed no incriminating manuscripts, the man demanded to know what had been done with them. François-Marie replied that he had stuffed them down the lavatory. Isabeau made a cursory inspection of the cesspool below the house in which Arouet had his apartment, and reported to his superior that no paper could be seen floating there. He was, however, commanded to make a thorough search. His men examined the cesspool with such enthusiasm that they damaged it, allowing the stinking detritus to flow into the landlady's cellar and destroy what she claimed was a valuable stock of fine wine. She thereupon sued the Crown, and won her case; damages were paid.

François-Marie was imprisoned for eleven months. Though no doubt at first he wondered just how severely he was to be punished for his impertinence, it soon became clear that his imprisonment was not to be too rigorous: he was allowed to receive visitors and take exercise on the bowling-green, and was entertained to dinner by the Governor. A note has survived which he wrote to the latter asking for some additional comforts:

> Two volumes of Homer, in Latin and Greek
> Two cotton handkerchiefs
> A small bonnet
> Two cravats
> A nightcap
> A small bottle of oil of cloves.[11]

His main deprivation was actually a positive one – he was denied the opportunity to waste his time. As a result he did some serious work, producing several cantos of his verse biography of Henry IV of France, *La Liugue*, later to be re-titled *La Henriade* (written on the endpapers and in the margins of the few books he was allowed) and a poem on the Bastille itself, as well as immersing himself in the classics. Outside the prison, when he was discussed at all it was as an impudent young fool who had overstepped the mark and been properly slapped down. This was not too remote from the truth: so far, his career – in as much as it could be described as a career – had been mainly an extension of the trait the Jesuit fathers had observed: he continued to be a show-off, and had given few signs of possessing a serious mind.

Suddenly released (on 11 April 1718, when the Regent presumably decided he had purged his contempt), he began to attempt to rehabilitate himself, once more writing fulsome apologies to Philippe and to the Chief of Police from his father's country house at Châtenay, where he had been sent. In October, it was decided that *'le Sieur Arouet de Voltaire'* could return to Paris and public life whenever he pleased,[12] although it was made very clear to him that if he caused any more trouble he could be sent again into exile. For the time being, however, he was not at all interested in attacking or making fun of anyone – at last there was the chance that his play, *Œdipe*, might be staged at the Comédie Française. The administrators of that august theatrical establishment were, however, rather backward-looking, and found his text far too 'realistic'; they wanted the story of Oedipus prettified so that it did not offend audiences by its horror.

Irritated and grumbling, François-Marie tinkered with his text until it was acceptable, and the play was produced on 18 November 1718 with Suzanne Livry as Jocasta. While he was in prison, she had decided that she really preferred Genonville as a partner (doubtless he was a more vigorous lover than his friend), and set up house with him. François-Marie took the betrayal well – he quite understood why Lefevre had found her irresistible:

> *Un cœur tendre, un esprit volage,*
> *Un sein d'albâtre, et de beaux yeux.*
> *Avec tant d'attraits précieux,*
> *Hélas! Qui n'eût été friponne.*[13]

> [A tender heart, a giddy mind,
> An alabaster breast, and beautiful eyes.
> With so many priceless attractions,
> Alas! Who wouldn't be mischievous?]

Œdipe ran for an almost unprecedented forty-five performances – an enormous success. It has been suggested that this was for reasons unconnected with the story of Oedipus, that audiences believed the play to be a thinly disguised anti-clerical attack on the late King. Certainly there are a few lines in the text that might be taken to suggest that the author was not a great admirer of hereditary monarchy, and one or two which might be interpreted as critical of the idea of an all-powerful, all-loving god: Oedipus, as he dies, complains that his crimes are really the gods', yet he is punished for them, and Jocasta, dying, accuses the gods of compelling her to commit incest. Some members of the audience seized on these lines, others on the couplet in the first scene of Act IV:

> *Nos prêtres ne sont pas ce qu'un vain peuple pense;*
> *Notre crédulité fait toute leur science . . .*

> [Our priests aren't what a silly people think;
> our credulity is all the argument they have.]

Other members of the audience seized on what they saw as a suggestive parallel between the incestuous theme of the play and the condition of the Duchesse de Berry, now assuredly pregnant – and not, it was suggested, by the Captain of her Guard, whom she was parading as her ostensible lover. Happily, almost everyone found something to applaud at one or other point of the play.

Descriptions of the first night vary: some intimate a scandal, others an immediate triumph, with Arouet senior beside himself with pleasure and pride, reconciled to and congratulating his son. What is clearly true is that François-Marie himself played a strange part in the success of the evening – he appeared on-stage, capering about and pulling at the train of the chief priest's costume at a tragic moment. In his fragmentary autobiography, he suggests that he was drunk, and this may have been the case. He could clearly have wrecked the performance, but by now audiences had taken – or thought they had taken – his measure, and were delighted by this fresh evidence of the puppyish behaviour of a show-off. He did, incidentally, achieve one particular triumph: taking great exception to the custom that those fashionable men and women who could afford an extra fee were allowed to sit actually on stage, not only at the sides but behind the actors, he insisted that the privilege should be discontinued. The stage was cleared for *Œdipe* and when his example had been followed by Diderot and other playwrights, the custom vanished for good.

For its time, the piece was a tremendous success, earning more money for its author than any other eighteenth-century play and having a longer run. The Regent did not take offence – or perhaps chose not to take offence; at all events, he presented the young author with a gold medal and a generous annuity (he had already granted him a small pension on his release from the Bastille, for reasons which have eluded biographers). The British Ambassador reported the success of *Œdipe* to King George I in London, and hearing this, François-Marie sent His Majesty one of the hastily printed copies of the text; the King returned the favour by a present of a gold watch and another medal. Attempting to seize the moment, François-Marie with incredible naivety asked the Regent if he might dedicate the published edition of the play to him. D'Orléans declined the honour, and the author had to be content with a dedication to the Regent's mother. It ends: '*Madame, de votre altesse royale le très humble et très obéissant serviteur Arouet de Voltaire.*' It was the first time he used the name by which he, was to become truly famous.

There have been many discussions about the provenance of the name and the reason why young Arouet took it. The most likely origin is in the nickname by which he had been known as an infant – '*le petit volontaire*', the little stubborn one. As to why he should so decisively have rejected his family name, that is anyone's guess but it may well have had something to do with the fact that for some reason he believed M. Arouet was not his real father. He alludes to the possibility several times, if somewhat obliquely, in letters and articles, but attaches no evidence to the assertions, and no evidence has ever been found. His already cultivated habit of obfuscating his birth and the history of his family suggests that he was not proud of it, although he had absolutely nothing to be ashamed of in a background of good, solid breeding, both on his mother's part and on her husband's. No doubt a desire for a more memorable name – to call him a snob would not be too much of an insult – played a part. And it is certainly true that his new name swiftly became far better known than his old one.

The success of *Œdipe* made the 25-year-old sought after and, to a degree, famous. He dined out, splendidly dressed and with a witty quip always on his lips, and was courted by the wealthy and fashionable, notably the Maréchal-Duc de Villars and his duchess, out at the Château de Vaux where the most cultivated men and women of the age collected. The maréchal was a genuine admirer and patron of the young man but the duchess, who had met him at the first night of *Œdipe*, made gentle fun of him and flattered his vanity by pretending to be in love with him (she was almost ten years older than he, and in fact was devoted to her lover, the impoverished but sturdy young Abbé de Vauréal, who at the same time was paying attention to a Comtesse de Guitaut; so adept was he at using his mistresses' influence to effect that he ended up as Bishop of Rennes).

Voltaire was thoroughly captivated by the duchess, and she certainly got good value for her flattery; he was a very personable young man who was always entertaining company at table and amply repaid her attentions. Though he as usual enjoyed showing off, and particularly enjoyed the pleasure of living in fine company, dining at luxurious tables and staying in comfortable rooms at great châteaux, he was conscious that what he should really be doing was working. Time was passing and although the success of his play had been considerable, he knew perfectly well that he should be building upon it rather than wasting time paying court to duchesses. He had also been wasting time and energy in less salubrious circumstances, back-stage at the Comédie Française, where his friend Suzanne Livry had not shared his success in *Œdipe*, being booed nightly for her efforts to portray Jocasta; in as much as she could act at all, she was an ingénue, and the tragic role was just too much for her. Another member of the cast, a M. Poisson, was infuriated by the nightly fiasco of her performances, and suggested that her casting as Jocasta had more to do with her having shared a bed with Voltaire than with her slender histrionic talents. She complained to Voltaire, who rebuked the actor in such terms that Poisson challenged him. Voltaire was far too wise to engage in a duel with an actor, and refused in even ruder terms. Poisson threatened to have him beaten up, whereupon Voltaire complained to the police. In the end the affair petered out, with no good done to the reputation of either man. It was the kind of broil Voltaire would have done well to avoid, but the affair was typical of his hot-blooded reaction to any disagreement, especially when it reflected upon his honour. He turned his attention to more serious matters, and by early 1720 had written a second play, *Artémire*. This was much touted, and Adrienne Lecouvreur expressed an interest in it; but an early production in February failed utterly; Voltaire quickly rewrote it and it was presented once more, but again failed, and no more was heard of it.

It was a rare failure. Many of his plays were spectacularly successful, though today, even in France, they are regarded as unperformable and almost unreadable. Modern readers are interested chiefly in Voltaire's philosophy, though they still delight in some of his prose with *Candide* being the obvious example. Turning the pages even of the best of them – *Zaïre*, say or *Tancrède* or *Mérope*, one soon becomes conscious of how hog-tied the writer was by the relentless thud of the alexandrines in which he was forced to write in order to conform to the style of the period (though it must be said that he showed no signs of wanting to break free – indeed, one of his objections to Shakespeare was the 'barbarous' style in which he wrote). Voltaire's plays were above all for performance – no one except a relentlessly faithful student has ever sat in the study reading them, or at least has done so without finally succumbing to boredom.

How, then, did he achieve his success as a dramatist? The truth seems to be that the without demanding anything too radical in the way of reform of theatrical values, the audiences of his day were beginning to grow bored with the plays with which they were continually presented – in particular, with those of the man regarded as the greatest theatrical stylist, Racine. The very slight outrages with which Voltaire presented them – characters drinking on-stage, for instance, or dying, or even the display of supposed corpses; the selection of plots that necessitated outlandish costumes and make-up – all produced just sufficient *frisson* to make his name. It is also fair to say that he moved his plays along with great speed and vigour – he did not have the patience for interminable monologue, and did not expect it from his audiences.

How much of this was planned and how much instinctive we cannot know; but the ingredients were needed, for the writing itself remains desperately pedestrian and the characterisation vestigial (Voltaire was so bad at this that his comedies failed completely). All the same, from *Œdipe* (written when he was eighteen) to *Irène* (written when he was eighty), he captured and held the stage. The feat was not inconsiderable.

The interest shown in *Œdipe* by the King of England gave Voltaire the idea that an international reputation might be achievable. He had already begun to believe that countries other than France might order their affairs rather better, both as far as religion was concerned, and where the freedom of the individual was in question. He began to talk freely to foreigners living in Paris. Sadly, he did not choose well, becoming the familiar of two adventurers neither of whom was precisely what he claimed to be: Baron Goertz was not really the representative in France of the Court of Charles XII of Sweden; nor was Baron Hogguers a bona-fide envoy of Austria or Switzerland (on occasion, he claimed to be both). Each, however, was apparently wealthy, dressed with panache and seemed to be in the swim of international diplomatic affairs, though they were in fact no more and no less than adventurers. Voltaire enjoyed the gossip they purveyed, and liked to feel that he was in the confidence of men who knew what was what. But neither association commended him to the French secret police. They reported the matter to the Regent, who in turn ordered the files to be salted away lest the silly young radical should again get above himself and make it necessary to take action against him.

By now it was 1722, and on the first day of the new year Voltaire's father died.

3

Religion and Royalty

The great consolation in life is to say what one thinks.

Letter, 1765

Monsieur Arouet died of dropsy on the first day of 1722, leaving his younger son one-third of his estate. A small fortune of about 150,000 livres was due to Voltaire, but it was to remain in trust until he was thirty-five. What this meant was that he was thrown on his own resources – we do not know whether his father had made him an allowance, but if so it ceased with his death. Happily, the young man was extremely shrewd when it came to money. He had made a considerable sum from *Œdipe*, and he now had two annuities from the Regent. Moreover, he made it his business to know a number of astute bankers, including the brothers Paris, who had been employed by the Regent to help resolve a financial scandal which had threatened to topple him.[1] They were able to assist Voltaire to a number of excellent investments. He became an unprofessional but keen money-lender, and despite his disappointment over his father's estate was by the mid-1720s a rich man, able to live comfortably within his means.

It was partly in the hope of financial gain that Voltaire turned his mind to the possibility of a diplomatic career, writing to the King's first minister, Cardinal Dubois, suggesting that he might go into Germany under the guise of a visit to his acquaintance – he might say colleague – Jean-Baptiste Rousseau, and there be of use to His Majesty as an agent (or, not to put too fine a point on it, a spy). The proposal was ignored. Meanwhile, there was an incident which provided the gossips of Paris with something to talk about. The Minister of War, a M. Le Blanc, invited Voltaire to dinner one evening at Versailles, where unfortunately another guest at table was a certain M. Beauregard, whom the writer immediately recognised as the police spy to whom he had unwisely confided the gossip about the Regent and his daughter which had resulted in his imprisonment in the Bastille. Unsurprisingly, he lost his temper and the following scene brought the entire evening to a halt. The spy, insulted with all the telling verbal skill which Voltaire could command, was furious and went to his master, Le Blanc, and asked permission to have Voltaire 'dealt with'. The Minister, to whom the spy was much more valuable than a fashionable scribbler, had no objection as long as the matter was discreetly handled.

A few days later Voltaire's carriage was brought to a stop in the street, he was pulled from it and severely beaten. The victim, and everyone else, knew perfectly well who was responsible (some even said that Beauregard handled the cudgel himself), but all attempts to bring the assailant to book came up against a brick wall. The spy had valuable friends, though he was to have his comeuppance later, when Le Blanc was dismissed and his main informant gaoled for some months. In the meantime, Voltaire gave up the unequal struggle against police and State, and early in 1723 set out for Brussels and The Hague, accompanied by a new friend, the young, red-headed, widowed Marquise de Rupelmonde. She was amusing and wealthy (the King of Spain, in whose military service her husband had perished, had given her a generous pension), but her reputation was not exactly golden, except in the sense that she was a blonde; she was popularly known as *Vaque-à-Tout*, which might be translated as 'busy body' and was widely taken in the literal sense. Voltaire may or may not have been her lover (it seems likely), but she was certainly an agreeable fellow-traveller; he wrote a number of verses in praise of her mature beauty (she was thirty-seven, and thus nine years his senior), and they discussed everything from religion to the sex life of the Regent.

They paused, *en route*, at Cambrai where there was a lively social scene to be enjoyed. Voltaire and his friend were not backward in letting the citizens know that a distinguished young writer was among them, and a performance of Œdipe was hurriedly mounted and well received. Praise for the play far outweighed the tittle-tattle about Voltaire's relationship with his companion, of which the more puritanical local dignitaries disapproved. The pair remained in the town until September, and then set out for Brussels in the marquise's lumbering coach. As it jolted over the notoriously bad European roads – road-sickness was quite as troublesome to travellers as sea-sickness – their conversation centred more and more on religion. The marquise was by no means entirely flippant and was troubled with a number of questions which she felt she could put to Voltaire, though it would be dangerous on grounds of blasphemy to mention them to a priest: how was it, for instance, that God made sex highly enjoyable to the men and women he had created, and then punished them for indulging in it? Why should He punish the ignorant savages who had never heard of Him, for disobeying laws of which they were perfectly ignorant? Why should children be punished for the sins of their fathers? Why should it be necessary that priests, who were after all only men, interpret the will of God to other men and to women?

Voltaire had himself been pondering such matters for some time, and was now so ready with answers – or if not with answers, then with forceful criticisms – that he began to write a poem based upon them. This turned into a trenchant critique of Christianity which at first he called *L'Épître à Uranie* (*Uranie* being the marquise herself) and then *Le Pour et le Contre* ('For and Against'), the title under which it was to be privately printed thirteen years later, when it caused a sensation, gaining for Voltaire a reputation for irreligion and blasphemy. Not so far from the truth, if one was a conventional Christian, for while Voltaire hesitated to say outright what he thought of God, he did point out that while he himself longed to adore Him, there were problems. How was it possible to love and honour a god who gave man a wicked heart specifically so that He could punish him for the evil he did, tormented men and women by making physical love important to them, created mankind only to drown the whole population of the world and replace it with worse sinners, and punished millions of people simply because they had never heard of the cruel death He had imposed upon His own son, allegedly for their good?

The poem actually ends with an impassioned argument in favour of readers making up their own minds what sort of God to believe in. Now, of course, the questions and reservations the poem expresses could be put from a pulpit by any clergyman, though the answers are as elusive as they were during Voltaire's lifetime.

For the moment, only the marquise read – or, more likely, heard – the dangerous poem, as the couple progressed to Brussels. There, Voltaire made the mistake of reading *Le Pour et le Contre* to Jean-Baptiste Rousseau, who later claimed to have been aghast at its profanity and blasphemy. At that moment they were still on speaking terms; his later gibes at Voltaire and his work stemmed partly from the fact that while the latter was happy to receive Rousseau's fulsome compliments about his own work, he was unable to return them, finding his senior's poetry at best indifferent and at worst downright bad. When Rousseau showed the younger man an ambitious poem entitled 'Ode to Posterity', Voltaire's only comment was that he doubted that the work would reach its destination. This, together with the fact that he was unable to resist repeating the remark to the literati of Brussels, put paid to any chance of continued friendship between the two writers, and it was war to the knife for ever afterwards. Naturally, the episode coloured Rousseau's recorded comments on *Le Pour et le Contre* and *La Henriade*; he is said to have found them profoundly shocking, with their attacks on religion, the priesthood and the establishment in general.

Voltaire seems to have had a remarkably pleasant time at Brussels and The Hague, playing tennis, riding, visiting a brothel, and working. Much concerned with the publication of the *Henriade*, he left the marquise in The Hague and returned to Paris via Cambrai and Orléans, where he spent some time at the home of Viscount Bolingbroke and his French mistress the Marquise de Villette, whom the Viscount was shortly to marry. The great Tory politician had been (at the age of twenty-four) Minister of War under Queen Anne, but was dismissed by King George because of rumoured treasonable connections with the Old Pretender (the rumours were entirely correct) and spent the years between 1714 and 1723 in voluntary exile in France. Voltaire had met him through the family of a school friend, and the two men established an instant rapport, Voltaire deeply impressed by the breadth of knowledge of his new acquaintance. 'I found in this famous Englishman all the learning of his country and all the politeness of ours,' he wrote to his friend Thiériot. 'I have never heard our language spoken with greater energy and precision. Although this man has spent all his life in pleasure and public affairs he has managed to learn and to remember everything. He knows the history of the ancient Egyptians as well as that of England; he has mastered Virgil equally with Milton; he loves English, French and Italian poetry, but he loves them in different ways, for he distinguishes to perfection their different natures.'[2]

Voltaire read the *Henriade* to Bolingbroke and his mistress and was much heartened by his new friends' praise. 'In the enthusiasm of their approval they put it above all the poetry published in France, but I know how much I must discount this excessive praise,' he told Thiériot. 'I am going to spend three months in justifying it in part.' Bolingbroke was perfectly honest in his admiration, and sent a copy of the poem to Alexander Pope in England, who acknowledging it suggested that Voltaire's 'Judgement of Mankind and his Observation of human Actions in a lofty and Philosophical view is one of [his] Principal Characteristics . . . who however is not less a Poet for being a man of sense . . . . I conclude him at once a Free thinker and lover of Quiet; no Bigot, but yet no Heretick: one who honours Authority and National Sanctions without prejudice to Truth or Charity; one who has Study'd Controversy less than Reason, and the Fathers less than Mankind.'[3]

It was a shrewd enough evaluation, though not one the French authorities shared, and indeed with censorship as it was, Bolingbroke's insistence that the poem 'must be published' rang hollow. The banning of any book which showed the slightest originality of thought or even form was almost automatic. The *privilège du Roi*, or royal permission to publish, was given only to books which offended neither Church nor State – and offence was easily taken by those almost indivisible bodies. The *Henriade*, Voltaire's epic poem the hero of which is Henry IV, beloved by the French for putting an end to the Wars of Religion, was already circulating freely in manuscript and was much quoted and praised, but when Voltaire approached the censor for permission to publish the poem by subscription, he met with a blanket refusal.

When he returned to Paris, his friend and possible mistress Mme de Bernières, wife of the President of the Rouen *parlement*, suggested clandestine publication of the *Henriade* by a press in Rouen. Voltaire began to make enquiries about the possibility. Meanwhile, he rented rooms in her house, and played host to Thiériot, who as usual was busy doing nothing. Voltaire decided to hand over to him half of the annuity he received from the Regent. Who can possibly explain his devotion to the man?

In the meantime he was working on a new play, *Mariamne*, a tragedy which he read in manuscript to a small party including Adrienne Lecouvreur, who was interested in playing the leading role. The event took place at Maisons, the home of Voltaire's friend Jean René de Longueil, Marquis de Maisons, who at the age of twenty-four had already been a judge for seven years. Unfortunately, on the very evening of the reading Voltaire was taken ill. Next morning it was confirmed that he had smallpox. His fellow guests vanished as if by magic. The author, always and in any event a hypochondriac, was sure of his demise (his suspicion confirmed by a servant kindly informing him that a coffin was being prepared for him), and after being bled made his will and his confession and prepared for death. He was saved by the intervention of a clearly skilled doctor, M. de Gervasi, and later described his interesting treatment to Nicolas de Tonnelier de Breteuil, Baron de Preuilly, head of protocol at the French Court. It is a detailed record of a procedure remarkably civilised and sensible for the age:

M. de Gervasi did not leave me for a moment. He studied attentively all the natural developments of my case, and never gave me anything to take without telling me why: he let me see the danger and gave me confidence, a method which is very desirable between a doctor and his patient, since the hope of being cured is half the battle. He was obliged eight times to give me an emetic; and instead of the cordials usually given in this illness, he made me drink two hundred pints of lemonade. This procedure, which will strike you as extraordinary, was the only one that could have saved my life . . . and I am convinced that most of those who have been killed by this redoubtable illness would still be alive if they had been treated like me.

The success of the lemonade treatment he explained by arguing that 'lemon-juice in a refreshing infusion softens the acrimony of the blood, soothes its heat, circulates with it through the miliary glands right into the pustules, resists the corrosion of the leaven, and even prevents the pocks the pustules usually leave on the face'.[4]

Voltaire's friend Génonville, with whom he had shared the delectable Suzanne, was not so lucky and perished in the same epidemic; the Marquis de Maisons was to die of the same disease in 1731. Voltaire felt Génonville's death keenly and was still missing his friend ten years later, when he wrote a poem in his memory. He spent some time recuperating in the care of Nicolas Thiériot, who at least bestirred himself on this occasion, making a long journey to Maisons to nurse his friend and staying by his bedside day and night until he was out of danger. Thiériot has been much criticised for his later disloyalty to Voltaire, and the avarice which led him to defraud the author; it is worth noting that on this occasion at least he played the part of a devoted friend.

Restored once more to reasonable health – not that Voltaire ever considered his health to be anything other than precarious – he resumed his social life in Paris. This was very different to the life he, or anyone else of his social circle, lived outside the city. As Charles Duclos[5] put it, anyone who lived a hundred miles from Paris was a hundred years away from it in thought or behaviour.

Women were at the centre of Parisian social life, and while he had men friends, it was on women that Voltaire concentrated his mind and his ambition. It was they who held the salons, they who provided the ears into which poets and prose-writers could read their latest work, they who through their lovers pulled strings and influenced not only fashions but events. They even influenced style. Denis Diderot pointed out that 'With women we have to express the dryest and most prickly subjects with charm and clarity. We talk to them all the time, we want them to listen, and we go out of our way to avoid boring them. Thus we develop a habit of expressing ourselves easily in conversation, and when we write this affects our style.'[6]

Voltaire could not make love to every influential woman in Paris; but if he was indeed the lover of Mme de Bernières, it was not because he found her particularly physically attractive. There were all sorts of ways in which she could and did help him. It is impossible to say that at this time he was absolutely devoted to any woman – or, indeed, man. He reserved his devotion for his work. He had a talent for friendship and a charm which made it easy for him to make friends (just as he had an audacity which easily made enemies). While he enjoyed both sex and romance, there is no mistress who at this point was capable of monopolising his time. This is true, too, of his friends; one would have to admit that the awful Thiériot was probably closest to him – certainly took up more of his time than any other acquaintance; but to call him a friend, in the face of the deceit and lying of which Voltaire was perfectly aware, would be going too far.

Apart from the salons of the wealthy and influential, the other place where Voltaire could frequently be seen was the coffee shop. Coffee had become almost as popular in Paris as wine; it was thought that it raised the spirits higher and quicker, and with fewer after-effects than alcohol. Every chemist sold ground coffee, and sometimes would serve it over the counter as a drink. In 1715 there were three hundred coffee-shops or cafés in Paris, and by 1750 six hundred. Voltaire often put on cloak and hat and went in disguise to the Café Procope (which some people called the Cave, because it was so dark) hoping to hear frank opinions on his latest play, above the noise of people playing dominoes and the general conversation.

Soon everyone at the Cave was talking about the *Henriade*, copies of which had finally come out in 1724 in 10 books and over 4,000 lines of verse. It had been printed and handsomely bound in Rouen and smuggled into Paris underneath a load of Mme de Bernières's furniture. 'Forbidden' books circulated with spectacular speed, and soon everyone with an interest in literature or politics had read this one and been astonished by its praise of England and Queen Elizabeth

I, its denigration of Protestantism (if by omission rather than commission – simply by failing to celebrate it), and its criticism of the late King's assumption of both spiritual and temporal power. Its religious and political opinions caused an immediate sensation. But it was also widely praised for its literary merits; one critic, Mathieu Marcius, wrote of it: 'It is a marvellous work, a masterpiece of the kind, as beautiful as Virgil. At last we have an epic in our own language',[7] while the philosopher Pierre Bayle addressed the ghosts of the classical authors Seneca and Lucian: 'You must learn to write and to think from this marvellous poem, the glory of our nation, and a reproach to you.'[8] Others compared the poet with Homer and thought him superior to Tasso and Milton.

But, of course, the great selling-point of the book was its content rather than its style. Voltaire traced the history of religious persecution through the ages – not simply that of the Christian religion, though the papacy was described in less than flattering terms, but of all religions. So he showed Agamemnon prepared to sacrifice Iphigenia to the gods, the Romans sending the Christians to the lions, religious fanatics of every hue persecuting those with whom they disagreed. The fairly ostentatious secrecy with which the book was published did it no harm – while it was a 'forbidden' work, it lay openly on the table of anyone who was anyone. Soon the whole of Paris was attacking its author, each sect contriving to find reasons for doing so, often imposing violent interpretations on a text which if anything was considerably less offensive than it might have been (the public had not yet had the opportunity to read *Le Pour et le Contre*).

Any work offering criticism of the establishment, of the small but infinitely influential world of Versailles, was highly apposite in 1724. In December of the previous year the Regent had died, and since the King at fourteen, though legally 'of age', was still a minor, the rulership of the State devolved upon the re-legitimised Louis de Bourbon, Prince de Conti.

Bourbon promised to be a good ruler. Much concerned at the poverty of the great majority of the King's subjects, he proposed wage and price controls, though like other politicians before and since he found that excellent idea next to impossible to implement. He did, however, impose income tax at 2 per cent on everyone, which bitterly upset the nobility and clergy, who conspired against him.

As for the King, that young man seemed disinclined to accept any advice from his new Regent, who was puzzled by the monarch's attitude until the true situation was explained to him. The Duc de Gesvres, disappointed in his own attempts to become a close confidant of the King, explained to the naive Prince de Conti that Louis was entirely under the influence of a homosexual coterie led by two of his most prominent courtiers, his tutor, Cardinal André Hercule de Fleury, and Jean Phélippeaux, Comte de Maurepas. From his youth the King had been discouraged from mixing with young women, and his invariable companions, the Duc de Boufflers, the Comte de Ligny, the Marquis de Meuse and the Marquis de Rambure, all in their late teens, had introduced him to enjoyable but hardly conventional sexual diversions. All four were eventually arrested on the Regent's orders and sent off to their country estates, with the exception of Rambure, who had been most enthusiastic in debauching the young King, and who was consequently sent to the Bastille. On enquiring about them, Louis was told they were being punished for pulling up the palings in the royal park (the expression 'arracheurs des palissades' subsequently became a popular synonym for 'pederast'). Their place was taken in the boy King's affections, until at least his sixteenth birthday, by the Duc de Trémouille, an attractive young First Gentleman of the Bedchamber and an even more predatory homosexual than Rambure.

Cardinal Fleury was to play an important part in Voltaire's life, and over many years was extremely influential in the affairs of the nation. Bishop of Fréjus since 1698, he had been made royal tutor in 1715. Tall, slim but muscular, with thick blond hair, the young King was taught by Fleury to regard physical enjoyment as not only a pleasure but a positive duty, which (as most people thought) weakened his character so that he became egocentric, reckless and careless of his role, preferring to play with his dogs, milk his cows, and spend hours at *petit point* rather than attend to his duties. Everyone who met him was impressed by the quickness of his mind, and he had no difficulty in obtaining a superficial command of history, mathematics and languages. But as a child he preferred to any kind of work the pleasure of catching, torturing and killing birds and small animals, and later hunting. In late adolescence he learned that girls could be as attractive as boys, and discreet courtiers recruited young women and trained them in sexual techniques before they were brought to his bed.

Though he must have known of Fleury's homosexuality and of the indulgence which weakened the young King's character, Voltaire nevertheless thought well of Fleury: he 'applied himself to mould the mind of his pupil to business, secrecy and probity, and preserved, amid the hurry and agitation of the court, during the minority of the King, the good graces of his own services, nor complained of others, and never engaged in cabals or intrigues of the court . . . . He privately endeavoured to make himself acquainted with the affairs of the kingdom at home and its interests abroad. In a word, the circumspection of his conduct and the amiability of his disposition made all France wish to see him at the head of the administration.'[9] Indeed, in 1726 he became in effect Prime Minister – at the age of seventy-three – and ruled the country for the following seventeen years.

Meanwhile, Voltaire's reputation continued to grow, though with a number of hiccoughs in its progress. In the spring of 1724, he supervised the production of *Mariamne*, which opened at the Comédie on 6 March with Adrienne Lecouvreur in the title role of a heroine poisoned by none other than King Herod. Against custom, Voltaire had her drink poison and die on-stage. Unfortunately, as she did so, a wag in the gallery shouted, 'The Queen's tight!', and the evening almost ended in the laughter which followed, though it was the play's obvious defects rather than the gallery humour which were responsible for its complete failure. Voltaire took to his bed with what was clearly a psychosomatic illness, and only cheered up when his friend the Duc de Richelieu (formerly Duc de Fronsac) took him off to the country, to the spa of Forges where he took the waters. He was not sanguine of their effect: they tasted like ink, and he was not convinced that ink was good for the health. He was almost recovered when news of the death in a hunting accident of another friend, the

Duc de Melun (one of Richelieu's lovers) plunged him into a new depression. He returned to Paris and tried to work on a new play, found the noise of the street outside the Bernières' townhouse insupportable, moved to furnished rooms, found them inconvenient, went back to the Bernières to find his rooms there had been ransacked and many books and papers stolen; then his skin broke out into irritating pustules which made work and rest seem equally impossible. Life had become a bad dream.

He was roused from a hypochondriacal torpor by the news that Jean-Baptiste Rousseau had the impertinence to be at work on a play on the subject of Mariamne, and that the Comédie had had the audacity to mount yet a third piece on the same subject, written by an obscure abbé (though it had happily failed even more catastrophically than his own). Working quickly and intensely, he rewrote his script, and his *Mariamne* was re-presented at the Comédie – and this time was a notable success. Its author was a happy but a sick man; determinedly sick. All those pustules and itches were symptoms, he was sure, of some fatal illness. He had never been healthy. He was only thirty, but he felt that his life was almost at an end. Death could not be far off. Relaxing as best he could with Mme de Bernières, he felt like one half of an old married couple approaching the end of their days together.

In August, Mme de Prie allowed him to mount for her a semi-dramatised reading of his latest play *L'Indiscret*, a squib which he had written while taking the waters at Forges and in which he himself appeared as a talkative village priest. She, and later the public, enjoyed it. The Queen saw *Mariamne* and was moved to tears. Voltaire must, she said, visit Poland, where his work would be much appreciated. Life might after all be worth living. But then came a problem which was common to many authors at a time when there was no such thing as the protection of copyright. A Jesuit abbé, Pierre Juyot Desfontaines, decided to make a little money by publishing his own edition of the *Henriade*, to which he added a number of frankly indifferent verses of his own. Voltaire was highly irritated, but could do little except protest that the edition had nothing to do with him.

The police then acted for him, but not on the grounds of

infringement of copyright. In April 1725, Desfontaines was arrested and accused of committing sodomy with two young chimney-sweeps. It was fruitless to deny the crime – he was not only known to be a pederast but had unwisely broadcast the fact. Now in prison, he contemplated the fact that it was not impossible that, convicted, he might be burned at the stake. Astonishingly, the only person to lift a finger to help him was Voltaire. Although (and as usual) feeling extremely unwell, he rode out to Versailles and personally implored Cardinal Fleury to spare the man. Fleury cannot have been unconscious that but for his position, he himself might have been sharing Desfontaines' imprisonment and possible fate. The abbé was released and within a month received a formal pardon. He wrote a grateful letter to Voltaire: 'I shall never forget the obligations I lie under to you: the goodness of your heart is still superior to your genius. I ought to employ my life in giving you proof of my gratitude.'[10] He did so by ever afterwards bitterly attacking Voltaire on every occasion that offered itself – proof that some men cannot be more alienated than by being forced to accept help from someone they consider an enemy.

Mme de Prie was not happy to hear that her favourite had been assisted by Fleury, with whom she and her lover the Regent were now thoroughly at odds. Knowing the Cardinal's sexual pre-dilections, encouraged by his mistress, the Duc de Bourbon started an anti-homosexual campaign, ordering the Commissioner of Police for Paris to arrest a friend of the Cardinal, a notorious sodomite, des Chaufours. Tried for sodomy, the unfortunate man was found guilty and burned at the stake. The backlash against de Bourbon and his mistress was much stronger than they had supposed possible. Their plan backfired, the Duc was exiled to Chantilly and Mme de Prie to Normandy. Her loss of power and the total boredom of life in the country so distressed her that she killed herself. Sniffing the air, Voltaire had been careful to begin to distance himself from her just before her fall from power.

Before that fall, Mme de Prie had interested herself in the matter of the young King's marriage. As a child he had been promised to Maria Ana Victoria, daughter of Philip V of Spain, who had indeed been brought to Paris when she was three years old in preparation for the promised wedding the moment she reached puberty. De Bourbon himself wanted to marry young Louis to his sister, the Princesse de Vermandois, but Mme de Prie was not entirely confident that once she was Queen the princess would be sufficiently malleable; her candidate was the penniless Maria Leszczinska, daughter of Stanislas Leszczynski, the ex-King of Poland. She persuaded her lover that his sister would be unwelcome to the influential Cardinal Fleury, whom it would be unwise to antagonise. Instead, she had Maria Leszczinska brought to Versailles, and saw to it that the girl pleased Louis in every conceivable way – so satisfactorily, indeed, that the King agreed to marry her. On 28 May 1725, Voltaire wrote to inform the Marquise de Bernières that 'yesterday at half-past ten the King declared that he would marry the Princess of Poland', and seemed very pleased. 'He gave his foot to kiss to Monsieur d'Epernon, and his arse to Monsieur de Maurepas, and received the congratulations of the whole Court.'[11] Meanwhile, the Infanta of Spain had been sent home, to the fury of King Philip.

The fifteen-year-old King and the 22-year-old Polish princess were married at Fontainebleau on 5 September 1725. He had not looked forward to the occasion, but found his bride extremely attractive, and the marriage seemed likely to be not merely satisfactory but perhaps even happy. At first, he was so enthusiastically uxorious that she employed a number of priests to attempt to persuade him to abstain from sex on saints' days. For seven years he was entirely faithful to her; then he found that his keen sexual appetite demanded more variety, and he took a number of mistresses. The first four were sisters – the Comtesse de Mailly, her sister Félicité, the less attractive Adélaide (whose wit amused him) and finally Marie Anne de Nesle de La Tournelle, the most attractive of them all; she insisted on occupying his bed in solitary state, and had her three siblings dismissed from the bedroom. Meanwhile, for five more years the Queen continued to endure a number of miscarriages and bear the King children (she had ten before illness released her from Louis's bed).

The new young Queen condescended to accept the dedication both of Œdipe and Hérode et Mariamne, as the successful later version was called. She addressed the author as 'my poor Voltaire', and granted him an unsolicited pension of 1,500 livres. By then Voltaire was beginning to establish a reputation as a wit and satirist, though as yet most of his humour was expressed in conversation rather than in writing. The intrigue of the Court was thus meat and drink to him, though it was not easy for him to satirise the goings-on, since he was in a sense part of the establishment, at least to the extent that he was by way of being a favourite of Mme de Prie, dined at her table, was much in evidence at her parties and dinners, and very probably spent some time in her bed. But if he offered no outright criticism, wrote no biting satire, he did nothing to deter readers of the *Henriade* from drawing their own conclusions about various parallels between his relation of historical events and the present state of things at Versailles. In the meanwhile, he had become a distinct favourite with the Regent's mistress.

In the summer of 1725, his position seemed as secure as it had ever been. If there were no more excellent dinners and fashionable gatherings at the house of Mme de Prie and the Regent, he was still in good odour at Court. He was able to relax and think about the future, which might perhaps involve a change of scene.

In October, he wrote from Fontainebleau to King George I of England asking permission to come to London and there to publish an edition of the *Henriade*, 'an epic poem dealing with Henry IV, the best of our kings. He is called the father of his people, and in that resembles you.' 'My work is written with freedom and truth,' he added. 'You, sire, are the protector of the one and the other, and I venture to flatter myself that you will accord me your royal protection to enable me to print in your realm a work which much be of interest to you, since it is the panegyric of virtue.'[12] No reply has been recorded, and soon enough Voltaire had other matters to attend to.

One evening an incident at the Opéra precipitated a quarrel which was to lead to an earlier visit to England than he had perhaps envisaged. A performance in December 1725 was attended both by Voltaire and by the Chevalier de Rohan-Chabot. The two men knew each other, if not well, and seem to have been reasonably friendly. But during an idle conversation in the dressing-room of the actress Adrienne Lecouvreur the chevalier addressed his acquaintance as 'Monsieur de Voltaire, Monsieur Arouet, or whatever your name is[13] . . .

I suppose you do *have* one . . . ?' Voltaire was understandably taken aback. It was a piece of gratuitous rudeness for which there was neither reason nor excuse. He made a quick reply, which has been variously reported, but which seems to have been along the lines that while the chevalier dragged his name behind him, Voltaire brought honour to his own. The chevalier raised his cane as though to strike the writer; Voltaire reached for his sword. The actress fainted, which for the moment put an end to the scene.

Voltaire's attitude to the insult is entirely understandable. He did not have the rank of chevalier, but he had every right to regard himself as a gentleman, and to take exception to the sneer. On the other hand, it might have been wise to have reined in his tongue, for the chevalier was extremely jealous of his name and family honour. A day or two later Voltaire was at dinner with his friend the Duc de Sully, when a message was brought that he was wanted at the door. Unsuspecting, he excused himself and went down – to be greeted by two bully-boys who beat him severely, while de Rohan-Chabot looked on from his carriage (and is said to have called out 'Be careful of his head – there might be something worthwhile in it!').

When the two men had finished with him, Voltaire went upstairs and appealed for help to de Sully, whom he had known since they had been schoolfellows twenty years previously. The duc shrugged his shoulders. He was not about to take sides with a mere writer against a fellow aristocrat, however long he had known Voltaire and however brilliant and entertaining he might be. Rohan was not only an extremely influential aristocrat, but members of his family held high positions in Church and State. The rest of the guests took a similar view. One of them, the Abbé de Caumartin, even made a little joke: 'Where should we be,' he asked, 'if poets didn't have backs for us to beat?' Perhaps some of the guests had actually watched the assault from a window, for the abbé had clearly noticed one of the most degrading aspects of the beating – it had been administered by a cane across the shoulders, the manner in which a naughty schoolboy would be beaten. The table sniggered. Voltaire left.

He was more angry than he had ever been in his life, his anger fuelled by the attitude of his supposed friends, whom he now saw in their true light. His anger was conspicuous, and it was soon clear that since no one seemed inclined to take his side in the quarrel, he was prepared to take his own revenge. He was seen taking lessons in swordsmanship in the company of roughs and assassins. A police report states that he was 'staying with a certain Leynault, a fencing-master in the Rue Saint-Martin, where he keeps very bad company. It is said that he is friendly with soldiers of the Guard and that various bullies visit him . . .'.[14]

In due course, the chevalier received a challenge which he was honour bound to accept, but he was careful to let a relative, Cardinal de Rohan, know of the coming duel; the latter privately complained to the Duc de Bourbon, and on the evening of 17 April 1726 Voltaire was arrested and taken to the Bastille.

The only voice raised in his favour was that of the Maréchal-duc de Villars. While agreeing that Voltaire should not have insulted the chevalier, he nevertheless rebuked the latter for having the young writer beaten, and took exception to the fact that it was the more injured man who now found himself in prison. Perhaps swayed by the argument, Louis de Bourbon wrote to the Governor of the Bastille instructing him to treat Voltaire with courtesy and respect, and the prisoner found himself in apartments furnished with tables and chairs from the King's own collection, and was allowed to receive visitors. One can only guess what his opinion was of the many Parisians who, having failed to sympathise with him – much less support him – in the recent argument, now vied with each other to obtain permission to call upon him in his luxurious prison cell. So many did so, indeed, that the numbers had to be limited and timed tickets issued. It is not unlikely that the sympathy which the public now seemed to be showing to an unjustly imprisoned man persuaded the government to agree to his request that he should be allowed to leave the country in order to visit England. It was also convenient for the authorities to release him rather than appear to countenance a duel between a commoner and an aristocrat. The order for his release was given on 29 April, and on 1 May Voltaire left the Bastille and was escorted by his friends Mme de Bernières and Nicolas Thiériot to Calais where he took ship for Greenwich.

4

England and Philosophy

*In England it is thought well to kill an admiral from
time to time to encourage the others.*

Candide

The 32-year-old who stood on the deck of a ship making its way
up the Thames to Greenwich on 28 May 1726 experienced
a strange mixture of emotions. Before leaving France, he had written
to a friend:

> It seems very likely I shall never see you again . . . . There are only
> two things left for me to do with my life: one is to risk it
> honourably when I can, and the other is to end it in the obscurity
> of some retreat consonant with my way of thinking, my
> misfortunes, and the knowledge I have of men.[1]

Yet as his ship sailed upstream, the river a-bustle with traffic, his heart
lifted at the sight spread out before him. The Thames was a city on its
own account: two rows of merchant ships were moored on each bank
for 6 miles upstream to Greenwich, where his ship tied up. Flags on-
shore and pennants on ship-board dipped as a barge of musicians
passed, leading the golden royal barge bearing King George I on a
sixty-fifth birthday outing, a crowd of little boats scurrying after, many
of them rowed by oarsmen in livery with the silver badges of the
rivermen on their shoulders. It was a perfect spring morning under
blue and cloudless skies, a soft west wind gently blowing, and he was

47

actually in England, the England he had celebrated in the *Henriade*, to the dismay of his fellow-countrymen.

Voltaire was unable entirely to free himself from the effect of Rohan's scornful gibe and the beating that had followed, indeed it still rankled so much with him that in August he crept back to Paris in the hope of finding and punishing the man; fortunately, he failed – 'the instincts of a poltroon hid him from me as if he had divined that I was on his tracks', he told Thiériot.[2] But what really rankled with him was the fact that the men whom he thought were his friends – the Duc de Sully, the Duc d'Orléans, the Prince de Conti and the rest – had shown so plainly that for them he was little more than a clever performing monkey. Even Mme de Bernières had let him down by appearing at the opera with Rohan not long after he had left Paris for London. His deep feeling of shame was based not only on his sense of betrayal, but on the fact that he had been so silly as to take his aristocratic acquaintances at face value. He did not make that mistake again.

His emotional confusion was increased by the feeling that he was now in middle life and had not yet achieved a solid reputation. He was being a little unjust to himself: his name, after all, was familiar throughout France, and sufficiently well known in England for the *British Journal* of 14 May 1726 to publish a paragraph announcing his arrival:

> On the 3rd instant M. de Voltaire was released from the Bastille and conducted as far as Calais, being allowed to go over into England, and forbid to come within fifty leagues of the Court. 'Tis said he will publish at London a large edition of his famous poem of the League, whereof we have only an imperfect copy.

Nevertheless, it was now eleven years since his early satires had brought him to the notice of those who enjoyed witty and slightly scandalous literature; eight years since the successful production and publication of *Œdipe* had made his name, and though this had been followed by *Artémire* and by the more or less public readings and clandestine publication of *La Henriade*, which had made him even better known ('celebrated' would be the wrong word), all that was somehow unsatisfying, unsatisfactory. When he suggested that he might end his life in obscurity, he was not merely dramatising.

His escape from France was a psychological as well as a physical one. He had no idea how long he was likely to spend there (it was to be almost three years), nor had he any particular plans apart, that is, from the ambition to publish the *Henriade* openly. But he needed a change, and a change which would lift his spirits. His first day in London did nothing in that way. After the brilliance of the scene which had greeted him at Greenwich, he found his first experience of society unappealing: the ladies to whom he was introduced (probably at Lord Bolingbroke's house in Pall Mall on his first evening in the city) made no attempt at interesting conversation, confining themselves over tea to slanderous gossip about people of whom he had never heard – when they were not talking about the weather. Next day he was taken to a coffee-house, where he was outraged when news of the suicide of a young woman was greeted with banter and sarcasm.

He went straight from Pall Mall to Wandsworth, to stay for several months with an Englishman whose acquaintance he had made in Paris. Everard, later Sir Everard, Falkener[3] was a silk and cloth merchant, an amiable collector of coins and medals. Though he was a commoner, his intelligence led to his appointment as British ambassador in Constantinople, and later still as confidential secretary to the Duke of Cumberland. In Wandsworth Voltaire led 'an obscure and charming life . . . quite given over to the pleasures of indolence and friendship,' as he wrote (in English) to Thiériot.[4]

The decade of the 1720s was in England not one of spectacular achievement, but there was quite sufficient going on in the field of the arts to keep Voltaire interested: Daniel Defoe published *Moll Flanders* and Sir Richard Steele produced *The Conscious Lovers*; James Gibbs had just seen his greatest achievement in architecture, the church of St Martin in the Fields completed; Lord Burlington and William Kent collaborated to produce the delicious fantasy which is Chiswick House, finished while Voltaire was in London, though the wonderful gardens Kent designed for it were still to be laid out; John Playford had all London dancing to the music from his *The Dancing*

Masters – a great compilation of no less than nine hundred dances. There was much to be seen, many people to meet, much to be done, and gradually Voltaire inserted himself into London society.

The first months of Voltaire's stay in England, however, brought nothing to lift his depression: he received news that his beloved sister Marie-Marguerite had died – he had always believed, in his hypochondriacal way, that he would outlive her; and then he faced a financial crisis when a Jewish banker on whom he had a letter of credit for 20,000 francs went bankrupt, and not yet in possession of the money his father had meant for him, he found himself short of funds. When the news got around, King George generously sent his distinguished visitor a present of 100 guineas (underlining for us the fact that the Frenchman really was well thought of in London). The generosity of other Englishmen matched that of the King. Falkener assured him that Wandsworth could be his home for as long as he wished to stay, and his other friend Lord Bolingbroke offered his hospitality should the visitor feel in need of a change of air. Voltaire was properly grateful, though perhaps faintly shocked to discover that his friend was cutting a swathe through the prostitutes of London. Bolingbroke was as great a whoremaster as he was a statesman, he noted; when the news got around that he had been made Secretary at War, the whores 'cried out with joy, God bless us, five thousand pounds all among us'. However, the rake was a sympathetic host who, as Voltaire already knew, shared many of his own views, in particular with respect to religion, regarding the Old Testament as a farrago of nonsense and lies,[5] and proposing that 'we ought always to be unbelieving . . . In religion, government, and philosophy we ought to distrust everything that is established.'[6]

Voltaire forced himself to relax and turned to the business of learning the English language. He seems to have done this, as Dickens was to learn French during the next century, by regularly attending the theatres – there are anecdotes of his sitting by the prompter at the side of the stage at Drury Lane with a copy of the text of the play being performed, and carefully following the lines as the actors spoke them. His diligence paid off very quickly; he was soon able to converse freely in English, and within four months of his arrival in the country was able to write a letter in the language. His command of spoken English made it easy, too, for him to move in society: he was presented at Court in January 1727, an event noted in the columns of the *Daily Journal* for 27 January:

> Last week M. Voltaire, the famous French poet, who was banished from France, was introduced to his majesty, who received him very graciously. They say he has received notice from France not to print his Poems of the League; a prosecution still depending against him, by the Cardinal de Bissy, on account of the praises bestowed in that Book on Queen Elizabeth's behaviour in matters of religion, and a great many strokes against the abuse of popery and against persecution in matters of faith.

Soon he counted among his acquaintances the Duchess of Marlborough and Lord and Lady Hervey. Lady Hervey, formerly Molly Lepell, was a great beauty, and Voltaire celebrated the fact by writing a set of verses in English:

> Hervey, would you know the passion
>   You have kindled in my breast?
> Trifling is the inclination
>   That by words can be express'd.
>
> In my silence see the lover;
>   True love is by silence known;
> In my eyes you'll best discover
>   All the powers you own.

He visited the Duchess of Marlborough at Blenheim. She had just quarrelled with her former great friend Queen Anne, and when Voltaire asked her if he might see the manuscript of her memoirs which she was said to be completing, he was told, 'One moment, I'm just altering my account of Queen Anne's character'. He was also received by the Prince of Wales; his Court was carefully separated from that of his father, whom he detested (the feeling was mutual).

This introduction was fortuitous, for later in the year George I died and Voltaire found himself on terms with his successor, George II, and with Queen Caroline who talked with him in excellent French.

He met, of course, many of the chief literary men of the time including Colley Cibber (who was to become Poet Laureate), John Gay, who had just finished the libretto of *The Beggar's Opera*, and read it to his visitor (who later went to a performance) and the playwright William Congreve. He read widely in the work of other English writers: Milton, Lord Hervey (so scathing about the state of the nation: 'any man of fashion or condition is almost as much ashamed to own himself a Christian as formerly he would have been to profess himself none'[7]), Edmund Waller, Sir John Denham, Sir William Temple and Lord Rochester.

His relationship with those English writers he encountered was cordial without being particularly close. He made an attempt to ingratiate himself with Pope, who some years before had been complimentary about the *Henriade*. Hearing of the collapse of a bridge which had thrown the poet in his carriage into a stream and damaged the fingers of his right hand, Voltaire wrote an extravagant letter in his still slightly imperfect English:

> The water you fell in was not Hippocrene's water, otherwise it would have respected you. Indeed J am concerned beyond expression for the danger you have been in, and more for your wounds. Is it possible that those fingers which have written the rape of the lock, and the Criticism, which have dressed Homer so becomingly in an English coat, should have been so barbarously treated . . . . J hope ser you are now perfectly recovered. Rely your accident concers me as much as all the disasters of a master ought to affect his scholar. J am sincerely ser with the admiration which you deserve, Your most humble servant, Voltaire.[8]

The hyperbole seems rather to have frightened Pope, who nevertheless invited the Frenchman to visit him at Twickenham. They did not warm to each other, though Voltaire always spoke of the poet with respect, and much admired his *Dunciad* (a mock-epic attack on those poets who were the favourite sons of the Goddess of Dullness) which came out while he was in England. Rumours that Voltaire's behaviour struck Pope and his mother as less than gentlemanly were chiefly put about by Dr Johnson, who suggested that he described problems with his bowels with too much freedom, and also blasphemed. One must remember that Johnson disliked Voltaire on account of his alleged atheism, though certainly Voltaire always enjoyed talking about his various ailments.

The visitor arranged to meet Isaac Newton, but the great scientist, whom Voltaire was to celebrate in the *Letters on England*, died before the meeting could take place. Voltaire attended his funeral in Westminster Abbey and was much impressed by England's celebration of the life and accomplishments of a man who, he was convinced, would have been treated with less respect in France, where the Church would have denigrated his achievements.

He went to the theatre for pleasure as well as to familiarise himself with the language, though he seems not to have enjoyed much of what he saw, allegedly complaining that 'English plays are like English puddings – nobody has any taste for them but themselves'.[9] He saw *The Beggar's Opera*, heard the popular singers Sensino and Cuzzoni in Handel operas at the Haymarket, and watched the fabled actress Mrs Oldfield perform Shakespeare, admiring her both for her acting and her majestic command of the stage.[10] The national poet presented him with a peculiar problem: he recognised Shakespeare's genius, but had very great reservations: 'He had a strong and fertile genius, full of naturalness and sublimity, without the slightest spark of good taste or the least knowledge of the rules', and believed that the only reason his plays continued to be performed was because 'there are such fine scenes, such grand and terrible parts interspersed in those monstrous farces called tragedies, that his plays have always been acted with great success'. Shakespeare was so bad, in other words, because he was so good.

Voltaire found it impossible to understand how an author could have written into *Hamlet* a scene in which 'gravediggers dig a grave, swallowing drinks and singing popular songs, cracking jokes typical of men of their calling about the skulls they come across', and in *Julius*

Caesar have included 'the jokes of Roman shoemakers and cobblers, introduced on the stage with Brutus and Cassius . . .'.[11] This in plays which were described as tragedies! It outraged all convention – really, Shakespeare had destroyed the English dramatic tradition! Infinitely preferable were such plays as Addison's *Cato of Utica*, which followed 'the rules' and was 'written from end to end with elegance . . . a masterpiece in diction and beauty of verse'. Shakespeare might have been a perfect poet had he lived in the age of Addison, rather than in the barbarous Elizabethan age.

Voltaire's view of the British dramatist's work was complex and has been the subject of much argument among critics.[12] This began as early as 1769, when Elizabeth Montagu, whom Dr Johnson called 'the Queen of the Bluestockings', published *An Essay on the writings and Genius of Shakespear, compared with the Greek and French Dramatic Poets. With some Remarks upon the Mis-representations of Mons. De Voltaire*. But it is at least certainly true that while he never hesitated to criticise what he saw as the writer's faults, Voltaire was almost singlehandedly responsible for making the French public aware of Shakespeare's existence and stature.

His judgement of the drama was sounder when it came to contemporary comedy. He greatly admired William Wycherley, the author of *The Plain Dealer* and *The Country Wife*. Wycherley 'moved in the highest society, knew all about its vices and painted them with the most firm hand and in the truest colours'. John Vanbrugh had also written well, but 'of all the English, the one who carried the glory of the comic theatre to the greatest heights is the late Mr Congreve . . . . The rules of the theatre are rigorously observed; the plays are full of characters differentiated with extreme subtlety, you don't encounter the slightest coarse joke, everywhere you find the language of well-mannered people with the actions of rogues, which proves that he knew his world and lived in what is called good society.'[13]

Voltaire was particularly pleased to meet Congreve (who had written nothing since his masterpiece, *The Way of the World*, was produced in 1700), though he rather disapproved of the playwright's attitude to his work: 'He had one failing, which was that he did not rank [himself] highly enough in his profession, that of a writer, which had made his reputation and fortune. He spoke of his works as trifles beneath him, and in our first conversation he told me to think of him as a gentleman who lived very simply. I answered him that if he had had the misfortune of being just a gentleman like any other I would never have come to see him, and I was very shocked at such misplaced vanity.'[14]

His comments on English literature in general are sparing and variable. He greatly admired Dryden, Rochester, Bishop Burnet (the author of A History of My Own Time), the Scottish poet James Thomson, and Samuel Butler – particularly the latter's satirical poem Hudibras (no doubt chiefly because of its unsparing attack on the Puritans). However, he thought the non-English-speaking French reader would forever be deprived of it, for though 'of all the books I have ever read, it is the one in which I have found the most wit . . . it is also the most untranslatable . . . it would need a running commentary, and a joke explained ceases to be a joke'.[15] This was why he considered 'the ingenious' Dean Swift also untranslatable.

He met Swift and was able to tell him how much he admired The Tale of a Tub, though he kept to himself the fact that he thought the second half of Gulliver's Travels tailed off badly, the writer's invention becoming strained and the wit less telling. All the same, Gulliver was a fine book, and he tried to interest Thiériot in translating it; but, constitutionally lazy, his friend ignored the suggestion. Voltaire and Swift liked each other, and Voltaire's compliments to the Irishman were more sincere than those to Pope (though he wrote frankly of the latter as 'the most elegant, the most correct and, what is much more, the most musical poet England has ever had [who] reduces the harsh blarings of the English trumpet to the soft sounds of the flute . . .').[16] Swift, he thought, was a greater writer than Rabelais, to whom he had been compared. 'He lacks, it is true, the gaiety of the earlier writer, but he has all the finesse, reason, discrimination and good taste lacking in our Curé of Meudon.[17] His poems have a strange and almost inimitable flavour, he is full of good fun in verse and prose alike . . .'.[18]

The homage paid by the English to their men of letters, and to their artists in general, much impressed Voltaire. In Westminster Abbey (where they had buried not only the great scientist Newton but the great actress Mrs Oldfield, who died not long after he saw her perform) there were not only statues to statesmen, aristocrats and royalty, but to authors. The English respect for the arts was something the French would do well to copy.

But apart from talking with the great men of the day, Voltaire spent many hours simply looking around at ordinary life in the country about which he had been so curious for so long, and meeting a number of humbler folk. He was especially interested in the conduct of religious life in England, and was to write amusingly and perspicaciously about it in *Letters on England*, or *Lettres philosophiques* as his collection of essays was called when published in France. The collection opens, indeed, with a delightful account of the life and manners of the Quakers, and in particular of a visit to the home in Hampstead of Andrew Pitt, an elderly Quaker at whom he could not resist poking a little gentle fun, though he found him enormously sympathetic – 'Never in my life have I seen a more dignified or more charming manner than his.'

Voltaire's description of their meeting and conversation is full of sympathetic humour and charm:

He kept his hat on while receiving me and moved towards me without even the slightest bow, but there was more politeness in the frank, kindly expression on his face than there is in the custom of placing one leg behind the other and holding in one's hand what is meant for covering one's head. 'Friend,' he said, 'I see thou art a stranger; if I can be of any use to thee thou hast but to say so.' 'Sir,' I said, bending my body and sliding one foot towards him as our custom is, 'I flatter myself that my natural curiosity will not displease you and that you will be so kind as to do me the honour of telling me about your religion.' 'Thy countrymen,' he replied, 'do too much bowing and scraping, but so far I have never seen one with as much curiosity. Come in and let us eat together first.'[19]

Describing their conversation in his book, which was heavily based on descriptive letters he wrote in English to Thiériot, Voltaire could not resist sarcasm (though never at the expense of the good old man):

I started with the question that good Catholics have more than once asked Huguenots: 'My dear Sir, have you been baptised?' 'No,' answered the Quaker, 'and neither have my fellow Friends.' 'What? Good God!' I went on, 'so you are not Christians?' 'My son,' he gently expostulated, 'do not swear. We are Christians and try to be good Christians, but we do not think Christianity consists in throwing cold water on somebody's head, with a pinch of salt.' 'God Almighty!' I said, outraged by this impiety . . . For the love of God, let me baptise you and make you a Christian!'[20]

The Quaker calmly enquired whether Voltaire had been circumcised, as Christ had circumcised Timothy. 'Friend, thou art a Christian without being circumcised, and I am one without being baptised.'

They went on to talk about the Quakers' dress code and archaic forms of address, and Voltaire was invited to attend a Quaker meeting, which he reported very fully, again with mild, sympathetic amusement: after a long silence

eventually one of them rose, doffed his hat, and after making a few faces and fetching a few sighs he recited, half through his mouth and half through his nose, a rigmarole taken from the Gospels, or so he believed, of which neither he nor anyone else understood a word. When this contortionist had finished his fine monologue and the assembly had broken up, edified and quite baffled, I asked my friend why the wiser among them put up with such silliness. 'We have to tolerate it,' he said, 'because we cannot tell whether a man who rises to speak will be inspired by the spirit or by folly. When in doubt we listen patiently to it all and even let women speak.'[21]

Voltaire remained in touch with Pitt for many years; they exchanged letters and even presents. He was less entranced by the Presbyterians and the way of life they recommended and attempted to impose – their influence was in his opinion perfidious:

These gentry, who have a few churches in England, have brought solemn and austere airs into fashion in this country. It is to them that we owe the sanctification of Sunday in the three kingdoms. On that day both work and play are forbidden, which is double the severity of Catholic Churches. There are no operas, plays or concerts in London on Sunday, even cards are so expressly forbidden that only people of standing and what are called respectable people, play on that day. The rest of the nation goes to the sermon, the tavern and the ladies of the town.[22]

Fortunately, however, the English were a tolerant and pragmatic people, and did not allow religion to interfere too considerably in their lives – particularly their business lives. At the Stock Exchange men of all religions did business happily together:

Here the Presbyterian trusts the Anabaptist and the Anglican accepts a promise from the Quaker. On leaving these peaceful and free assemblies some go to the Synagogue and others for a drink, this one goes to be baptised in a great bath in the name of the Father, Son and Holy Ghost, that one has his son's foreskin cut and has some Hebrew words he doesn't understand mumbled over the child, others go to their church and await the inspiration of God with their hats on, and everybody is happy. If there were only one religion in England there would be danger of despotism, if there were two they would cut each other's throats, but there are thirty, and they live in peace and happiness.[23]

There was one more encounter, rather more unusual, which is worth recording: he met again the delicious Suzanne Livry. She had been dismissed from the Comédie Française for her lack of talent as an actress and had come to England determined to succeed there. Alas, she found no one to employ her in the theatre, but she did find herself a suitor, the French Marquis de Gouvernet, whose offer of financial assistance she refused. He gave her three lottery tickets, and had a false list of winners printed which showed her as one of them. Whether captivated by his ingenuity or his generosity, she agreed to marry him, became the Marquise de La Tour du Pin-Gouvernet and lived happily ever after. Her relationship with Voltaire was never renewed, however; when he called on her and her husband in Paris, servants sent him packing. He was puzzled, but it seems likely that she had been offended by his poem *Le Tu et le Vu*, in which he had gently chided her for her snobbishness (she had continually insisted on her aristocratic lineage) and teased her by addressing her by the familiar '*tu*' instead of '*vous*'.

He found the English as a whole rather cold, their characters difficult to grasp. In his poem about Joan of Arc, *La Pucelle*, he spoke of their having '*dans leur caractère / Je ne sais quoi de dur et insulaire*' – 'something hard and insular in their character'. And in the same poem he observes the '*Parfait anglais, voyageant sans dessein / Achetant cher des modernes antiques; / Regardant tout avec un air hautain . . .*' – 'the perfect Englishman, travelling purposelessly, buying expensive fake antiques; looking haughtily around at everything . . .'.

But he nevertheless enjoyed meeting and talking to people from all ranks of life, while still finding time to work – he was diligent in making notes about the Quakers, the Presbyterians, the Anti-Trinitarians, the theatre, the strange English habit of inoculating babies against smallpox and other aspects of public life and culture,[24] and in particular the work of Newton and Locke. At the same time he began an abortive play in English on the subject of the Roman consul Lucius Brutus, the legendary figure who supposedly founded the Roman republic, and a translation of Shakespeare's *Julius Caesar* which never got beyond the second act. He also began to block out the biography of Charles XII of Sweden which he was intent on writing (the Duchess of Marlborough helpfully told him of the Duke's meeting with King Charles, and Bolingbroke introduced him to a Baron Fabrice, who had known him). An absolute monarch who ruled his kingdom between 1697 and 1718, Charles appealed strongly to Voltaire as a subject for biography not only because of the remarkable domestic reforms he put into force, but because of his character – he had been interested not only in architecture, painting and poetry but also in mathematics and science. He also wrote and published in 1727 a lengthy essay on *The Civil Wars in France*, which was actually a sort of prologue to the *Henriade* and indeed was advertised as such: for it announced that the latter was now 'almost entirely printed, nothing being wanting but the printing of the Cuts,[25] which I must recommend here as particular Master-pieces of Art in their Kind: 'tis the only Beauty in the Book, that I can answer for'.

He worked hard at raising a subscription for the publication of the *Henriade*, with some help from the Duke of Newcastle, who had been encouraged to assist him by Horatio Walpole (Sir Horace Walpole's brother) who contributed a note explaining that no one should be put off by the fact that Voltaire had been imprisoned in the Bastille, for that had been the result of a personal quarrel rather than for any political offence. The subscription list opened in January 1728. Three hundred and forty-four subscribers paid one guinea in advance and two more on publication – a very considerable sum – and George II gave Voltaire a generous present (said to amount to 500 guineas) towards publication. The book itself, splendidly bound and with magnificent illustrations, came out in March, gracefully dedicated to Queen Caroline:

> Madame, it is the fate of Henry the Fourth to be protected by the Queens of England. He was assisted by that famous Elizabeth, who was in her Age the Glory of her Sex, and the Pattern of Sovereigns. By whom can his Memory be so well protected, as by her in whom Elizabeth revives?

The publication was an enormous success. A certain amount of notoriety accompanied it, and the fact that the book had been banned in France as anti-Catholic certainly did it no harm, though some of those who read it regretted the fact that Voltaire failed actually to condemn Catholicism. The Duc de Sully was none too pleased with it when he eventually saw it, for every single reference to his great ancestor, the friend and minister of Henry IV, had been removed – there was not a single mention of him in the book, despite his importance to the age. So Voltaire revenged himself on the descendant who had betrayed him. The publication alone made Voltaire's visit to England very well worth while. When he returned to France in March 1729 he was able to feel himself financially secure.

From a different perspective, the visit had also been successful –

perhaps even more successful than Voltaire appreciated at the time. He had arrived in England with great expectations – one might suppose they were even too high to be fulfilled; but this was not the case. If he had fallen in love with the country before he ever left France, that love was consummated during the years he spent abroad. One of the reasons for this was negative: the contrast between the social and political atmosphere in England and that of France. Exchanging the intolerance of his native country for what he saw as the almost complete freedom of the people of England was an inspiriting experience. Repression of original thought, religious intolerance and a general denigration of the creative artist were exchanged for relative freedom of expression, religious tolerance and, despite certain restrictions placed on authors (Defoe, for instance, had been pilloried for a satirical pamphlet), an enviable degree of freedom for the country's writers and thinkers. Voltaire was also struck by the difference in the law relating to taxation: in France, the aristocracy and higher clergy were relieved of all payment of taxes, while in England they were forced to play their part in supporting the social and financial fabric of the country.

The main achievement of Voltaire's years in England was his development as a philosopher and thinker, and the crystallisation of his views on two subjects: religion and science. He had long disliked the Catholic Church's intolerance in France, his detestation of religious bigotry fuelled by his experience of its apogee in the behaviour of his Jansenist brother. In England, the established Church was not perhaps greatly to be admired, with its often indolent, rich clergy and its great stores of wealth. But at least in that country different religious views were tolerated. 'This is the land of sects,' he was to write; 'an Englishman, as a free man, goes to Heaven by whatever route he likes.'[26] Quakers and members of other sects were free from oppression. Since the one certain thing about God was that if He indeed existed His nature was unknowable, it was surely ludicrous that any man or organisation should impose their view of Him upon anyone else. For his part, Voltaire was inclined to believe that there probably was a God, and that at all events it was necessary in the interest of sanity for man to live as though there were – for otherwise the meaninglessness of the universe would be crushing. In fact, as he famously put it, 'If God did not exist, it would be necessary to invent Him.'

He could not have expected this view to be welcomed in France; but he had some hope of impressing his fellow-countrymen with another aspect of life in England – the respect of the best men in that country for forward-thinking philosophical and scientific thinkers. Voltaire had been especially impressed by the work of three men: Isaac Newton, John Locke and Francis Bacon, all of whom he was to celebrate in his *Letters Concerning the English Nation*, published in England in 1733, and a year later in France as *Lettres philosophiques sur les Anglais*.

5

Dignity and Impudence

The composition of a tragedy requires testicles.
On being asked why no woman had ever written a good tragedy;
quoted in letter from Byron to John Murray, 2 April 1817

Voltaire returned to France on 15 March 1729. For some reason known only to himself he avoided Paris and settled down instead on its outskirts, in a hovel in Saint-Germain-en-Laye, a little town on the Seine.

It would have been pardonable had he been in an extremely bad temper. While in England he had continued to keep in touch with Thiériot, the nondescript, talentless, lazy ne'er-do-well who had shared his student days in Caen. Unwisely, in 1728 he had entrusted him with the arrangements for the official publication in Paris of the *Henriade*. Thiériot had managed to raise only eighty subscriptions; then when one Sunday he uncharacteristically decided to go to mass – an exercise he very rarely performed – there was an alleged burglary at his apartment and every copy of the book vanished, later to be sold to the public by some person or persons unknown.

There seems little doubt that Thiériot himself stole the edition and profited considerably from it, but Voltaire, who had returned from London on 15 March, did nothing, instead sympathising with his friend about the burglary, giving no hint that he thought the story was contrived, and had enough extra copies of the poem printed to make sure that every subscriber received one. No more was said about the unfortunate affair. This was typical of his relationship with Thiériot;

however often he was betrayed or let down by that dishonest man, he forgave him again and again, describing him right up to his death as 'my old friend'. When someone later suggested that Thiériot might have been less than honest, Voltaire simply said that he had after all been very young at the time. In 1728, the man was thirty-three. One would hesitate to accuse Voltaire of sentimentalism, but certainly his feeling for his 'old friend' time and time again overcame his common sense.

Despite the difficulties of publication and the consequent restrictions on circulation, it was the *Henriade* which made Voltaire's reputation; nothing before, and nothing after – with the possible exception of *Candide* – had quite the same effect. Until the poem became known, Voltaire had remained a promising but lightweight writer of plays and occasional poems; now those who read it immediately recognised a major talent, and the author was on his way to becoming what in a very few years he was generally recognised to be – the first writer of Europe.

If it is difficult for any reader, even a French reader loyal to his great compatriot, to read the *Henriade* with pleasure today, it is because Voltaire is not to twenty-first-century taste a great, or perhaps even a good poet, though he was revered by almost every contemporary critic. Lord Chesterfield thought the *Henriade* unparalleled by any contemporary work and the view was not uncommon up to the middle of the nineteenth century, with such punctilious critics as Matthew Arnold considering Voltaire a great poet. Our trouble – the difficulty for twenty-first-century readers – is that he was wedded to 'good taste' in prosody: to a style largely devoid of imaginative imagery and metaphor. His lines march forward uniformly and with a remorseless, suave rhythm, his meaning never in doubt, but with never a touch of imagination, rarely a memorable image. Even when his arguments are at their most impassioned, there is an almost complete absence of emotion. That is replaced by irony and cool conviction. It is difficult today to understand the very real veneration for Voltaire as a poet which the *Henriade* stimulated, but that it was the foundation-stone of his reputation cannot be doubted.[1]

In Saint-Germain-en-Laye, he waited to hear what sort of reception awaited him in the city. Then he managed to persuade

Maurepas to give him permission to live in Paris, and for a while settled in a house in the Rue de Vaugirard, which does not seem to have been especially salubrious. There was, though, evidently plenty of street entertainment, for Voltaire composed on behalf of fifteen of his neighbours a letter of complaint to René Herault, head of the Paris police, about a woman called Travers, who 'continues to create a public scandal pushed to the last extremity, getting drunk every day, beating her neighbours, calling on the name of God, which she interjects into the most infamous talk, entirely uncovering her nakedness, and showing that which decency forbids to name . . .'.[2] He was by no means short of money, and it may be that he thought a display of poverty might prove helpful in persuading the King to continue his pension. He was not long left in doubt: almost immediately he heard that this useful income was to cease.

He set about repairing the damage, and almost immediately brought off a financial coup of the first order. He was at dinner one evening when the conversation turned to the reorganisation of the state lottery. The mathematician La Condamine argued that anyone who bought all the tickets would make a fortune. Forthwith Voltaire set up a syndicate which collected over 1 million livres, with which they did indeed buy up all the tickets. His share of the profits – as 'onlie begetter' of the scheme – was 500,000 livres, or about a million francs. The lottery organisers were furious and refused to pay, but were forced by law to hand over the money.

Probably wisely, Voltaire decided that this might be a good time to travel for a while, and so went to take the waters at Plombières. On the way, he heard that the Duc de Lorraine had issued some bonds which had become so profitable that no one outside Lorraine was permitted to buy them. He instantly turned off the road to Plombières and made for Nancy, where he spent several days attempting to negotiate the purchase of a bundle of the bonds in spite of being unwell. At first nothing he said or did worked, but then 'after pressing entreaties they allowed me to subscribe for fifty shares, which were delivered to me a week later because of the lucky similarity of my name to that of a gentleman of His Royal Highness's; for no foreigner was allowed to buy them. I profited at once by the demand for this paper; I tripled my gold.'[3] At the same time he succeeded in obtaining his share of his father's estate, and moreover managed to persuade the Queen to restore the pension she had formerly given him.

These sums were welcome additions to his capital, and he was always concerned to bolster both income and capital when he could. He could not exactly be described as a miser – he spent very freely when he felt either the need or the inclination; papers discovered late last century revealed that between 1759 and 1768 he spent well over a million francs.[4] But he was always concerned to make sure that he was at least comfortably off, and exercised great shrewdness to that end. Apart from his careful investments, often made on the recommen-dation of friendly advisors, he lent money on excellent terms; later, when he had room at the château of Cirey, he collected pictures on a grand scale – works by Tiepolo, Watteau, Teniers, Albani and others. He died a rich man, after a lifetime of careful investment.

Well satisfied by his two financial coups, he now gave up the idea of a cure, and returned to Paris, where he began negotiations to stage his play *Brutus*, which had largely been written in England.

The Brutus in question was not Julius Caesar's friend, but Lucius Junius Brutus, the fifth-century Roman consul. The main thrust of the play was republican, and such an argument for democracy as had never before been staged in France. This upset the theatre management. Moreover, the Chevalier de Rohan, who had been responsible for his exile, had heard of the attempt to stage it and intrigued to prevent it. In the end, the play made its way on to the stage on 11 December 1730, when it was only a moderate success (though later it was recognised as one of Voltaire's better plays). A main part was played by a fifteen-year-old actress, Marie Anne Dangeville, who made a greater success than the play itself, and was thanked by Voltaire. On the morning after the first night he wrote to her in appreciation and with some good advice:

The play is unworthy of you, but be sure that you are going to acquire much glory in clothing my rôle of Tullie with your charms. The success of the play will be due to you. But to achieve this remember not to rush everything, to animate everything, to mingle sighs with your declamation, to leave long pauses. Above all perform the final couplet of your first act with much feeling and fire. Act the last curtain with terror, tears and long pauses. Appear desperate, and all your rivals will despair. Goodbye, prodigy . . . . For heaven's sake be calm. Even if things do not go well, what matter? You are only fifteen, and all that they could say would be that you are not yet what you will be one day.[5]

Meanwhile, Voltaire had received permission (the royal '*privilège*') to publish his *Histoire de Charles XII, roi de Suède*. He hoped that it would attract the favourable attention of the Queen, whose father Stanislas was mentioned favourably in it. And surely neither Church nor King could complain about its content. There were 2,500 copies printed, but before they could be distributed permission was withdrawn, the copies were seized by the censors and the book banned. The reason given was that France needed to placate the present King of Poland, who had been Charles's antagonist.

Voltaire decided to have the book quietly reprinted in Rouen and circulate it clandestinely, as he had successfully done with the *Henriade*. He gave out that he was making another visit to England to stay with friends in Canterbury, and went off to the Hôtel de Mantes, under the shadow of the Cathedral, and lived quietly in the guise of an English tourist while correcting the proofs, at the same time working on a final draft of *Le Mort de César* and writing a new play, *Ériphyle* (later produced, but a complete failure). The biography of Charles was issued, and was a great success with the public.

He had been much affected by the sudden death in March of the handsome and talented Adrienne Lecouvreur; she had died in his arms, only three days after she had played Jocasta in his *Œdipe*. As an actress, she was not allowed burial in hallowed ground, although on her deathbed she had signed a paper promising never to appear on any stage again – a priest attending her falsely guaranteed that this would ensure her a Christian burial. Upon the midnight after her death, when Voltaire and her lover the Comte d'Argental had left the house, the body of the pre-eminent tragedienne of her time, who was beloved by everyone in Paris with an interest in theatre, was taken on the orders of the Church to waste land near the Seine, placed in a hastily dug grave, covered with quicklime and buried.

Voltaire was outraged, not least because he was vividly aware of the contrast between the ignominious disposal of his friend's body and the magnificent funeral accorded Anne Oldfield in Westminster Abbey. He wrote a scathing poem on the occasion, *La Mort de Mlle Lecouvreur*, in which he condemned the Church for its actions, speaking of ' . . . *la flétrissante injure / Qu'à ces arts désolés font des prêtres cruels*' – 'the degrading injury done to the mourning arts by cruel priests', and pointing out that in England Lecouvreur would have been interred in the company of kings and heroes.

> *Ah! Verrai-je toujours ma faible nation,*
> *Incertaine en ses vœux, flétrir ce qu'elle admire . . .?*[6]

> [Ah! Shall I always see my wretched country
> Uncertain in its aspirations, defile what it admires?]

The ordinary people of Paris passed the verses approvingly from hand to hand. The clergy were furious and attempted to persuade the authorities to arrest Voltaire, though he denied authorship and in any case it was obvious that opinion was so strongly on his side that any action against him might well have resulted in public disorder. He thought it wise to go into hiding until the dust settled, but by 1731 was back in Paris reading his *La Mort de César* to his friend René de Maisons and at the same time making clandestine arrangements for the circulation of 2,500 copies of *Charles XII*, which were smuggled into the city by barge. It was avidly read from the start and reprinted ten times during the following decade. Generally seen as a new departure in biography, certainly in retrospect it marked a new approach to the subject.

Previously, when authors wrote the lives of kings they did so, so to speak, on their knees. The events of a royal life were baldly set out (or manipulated or suppressed when they showed their subject in a bad light); little background was supplied, and a dumb air of respectful congratulation lay over the pages. Voltaire was perfectly willing to be disrespectful, and bearing in mind that he had at the same time to consider carefully whether he was providing the authorities with material for another suppression or prosecution, he was extraordinarily critical of the whole idea of kingship. His attitude to biography was much nearer that of Lytton Strachey in England (the comparison has been made before) than that of any previous French writer.

For the following twelve months he lay very low and concentrated on his writing. Of all the work he did during that time, the most significant was a play which was to become the greatest theatrical success of his lifetime. He is said to have written *Zaïre* in just over three weeks, very probably at the Paris mansion of the Comtesse de Fontaine-Martel, a rather unattractive old lady troubled with eczema but an admirable hostess – and nowhere near as unsympathetic to Voltaire, that admirer of beautiful women, as some people might have thought, for she was an atheist and freethinker, an enthusiastic theatre-goer, disliked going to mass as much as she loved going to the opera, and was an enormous admirer of his.

Zaïre caught the public by the ear from its first performance; the story of the desperate love of the Sultan of Jerusalem for his Christian captive Zaïre was just the thing to tug at the susceptible heart-strings of a sentimental audience, and when the play opened at the Comédie Française on 13 August 1732 there was not a dry eye in the house. The play was an immediate hit, speedily translated into several European languages, and remained popular until well after Voltaire's death. He now shared a pedestal with Racine and Corneille as the greatest playwright of his age and the catch-phrase '*Vous pleurez, Zaïre*', which occurs at a seminal moment, became as much common currency as any phrase of Shakespeare in England.[7]

Indeed, *Zaïre* itself was soon on-stage in London, even if the first performance was a somewhat strange one. An actor called James Bond got hold of a copy of the play, was eager to produce it, and commissioned a translator to prepare an English version. Failing to persuade the management of Drury Lane to mount it, he staged a private performance in a concert-room in York Buildings, off the Strand, with himself in the leading role. An anonymous reporter describes the result:

Neither pains nor expense were spared to render the performance respectable, and the assembly was numerous and elegant. Bond's acting excited, by its excellence, universal admiration; so passionately did he identify himself with the character [of Lusignan] that on the discovery of his daughter he fainted. Here the applause was redoubled, but finding his swoon prolonged, the audience grew uneasy. With some difficulty he was placed in his chair, when he faintly spoke, extended his arms to receive his children, raised his eyes to heaven, and died.[8]

Voltaire, when he heard the anecdote, professed to regard it as a considerable tribute to his drama.

Meanwhile he was busy completing the *Lettres philosophiques*, conscious of the scandal it would cause and already taking precautions to see that it was not banned before publication: he read some innocuous passages, for instance, to Cardinal Fleury, in order to be able to say that the Cardinal found the work completely innocent. He also wrote and published *Le Temple du goût* – 'The temple of taste' – an essay in which he did not spare those who set themselves up as arbiters of contemporary culture. In particular, he pours scorn on a cardinal and an abbé who protest at being taken to the temple, because they object to taste on principle: they approve of what has always been said about matters of culture – it is not for them to think for themselves. There are portraits of a fat, somnambulant patron of the arts, who knows nothing and is uninterested in learning; of crowds of pseudo-artists; of artists who believe they have a right to live in the temple simply because they have been praised by critics; and of the critics themselves, notable not because they are intelligent but because they know how to sting. It was they, after all, who pretended that Scudéry, a thoroughly indifferent writer, was greater than Racine. There is also a considerable slap at Jean Baptiste Rousseau, whose voice has changed to that of a frog.

There are some heroes and heroines in the poem, notably the famous correspondent Mme de Sévigné (Voltaire quotes her famous line, 'The more I see of men, the more I admire dogs') and Ninon de Lenclos, who praises sensuality. Perhaps surprisingly, the Jesuits are among the few lay visitors to the temple who are applauded (for writing good prose), while there is applause for some writers, including Corneille, Racine, Pascal, La Fontaine, Boileau and Molière. Lully is approved for his operas (though his tunes might be more fetching), Poussin, Lebrun and Le Sueur for their paintings. Some architects are complimented – for example, Perrault for the *court carrée* at the Louvre, while Voltaire greets with love and honour the great Réné de Maisons, wishing that he himself had died instead of his friend (who had recently perished of smallpox at the age of only thirty. His death affected Voltaire strongly: 'I have lost my friend, my support, my father,' he wrote to a friend[9]).

There were in *Le Temple du goût* comments designed to offend almost every instinct of any reader who considered him- or herself to be an arbiter of good taste. Voltaire referred to Notre Dame as 'scattered with rubbishy elaboration', criticised the Chapel at Versailles and called the church of Saint-Sulpice, then being built, 'a monument of bad taste'. The Church (because of a disrespectful allusion to the Pope) and the State were both highly critical of the poem – but it was widely read, and from time to time Voltaire revised it, adding a dig here and a dig there, as new topics for his satire occurred to him.

It was at this time also that he began an epic poem about *La Pucelle*, Joan of Arc. The only other author who might have written this highly irreligious and ribald work is perhaps Byron; certainly it may be compared to *Childe Harold* or *Don Juan* in style – witty, quick-moving, elegant and in wonderfully bad taste. It is all highly amusing, ingenious and beautifully written in often complex verse-forms. A *tour de force*, in other words. Voltaire could always count on it as an after-dinner entertainment when he recited it for his friends. It is perhaps his best poem, all the better for being 'light verse', unfettered by too much regard for literary 'style', full of wit and pointed ridicule. It has something of the 'cruelty' of *Candide* but as in that work, the horrors are heavily mitigated by the satiric use made of them, so the rape of a whole convent of nuns in *La Pucelle* is rendered anodyne by the humour which compares the loss of their useless virginity to the loss of spurious superiority.

He tinkered with the poem for many years; it was a way of relaxing without actually stopping work (always difficult for him unless he felt very ill indeed, and sometimes even then). It amounted in the end to twenty-one books containing 8,300 lines of verse, and from the first moment when he read it, it was a *succès de scandale* with everyone who came across it – everyone, that is, except strictly conservative members of the clergy. It was even rumoured that the King's mistress, Mme de Pompadour, got hold of one of the many manuscript copies in circulation and read it to the King. There were believed to be well over five thousand such copies doing the rounds in Paris in the 1750s, and Voltaire was forced by the sheer volume of demand and by a number of spurious editions, to publish the whole poem in 1762.

Though she was not canonised until the twentieth century, most French people admired and revered Joan – and Voltaire was among them; but he simply could not resist making fun of the supposition that it was the fact that she was a holy virgin which had enabled her to defeat the English: as he put it,

> *Quand il s'agit de sauver ma ville,*
> *Un pucelage est une arme inutile,*[10]

> [When you've got to save a city,
> Virginity isn't much use.]

His Joan is a fetching piece:

> *Ses tétons bruns, mais fermes comme un roc,*
> *Tentent la robe, et le casque, et le froc.*[11]

> [Her brown tits, firm as rocks,
> Tempt the aristocrat's robe, the soldier's
> helmet and the clergyman's frock.]

Various incidents in St Joan's life, legendary and invented, keep the reader – as they kept the writer – amused: slipping into the tent of John Chandos, one of the most prominent of English knights, she steals his breeches and draws a fleur-de-lys on his page's bottom to prove that she was there. Any lingering doubt about her virginity is dispelled when she is examined by teams of doctors, scholars, respectable married women and apothecaries, and awarded a certificate of chastity. Dunois, the Bastard of Orléans, managed to resist those nut-brown breasts by continually reminding himself of the importance of her 'hidden jewel', on which the fate of France depended. The poem is spiced with erotic incidents – a duel between two naked knights; a torrid incident involving Agnes Sorel; a narrow escape for Joan's virginity at the castle of Hermaphrodix – after which she meanders about the countryside, naked and mounted on an ass. The Devil, seeing this tableau as promising, takes possession of the donkey and attempts rape, but is foiled by St Denis.

While toying, off and on, with *Pucelle*, Voltaire cared for his hostess, who was mortally ill. On her deathbed she consented to receive a priest, in order to exculpate Voltaire, who as a well-known sceptic might otherwise have been accused of denying her religious consolation at the end. She died well. She asked what time it was, as the end approached, and was told it was two in the morning. According to some reports, she said, 'Thank God – whatever time it is, I always have an engagement.' According to others, she remarked upon how consoling it was that at any time of day the human race was at the business of perpetuating itself.

Shortly afterwards, Voltaire was once more accepted at Court, when the King and Queen could not resist having the highly successful *Zaïre* presented at Fontainebleau. He busily ingratiated himself with everyone he contrived to meet there, again with a view to the successful publication of the *Lettres*. There was, however, a setback in store, for without his permission or even knowledge *Le Pour et le Contre* had been printed and circulated, provoking considerable complaints from the clergy. At the behest of the Archbishop of Paris, the superintendent of police, M. Hérault, called on Voltaire to demand whether he was actually the author of the poem. Voltaire denied it; the author was, he said, in fact the Abbé de Chaulieu (who could not deny it, for he had been dead for fifteen years). The superintendent believed, or pretended to believe him; all the same, the edict went forth denying M. de Voltaire the right to print or publish anything at all for the foreseeable future.

This, of course, did not stop him writing, but he did begin to retire from the public stage, and as a first step took lodgings in an even more disreputable street than the Rue de Vaugirard – in a dirty alley, the Rue du Long Pont, near the church of Saint Gervais behind the Hôtel de Ville. In the same street lived a M. Demoulin, who had recently invented a way of making paper from straw; Voltaire supplied the capital, and soon a thriving and profitable little business making wrapping paper brought him in a steady and by no means negligible income. Whether he moved to his wretched lodgings before or after meeting M. Demoulin one cannot tell; but his native shrewdness suggests that the two events were linked.

It was while he was living in such mean quarters that one of the most important events of his life – certainly of his emotional life – occurred.

6

Love and Domesticity

*It is one of the superstitions of the human mind to
have imagined that virginity could be a virtue.*

Notebooks

Voltaire's lodgings in the Rue du Long Pont may have been insalubrious, but because of his reputation he would have had callers wherever he lived, and his friends certainly did not desert him. One evening in the summer of 1733 a pair of lovers, the Duchesse de Saint-Pierre and M. de Fourqualquiers, presented themselves and, since he kept no cook and his lodgings were in any case scarcely fit for entertaining, insisted on taking him out to supper with their mutual friend Emilie, Marquise de Châtelet.

He had known Emilie for many years. Her father, the Baron de Breteuil, had been attentive to him when he was imprisoned in the Bastille, and was considered a friend. Meeting the daughter again now that she was no longer a child, Voltaire no sooner got to know her than he came to the conclusion that no other woman was so worthy of his attention and (he quickly concluded) his love.

She was not celebrated as a beauty, comely rather than beautiful – some people actually called her ugly – but with one asset on which everyone remarked, her piercing, intelligent sea-green eyes. She loved jewels as much as she loved gambling, but seems to have had no idea how to dress, and on special occasions turned herself out like a Christmas tree or, as one observer put it, 'like a mule in fancy dress carrying relics in a religious procession'.[1] But her charm and intelligence were a nonpareil, and these were the qualities that captivated Voltaire.

Because she was to become one of the most important people in his life, she merits a proper introduction. Gabrielle-Emilie Le Tonelier de Breteuil was born on 17 December 1706, and was thus not quite twelve years younger than Voltaire. She was one of the five children of the baron, himself a fashionable member of the 'new nobility', head of protocol at the court at Versailles and an administrative magistrate, the latter post being of far greater importance and considerably more profitable than we might today suppose. A magistrate was a member of one of the thirteen *parlements* that served as city law courts, and was proudly of the *noblesse de robe*, their dignity marked by scarlet robes with generous mantles, shirts with frilled sleeves, powdered wigs and plumed hats. The high fees he and his colleagues charged frequently made them extremely rich. Breteuil's wife was a member of the 'old nobility', her family like many others much impoverished through inflation and, sometimes, centuries of mismanagement of their affairs. The family house overlooking the Tuileries gardens was divided into apartments which were occupied by a number of her relatives, including the widowed marquise and comtesse, the Commander de Breteuil and the Bishop of Rennes. The baron had the largest apartment, in which he and his wife lived with their five children.

Emilie's four sisters were indistinguishable from any other young women of their class – that is, they paid attention to their manners, to how they looked, to the art of taking tea and making conversation, and to their marital prospects. Their mother was particularly attentive to the social niceties: 'Do not blow your nose on your napkin . . . I have seen the Montesquiou brothers blow theirs on the tablecloth, which is really too disgusting. Break your bread and do not cut it. Always smash an egg-shell when you have eaten the egg, to prevent it rolling off the plate. Never comb your hair in church. Be careful with the word Monseigneur – it is pronounced differently for a Prince of the Church and for a Prince of the Blood. If there is a priest in the room always give him the chair nearest the fire and serve him first at meals, even if he has modestly set himself at the bottom of the table.'[2]

Emilie, though obedient, was not interested in such things. Her father (not otherwise notable for his good sense) recognised when she was very young that she was extremely intelligent, and saw to it that while her sisters were being taught the social graces, she was learning Latin, Italian and English, reading Tasso, Milton and Virgil, translating the *Aeneid* into French couplets, learning Horace by heart, and becoming engrossed with mathematics, which were to be a passion all her life.

At nineteen, she married the Marquis de Châtelet, an impoverished aristocrat and professional soldier who brought her no money but a certain social position: she inherited, for instance, the privilege of sitting in the presence of the Queen. He was often away from home on army duty, leaving the marquise to care for their two children, a boy and a girl (the former would become ambassador to England before being guillotined during the Revolution). She did not hesitate to take her pleasure where she might – and not only during her husband's absence. Evidently a kind and nice man, he was not highly sexed, which his wife decidely was. Her servants clearly found service in her house embarrassing: one man presenting himself for an interview for a position as footman was summoned to her bedroom, where she stood completely naked before him while questioning him about his references. Given the position, one of his first tasks was to carry hot water to her room and to pour it into the bath while she lay spreadeagled in it. He was greatly flustered.

She took a number of lovers early in her married life, the first of whom was the Marquis de Guébriant. When he deserted her, she took an overdose of opium, but not before writing him a farewell letter which brought Guébriant to her house in time to summon help and save her life.

Next, she turned among 'several others' (as Voltaire himself recorded in his fragmentary memoirs), to the Duc de Richelieu, a happy, mischievous, attractive vagabond intelligent enough to be able to talk with her and certainly sufficiently physically attractive and attentive to satisfy her sexual appetite (his mistresses were legion – indeed, it was said in Paris that no woman could call herself experienced if she had not been to bed with him). Their relationship was a happy one, and after it had ended they remained friends until the end of her life.

When Emilie got to know Voltaire, she was as swiftly smitten by him as he by her. He was no more conventionally handsome than she beautiful; but like hers, his appeal was immediate. His face was lively and intelligent, his black eyes bright, his lips always ready to curl into a sardonic but only rarely bitter smile. He dressed with extreme care, always looked elegant, moved with the grace of a dancer, had the most cultivated manner – and was the greatest conversationalist of his age. But while he used this talent to captivate half of Europe, he was perfectly able to subdue his wit and converse seriously and intelligently about philosophy and politics.

In short, he and Emilie seemed made for each other, and recognised the fact the moment they began to converse: when Voltaire talked of Locke and Newton, she not only recognised the names but understood what he found to admire in their work. They could talk together on equal terms – though it seems improbable that he was able to meet her on equal terms in the bedroom. Only a short while before they met he was complaining that he was too ill to make love. Emilie must have realised fairly rapidly that she was not destined to be the mistress of one of the world's great lovers.

Apart from the fact that sex does not seem to have been particularly important to him, there was the matter of his health. If he was free of pain for more than two hours at a time, he said, it was something of a miracle. From time to time during his long life he complained of paralysis, blindness, neuritis, loss of voice, insecure teeth, dropsy, indigestion, deafness, stranguary, rheumatism, herpes, scurvy, inflammation of the lungs, apoplexy, gout, erysipelas, chronic colic, fever, grippe, smallpox, itch, dysentery and catarrh. How far his illnesses were 'real' is questionable (he told one correspondent, 'I am always complaining, in accordance with my custom, but by and large I am quite comfortable'). On the other hand a distinguished physician who carefully studied his symptoms suggested that his mother was tubercular and that he inherited the disease from her.[3]

There is no doubt that Emilie became his mistress in every sense of the word, but also no doubt that the intellectual side of their relationship was the most important. Within a few weeks of their first meeting he was teaching her English, while at the same time she was learning algebra from the handsome and much more virile Pierre-Louis Moreau de Maupertuis, a mathematician and astronomer who later checked and corrected Voltaire's essay on Newton for him for the *Letters philosophiques*. A few notes which she addressed to her teacher suggest that the handsome young man was not only more ardent by nature than Voltaire, but was given frequent opportunities to prove it. Voltaire know about this, and was complaisant; he was entirely devoid of sexual jealousy (his later hatred of Maupertuis had nothing to do with the man's affair with his mistress). Though Emilie was without question the love of his life, her liaisons with other men never disturbed him over-much; in fact it was something of a relief when she looked elsewhere for satisfaction. Her intellect, insight and wit were what mattered to him, what captivated him and kept him captivated.

Looking at his workload during the period when they were getting to know each other, it is difficult to conceive where he could have found the time to write all the verses he showered on her. Managing the paper-making project, he was at the same time writing the libretto for Rameau's opera *Samson*, rehearsing his romantic, almost Shakespearean play *Adélaide du Guesclin*, attending the theatre virtually nightly, researching French history, continuing to study philosophy, beginning what was to be a remarkable correspondence with correspondents all over Europe – and concerning himself with a new protégé, a certain Abbé Michel Linant.

Linant, a chubby young aspirant poet with a stammer, was the son of a inn-keeper at Rouen, and when Voltaire came across him was writing a tragedy set in ancient Rome. He resembled Thiériot in that he was hopelessly untalented, lazy and demanding. Why Voltaire burdened himself with these two men is a mystery. Nancy Mitford, in her delightful *Voltaire in Love*, goes so far as to suggest that he 'had a little fancy' for Linant, but if she meant by that any kind of homosexual leaning on Voltaire's part, the suggestion is, indeed, highly fanciful. However, he certainly took the young man up with surprising enthusiasm, asking his friend and former schoolfellow Pierre Cideville, President of the Rouen *parlement*, to propose him as a secretary to the

Archbishop of Rouen (although admitting that he was slothful and that his handwriting was illegible). The idea was a non-starter, and Voltaire himself was to be burdened with the young man for some years – as irritating a hair-shirt as Thiériot, but the object of the same unquestioning patronage.

Voltaire's major undertaking at this time, however, was the final editing of the *Lettres philosophiques*, which he was making ready for publication in France by Claude-François Jore, a printer who had hidden him when his poem on the death of Adrienne Lecouvreur upset the authorities, and whose father had himself been three times imprisoned in the Bastille for publishing prohibited books. In 1731 Voltaire had intervened when the son was threatened with prison for publishing an account of an ecclesiastical trial. But the younger Jore had always complained that Voltaire had been insufficiently grateful for his help, and was now irritated by what he saw as the author's over-cautious approach to the preparation of a French edition. He should have known better – the police raided his print-works while the book was in preparation. Fortunately, Voltaire had been tipped off, and the work was hidden – but it was a close-run thing.

Jore then let his author down badly by putting out the book in Paris without even letting Voltaire know he had done so. The work was immediately reviled, even by Voltaire's former admirers. The outrage was not, of course, caused only by Voltaire's comments on religion in general and Pascal in particular. It was his comparison between the relative liberty of the subject in England and the relative servitude of the subject in France which gave the greatest offence. Naturally, it was not to be expected that the establishment would take pleasure in reading that the English enjoyed 'wise government in which the prince, all powerful to do good, has his hands tied against doing evil', while in France 'the blood shed in the cause of liberty has only cemented the servitude of the people'.[4] Voltaire emphasised the separation of powers between monarch and people, and pointed out that in England no taxation could be imposed without the permission of Parliament, while no man was exempt from paying taxes because he was a member of the clergy or the nobility.

It was his emphasis on liberty and 'natural rights' which so annoyed the upper classes, and his (one has to admit exaggerated) account of the excellence of the English constitution, under which the people enjoyed 'entire liberty of person and property; freedom of the press; the right of being tried in all criminal cases by a jury of independent men; the right of being tried only according to the strict letter of the law; the right of every man to profess, unmolested, what religion he chooses'. This was heady stuff, and was read with passionate interest by those upon whom his chapters on Bacon, Locke and Newton were lost.

The tone in which the author appeared to celebrate everything English while denigrating everything French was wounding to the national sensitivity. He seemed to make fun of Church and State, to criticise French institutions with a sense of irony which could actually damage the establishment. In fact, his book was too clever by half: much of what he said had been inferred, or even said, before but in a manner which was acceptable because the criticism was too mild to result in change. It appalled authority to realise that Voltaire's arguments might actually have an effect: as the secretary of Chancellor d'Aguesseau remarked: 'This man is capable of destroying a state'.[5] One authority has called the book 'the first bomb thrown at the *ancien régime*'.[6]

Apart from this, it was his attack on Pascal which really upset the religious community.[7] Voltaire did not attack his stature as a great Christian apologist, suggesting merely that the *Pensées* could have been much improved had the writer lived to work them into a coherent argument. As it stood, Pascal's writing seemed to him often to be wilfully obscure – indeed, it argued *for* obscurity, suggesting that the truth of religion must be acknowledged to be shrouded in mystery, and that one should recognise that fact, and celebrate it, or at least be indifferent to it. Voltaire also intensely disliked and criticised Pascal's dogmatism, intolerance and despairing attitude to life.

As was so often the case, the French authorities missed the main point of the book; it was not so much a criticism of the French way of life as opposed to the English as a celebration of English philosophical thought and scientific knowledge, the core of the argument being that empirical thought could release humankind from the damaging vagueness of 'belief' (religious or otherwise) which rested on speculation and metaphysics rather than on observable fact. The book is a record of Voltaire's coming-of-age as a serious thinker. The Church, of course, would rather have continued to consider him an irritating gadfly.

In June 1734, Voltaire and his new mistress travelled to the château of Montjeu for the wedding on the 10th of her former lover the Duc de Richelieu and a Mlle Marie de Guise. Voltaire had made the match and everyone was happy with it except the family of the bride, who considered Richelieu (whose title dated only from the fifteenth century) to be beneath them because his family had become ennobled by marriage, whereas the Guise were of royal blood, though now much impoverished. Two Guise cousins, the Prince de Lixin and the Prince de Pons, refused to attend the wedding, and the former later made trouble.

It was at Montjeu that Voltaire heard Jore had been arrested and thrown into prison. The news prompted his return to Paris, despite the danger, to attempt to get his duplicitous printer and publisher released. His attempts were fruitless and he was greatly inconvenienced when, under pressure, Jore revealed the whereabouts of the remaining copies of the edition of the *Lettres* which he had prepared. The books were seized, together with manuscripts and a considerable amount of money. Meanwhile the *parlement* condemned the book as 'scandalous, contrary to religion, to good morals and respect for the powers that be' and 'the greatest danger to religion and public order', and ordered it to be 'burned by the executioner at the foot of the great stairway' – the stairway at the Cour de Mai of the Palais de Justice, where on 10 June 1734 the public hangman duly tore up and burned *Lettres philosophiques*. Meanwhile the police had been ordered to search diligently for the missing author and to execute the *lettre de cachet* which was to hang over his head for ten years. This sent Voltaire hurriedly back to Montjeu.

Richelieu was no sooner married than he left the château to return to his duties as colonel of a regiment serving with the French army besieging Philippsburg in Germany. Emilie (who incidentally had lately borne her husband a son) returned to Paris, and becoming aware of the extent of the authorities' determination to arrest

Love and Domesticity

Voltaire, sent a messenger to Montjeu counselling flight. Voltaire needed no encouragement; he had already had experience of the Bastille, and was convinced that another period of imprisonment would be the death of him. He took horse to Lorraine, where Richelieu was recovering from serious wounds resulting from a duel in which he had killed the Prince de Lixin, who had insulted him and his wife. The bridegroom's life had for some time been despaired of, but he was now well enough to welcome Voltaire as his personal guest. He lived in some state, his lodgings made tolerable by his own furniture, carried with him by seventy-two mules, and his comfort ensured by a multitude of valets.

Voltaire was made equally comfortable – a fact which infuriated his enemies at Versailles, who determined by one means or another to get their hands on the impertinent philosopher. Emilie kept sending messages urging him to flee – to Brussels, to London, anywhere. He was not interested, confident that one way or another he could stay a pace or two ahead of his enemies. The siege of Philippsburg provided him with his first experience of war, and the slaughter which he observed left a deep mark on him, later manifested in *Candide*, among other works.

He next accepted for a while the hospitality of a friend, the young Comtesse de Neuville, at her house in the country near Cirey, in Champagne, fifty miles or so from Nancy. Then came an invitation which seemed a godsend, to take refuge for as long as he liked at the château of Cirey, the property of the Marquis de Châtelet, the complaisant husband of his mistress. There seems little doubt that the suggestion originated with Emilie.

The château was a thirteenth-century ruin, deep in woodlands; it had been unoccupied for years, and when Voltaire arrived he had to install basic furniture before he could be even moderately comfortable. He then began to equip the house for what he thought might be a long occupation (though he could not in his wildest dreams have thought that he would live there for fifteen years). He brought in painters, decorators, plasterers and masons and within two or three months had prepared a fine suite of rooms for himself and Emilie. All this was paid for by the marquis with money loaned to him by Voltaire (he charged 5 per cent interest, but never required his host to pay it). The rest of the house remained more or less uncared for, and the many visitors who spent time there during the following decade often complained bitterly about the discomfort they were forced to endure while their host and hostess lived in considerable splendour.

While work was going on on the house, Voltaire worked in any quiet corner he could find on his new play *Alzire, ou les Americains* (which was to be an enormous financial success when produced two years later) and on a new canto of *La Pucelle* (which, dangerously, had begun to circulate in manuscript, and which both friends and enemies alike were describing as the most sacrilegious poem ever written – not something inclined to repair Voltaire's reputation in the eyes of authority). At a distance, he enjoyed hearing of the outrage the *Lettres* was causing in Paris.

'If you want to have some fun,' he wrote to his friend the Marquise du Deffand, 'talk to some Jansenist about that book of mine which is only fit for burning. If I had written that there is no God these gentlemen would have had high hopes of my conversion, but since I have said that Pascal was sometimes wrong . . . that it is not absolutely demonstrated that we must believe in religion because it is obscure, that the existence of God should not be decided by tossing a coin, in short, since I have published these impious absurdities, there is no good Jansenist who would not like to burn me in this world and the next.'[8]

He was not lonely, not only because his own company was often enough for him, but because he found that he had some attractive neighbours, with whom he exchanged compliments. In July, he sent the Comtesse de la Neuville a boar's head:

This gentleman has just been murdered so as to give me the opportunity of paying you my court. I sent them to get a deer, but none could be found. The boar was destined to give you his head. I swear that I attach very little importance to the head of a wild pig, and I really believe it is eaten out of snobbishness; but I have nothing else to offer you. If I had caught a lark I would present it to you in the same way with the confidence of a man who believes that the heart is all.[9]

Love and Domesticity

Emilie arrived at Cirey in October 1734 (with two hundred pieces of luggage) shortly after the death of her baby, aged sixteen months, an event which saddened but fell short of devastating her; the death of infants was common. She immediately took an interest in the repair of the château and began working on her own plans for the estate, which all too often ran counter to Voltaire's. He complained to Thiériot that he and Emilie had to live in the entresol while she busied herself by planting terraces 50 feet wide, installing porcelain baths, planning 'yellow rooms' and 'silver rooms' and 'des niches en magots de Chine'.

The fact that he was living in the country did not mean that he had retired from the literary fray. He was perfectly willing and able to engage in verbal skirmishes with anyone who upset him. The first of these was the Abbé Desfontaines, whom Voltaire had saved from burning some years previously, and who now published a play of his without his permission and in an edition profligate with errors. Voltaire wrote to Desfontaines and asked him to make it clear that the edition had been published without the author's knowledge. Far from doing this, the man wrote a critique of the play emphasising all the errors as though they were Voltaire's own. Not only that, but he revealed the fact that the playwright was at Cirey, which could have had dire consequences.

Voltaire, not unreasonably, was outraged and wrote an article for Le Mercure which became famous for its spleen, in turn exposing the mistakes Desfontaines had made as a translator, referring to him as 'il buggerone abbate' and slyly alluding to 'les petits Savoyards', by which he meant the young chimney-sweeps for whom the abbé had such a predilection. Yet even in his fury, Voltaire was not uncharitable and when, understandably, the Marquis de Châtelet expressed his own annoyance that the abbé had written about the odd business of his sharing of his marital bed with an atheist writer, and threatened to prosecute, Voltaire pleaded with the marquis to refrain from having Desfontaines imprisoned, which he could easily have done.

Another spell of illness – these are so regular that it would be supererogatory to mention them all – laid him low for a few weeks; he wrote to Thiériot that he had but a few years to live. In fact his life was only half-spent; he was forty-one years old and would live another forty-three. While hypochondria and genuine sickness ruled his physical life, he was in fact extremely sensible about his health. Sébastien Longchamps, variously described as his footman or his secretary, recalled that his master always maintained that one's health depended entirely upon oneself, writing: 'Its three pivots are sobriety, temperance in all things, and moderate exercise; in almost all diseases which are not the result of serious accidents . . . it suffices to aid nature, which is striving to restore us; it is necessary to confine ourselves to a diet more or less strict and prolonged, suitable liquid nourishment and other simple means. In this manner I always saw him regulate his conduct as long as I lived with him.'[10]

In March 1735 he once more received formal permission to return to Paris, though the *lettre de cachet* remained in force in case he ignored the suggestion of the superintendent of police, Réné Hérault to 'act like a sensible man who has reached middle age'.[11] He made a brief visit to the capital, just to establish the fact that he was still alive and kicking (one of the people he kicked was Jore, who attempted to bring a court action against him for money the printer claimed was owed to him; the claim was rejected by the courts). He then happily returned to Cirey, his mistress, her son and – astonishingly – the awful Linant, whom he had persuaded Emilie to engage as a tutor (on condition that he withdrew from the Church: 'We'll have no priests at Emilie's house,' Voltaire insisted). He was not, as anyone but Voltaire might have foreseen, a success; Emilie had to teach him Latin so that he could pass the lessons on to the boy; then he made a spectacularly clumsy pass at Mme de la Neuville, and Voltaire had to write a placatory letter to his friend.

Voltaire continued to prove that wherever he was, there could be no question of leisure. He continued to plan the decoration and to some extent rebuilding of the château, with the help and hindrance of Emilie, who disputed almost every decision and contradicted almost every order. He continued, too, to add stanzas here and there to *La Pucelle*, and finished *Alzire*, which when it was produced in January 1736 ran for twenty performances and made a considerable profit – no less than 53,000 livres (a proportion of which the author gave to the actors).

Love and Domesticity

Gradually, everyone came to know where Voltaire was living and under what circumstances. At first he was cautious about revealing his whereabouts, but gradually, as it became clear that he was not now going to be pursued by the authorities, who had perhaps come to the conclusion that capturing and prosecuting him would be more trouble than it was worth, he stopped taking any precautions and lived openly as a country gentleman. This caused a few raised eyebrows: cutting oneself off from the pleasures of Paris, the intrigues of court life, the conventional life of a man of letters, was almost scandalous.

But Voltaire was extraordinarily content with his life and so was Emilie. The château was now quite comfortable (at least for its two main occupants). The gardens had been redesigned, the chief rooms painted and decorated, a number of porcelain baths had been installed (bathing, Longchamps remarked, cooled Emilie's ardours. He may have had personal evidence of this). By the middle of 1730 a daily regime had been established – which included the occasional presence of du Châtelet, the very model of a complaisant husband, who kept out of the lovers' way (he disliked the hours they kept, anyway) and always seemed happy to leave to rejoin his regiment.

An account of the décor and furnishings at Cirey was left by Mme Françoise Paule d'Issembourg Graffigny, an impoverished aristocrat to whom Voltaire and Emilie were kind. She arrived at the château in 1738 as a more or less permanent guest, and two days later described the house in detail to a correspondent. The lovers had separate apartments. Mme de Châtelet's were ravishingly beautiful – a bedroom decorated in light yellow and pale blue, paintings by Veronese and Watteau hanging above a bed covered with blue moiré, matched by the dressings of the dogs' baskets. A small dressing-room was even more beautiful, with a marble floor and panelled walls painted light grey, more charming paintings and an exquisite ceiling. A large armchair, two stools covered in white taffeta and an amber desk was all the furniture (it was there that Emilie showed her guest her jewel box and its ravishing contents).

As for Voltaire, he had a wing of the house to himself, with a small anteroom hung with crimson velvet, a reception room, and a 40-foot long panelled gallery with statues of the Farnese Venus and Hercules standing between the windows which gave on to the garden. Opposite the windows were cupboards containing books, and between them a stove which kept the large room at a comfortable temperature (unlike poor Mme Graffigny's own rooms, which were freezing). There were many paintings by, among other artists, Titian, Watteau, Lancret, Albani, Boucher, Teniers and Tiepolo,[12] mirrors, writing-desks, tables, a sofa, pieces of porcelain, handsome clocks . . . and how *clean* everything was! (Unlike many of his contemporaries, Voltaire was almost obsessively clean, both in his person and in his surroundings.) In the corner (perhaps not shown to the guest) was a private staircase to Emilie's rooms, and between the two suites was a large laboratory for chemistry and physics, equipped with thermometers and crucibles, microscopes and telescopes, scales and compasses, air pumps and a furnace.

There was also a specially designed little theatre which the couple built for the amateur performances which were a part of the life of the château.[13] Where recreation was concerned, this was the centre of their world. They dragooned guests and neighbours into taking part in performances of comedies and tragedies, even operas (Emilie was an excellent musician and if no other guests were musical could – and would – sing a whole opera, playing all the parts herself. She had, Mme de Graffigny said, a '*voix divine*').

The atmosphere was on the whole extremely placid, except when Voltaire and his mistress disagreed about something. When they quarrelled, they tactfully did so in English, and in picturesque rhetoric (Boswell, visiting Voltaire years later, was extremely impressed by his command of English obscenities). Both were capable of small pettiness: Voltaire once sulked for a whole evening and refused to recite a new canto of *Pucelle* because Emilie had refused him a glass of Rhine wine which he fancied. On another occasion (as one of their servants reported to the police, who were always interested in Voltaire's doings), the sounds of a quarrel were heard from the couple's bedroom for most of a night, all because they had disagreed about where supper should be served. But on the whole guests were conscious chiefly of the two lovers working away happily in their respective corners, Voltaire at his writing, his mistress 'at her triangles' in a house the atmosphere of which was full of gaiety and romance.

There are various accounts of how life went on at Cirey, some portraying it as an idyll, others less enthusiastic. Some thought the place inordinately isolated: Mme Denis, Voltaire's niece, thought that he lived in 'terrifying solitude' – four leagues from the nearest neighbour, with nothing to be seen from the windows of the château but mountains and moorland. But she was obviously jealous of the hold that Emilie had on her uncle: 'he is lost to his friends, and will never get away,' she said. Emilie 'employs all the art imaginable to seduce him'.[14] Another visitor who had no axe to grind, and one neither extravagantly fond of Voltaire nor in any way antipathetic to him, was the Chevalier de Villefort, a gentleman-in-waiting to the Comte de Clermont.

He arrived one evening, as the light was fading, and passed from courtyard to courtyard looking for signs of life. Eventually, he found a bell and rang it. Silence. He rang again. Continued silence. Somewhat later, the noise of footsteps behind the door, and the appearance of a chambermaid carrying a candle. He followed her down the hall, along corridors, through large echoing rooms empty of furniture. At last they came to a stop in a room which seemed devoid of identity, when at last the maid asked him what he wanted. He asked to see Emilie.

The maid left, taking the candle with her and Villefort groped his way to a chair and waited. More time passed, then a door was thrown open from a neighbouring room and light flooded in. He saw what seemed almost a set from the theatre, with the figure of his hostess centre-stage, 'wearing so many diamonds that she would have looked like a Venus at the opera if, despite the indolence of her attitude and her richly bejewelled attire, she had not been leaning over papers covered with xs and ys, at a table strewn with instruments and books on mathematics'.[15]

Reluctantly Emilie tore herself away from her calculations just long enough to instruct the maid to take the visitor to Voltaire. He followed her to the fireplace, where there was an ingeniously concealed door. Handed a candle, he was left to climb a narrow winding staircase for what seemed at least two storeys. He came to a door and knocked. There was no reply. He knocked again, and at last a footman answered, and took him into an anteroom. M. Voltaire, he was informed, could not see him immediately; it was not the time for conversation. He sat uncomfortably for some time, until what sounded like the ringing of a school bell. The footman returned to announce that dinner was served.

There were no servants in the dining room, where there were a few other guests. The food, which was at least plentiful and beautifully prepared, arrived on one or the other of two dumb-waiters, one at each end of the room, and the guests served themselves. After dinner, de Villefort selected a book from among the piles which lay on each table of a sitting room next to the dining room and read. Then the school bell rang again and it was time for bed, and an uneasy sleep which was disturbed at the ungodly hour of 4 a.m., when a servant announced that a poetry-reading party was about to convene in the gallery. Villefort hurried into his clothes and went down to the desperately cold gallery where Voltaire and Emilie presided over a selection of poetry-readings from the best authors (*'l'exercice de poésie et de littérature'*, as another visitor, the Abbé Le Blanc remembered). In winter although wood fires blazed in thirty-six fireplaces, they failed to dispel the chill wind that crept into the rooms through cracks in the wainscot and windows. Villefort dined out for weeks on his account of his uncomfortable visit to Cirey, though it is well to note that his hosts dismissed his account as fiction. The sound of the school bell, however, has been too often remembered by too many visitors to be a fiction. Voltaire liked to live by the clock.

Guests at the château were also expected to do so. They had to remain in their rooms until it was time for coffee, which was served in Voltaire's gallery between 10.30 and 11.30 a.m. They dined at noon, and if Voltaire decided to be present at table, general conversation took place until he rose and bowed, at which everyone else was expected to make their bows and leave. Occasionally a light meal was offered at four, but one was unlikely to see the host again until nine, when supper was served; and he was usually unpunctual, since he ignored mealtimes until he had finished the piece of work on which he was engaged. Emilie liked to work at night – often until five in the morning, sometimes even later; but she was still up and about by nine or ten at the latest. Except when they were at meals or on some special occasion both she and Voltaire spent their days and nights at their desks, only occasionally taking the air, Emilie on horseback, Voltaire on foot. He tried to become some sort of a sportsman, but his attempts to shoot deer were farcical – he was as likely to shoot a human companion as the animal at which he was aiming.

The remnants of letters from Voltaire to his man of business in Paris, rescued and published by Theodore Besterman,[16] provide some details of daily life: Voltaire gives instructions for the buying and selling of shares – 1,200 francs-worth were sold to pay for a dressing-case for Emilie; orders tweezers for attending to bushy eyebrows; asks for thermometers and barometers, feather-dusters, a good reflecting telescope and some slippers ('my feet and my eyes are very much obliged to you'), powder-puffs and sponges; sends ten *pistoles* to a needy young woman who lives near Cirey ('I don't know her at all, but she is in great need'); commissions 'a small Bohemian crystal chandelier costing about 250 francs . . .'.

Meanwhile, the work went on – finishing *Alzire*, composing a poem entitled *Discours sur l'homme* (clearly suggested by Pope's *Essay on Man*), and writing a book by which he intended to familiarise the French with Newton's work.[17] Emilie concentrated on science, studying kinetic energy and translating Newton's *Principia* from Latin into French, while also finding time to read Cicero and Virgil in Latin and Ariosto and Tasso in Italian (she read Newton in English). She completed a six-volume book exhibiting and denouncing the immorality and injustice of the Bible, which needless to say remained unpublished. Her *Traité de Bonheur*, or essay on happiness, was published – it argued that health, love, sensible self-indulgence and the pursuit of knowledge were the true basis of a good life. She was a genuine scholar. But amid all the work that went on in the separate apartments of the château, there was still time for playfulness, Voltaire pausing in his more serious endeavours to write the occasional whimsical verse to Emilie:

> Sans doute vous serez célèbre
> Par les grandes calculs de l'algèbre

Où votre esprit est absorbé:
J'oseraus m'y livrer moi-même;
Mais, hélas! A + D – B
N'est pas = à je vous aime.

[Undoubtedly you'll be well known
For these fine algebraic calculations
By which your mind is absorbed:
I'd have a go at them myself;
But alas, A + D – B
Doesn't = I love you.]

Apart from work, the years 1734–5 were the time when Voltaire really consolidated his reputation as a brilliant correspondent; more or less isolated in the country, he wrote daily to a large number of friends and correspondents all over Europe. One in particular, from whom he received a letter at the end of August 1736, was to become one of the most important men in his life.

7

King and Commoner

*It is the triumph of reason to get on well
with those who have none.*

Letter, 1754

Frederick, Crown Prince of Prussia, seemed as a youth unlikely to become one of the world's most memorable monarchs, the 'Frederick the Great' whose name reverberates through the history of the eighteenth century.

In 1736 he was twenty-four years of age, and had lived through a literally tortured adolescence at the clumsy and brutal hands of his father, the maniacal King Frederick William I. His mother was kind and while his father remained uninterested in him, until the age of about twelve, his childhood was reasonably pleasant. He had a good tutor who impressed on the boy his own respect for and love of French literature, and clandestinely taught him Latin (his father forbade the language as unsuitable for a future Prussian officer). When, however, the King discovered Frederick's love of reading and of music, he was beside himself with fury that his son was so effete and effeminate as to want to spend his time with books and learn to play the flute. In an attempt to cure him of what he considered unmanly intellectual attitudinising, his father struck the boy repeatedly in the face, and if he gave unsatisfactory answers to any question put to him, perhaps about military strategy, knocked him down, and was even seen to drag him across a muddy parade-ground by his hair. The fact that it became clear that the boy was homosexual did not endear him to the King.

One day during his eighteenth year, while bring driven from Berlin to Potsdam, the Crown Prince heard the sound of a flute. Stopping the carriage, he discovered a young army lieutenant, Jean-Hermann von Katte, playing in a clearing among the trees. Katte became an intimate friend, possibly a lover, and when Frederick explained that he believed his father was trying to drive him to suicide, and that his only hope appeared to be in escape from the country, perhaps to France, introduced the Prince to a number of other young officers with whom a plot was laid to enable him to flee the country.

The plan was discovered, and Katte and two of his friends were arrested. Frederick was cashiered, deprived of the title of Crown Prince, and thrown into prison. On 5 November 1730 two officers entered his cell, and held his face to the window to force him to witness Katte being led to his execution. He shouted to his friend to forgive him; Katte called back that he was happy to die in the service of his Prince. He was then beheaded in the courtyard below the cell. Frederick fainted at the sight, but was brought round and lifted again to the window to see Katte's head lying in the blood-stained sawdust. He was then imprisoned in the fortress of Küstrin, and it seemed for a time that the King might even go so far as to kill the heir to the throne. Instead, he was released after some months and set to work as a civil service clerk.

In November 1732, after he had made humble obeisance to his father, it was assumed that his spirit had been broken, and he was once more allowed to wear uniform and attempt to prove himself a true Prussian soldier. The following year he reluctantly married Princess Elizabeth-Christine of Brunswick-Bevern, a plain young woman whom he found physically repulsive and could not even bring himself to like. But at least he was now allowed to live on his own estate at Rheinsberg, to decorate his small château with paintings and *objets d'art*, to read philosophy and enjoy music. He spent seven happy years there, delightfully neglected by the King. He specially loved French literature – he loved everything French; indeed, he invariably wrote and spoke that language. He could not spell in German and spoke it 'like a coachman'; it was, he thought, a coarse, primitive language, and to believe that it could have a literature was ludicrous.

King and Commoner

Among the French authors he most revered was Voltaire, for whose books he conceived a passion. On 8 August 1736 he sat down and wrote what can only be described as a fan letter, in which he complimented the author on the wonderful style of his writing, by which he was so entranced, he said, that he read those books of his which he possessed (including the *Henriade*) again and again, and asked him to be so kind as to send him his complete works, in particular the *Pucelle*, of which he had heard much. He hoped one day to be able to meet so eloquent an author and converse with him face to face. Meanwhile, he enclosed a small gift: a French translation of some essays by Christian Wolff, a follower of the philosopher Leibniz whose views were to be the subject of Voltaire's attentive wit in *Candide*. The Crown Prince signed himself, 'I am, with all the consideration due to those who, following the torch of truth, consecrate their efforts to the public good, Monsieur, your friend Frédéric,[1] P.R. de Prusse.'

In the second of almost a thousand letters the two men were to exchange, Voltaire responded enthusiastically to Frederick's compliments. He was touched and flattered, he said, by the Prince's letter, and overjoyed that there existed in the world a 'philosopher-prince' who would make his subjects happy. The thoughtfulness with which Frederick was educating himself would make him adored by his people. He, Voltaire, was more than grateful for the book (which in fact he found ridiculous) and would certainly hope one day to greet Frederick face to face: 'One goes to Rome to see churches, pictures, ruins and bas-reliefs. A prince like you is far more deserving of a journey, he is a much more marvellous rarity. But friendship, which keeps me in my retreat, does not allow me to leave it.'[2]

He was careful not to suggest that it was impossible that he should visit Prussia.[3] He must indeed have been attracted by the idea: censorship in France made publication there tedious, and attempts to evade the censors were dangerous. The thought of writing and publishing freely abroad and under royal protection was surely extremely tempting, and a notion by no means to be dismissed out of hand. Voltaire was always under threat in France – the *lettre de cachet* was still in effect; life at the Court of a distinguished intellectual prince who would eventually become king had very obvious attractions. The very thought of it was enough to suggest modifications to the inflexible anti-monarchist, republican views expressed in the *Lettres philosophiques* and *Brutus*.

Their correspondence was, from the start, a warm and discursive one. Frederick looked on Voltaire as a sort of tutor on whom he could try out his ideas about a range of subjects, and whom he believed would appreciate his odes and verse epistles; the latter responded no less enthusiastically, complimenting the Prince on the range of his interests, and at first happy to correct the metre and errors of syntax in the Prince's turgid French verses. As time went on, Frederick stopped addressing Voltaire as 'Monsieur', proceeding to 'Mon cher ami', and then 'Mon cher Voltaire'. Voltaire confined himself, very properly, to 'Monseigneur'. His flattery was perhaps excessive: he compared Frederick to Marcus Aurelius, Alcibiades, even Apollo, telling him that it seemed as though the world should celebrate 'the re-birth of the talents of Virgil and the virtues of Augustus'. Frederick on his side assured the philosopher that there was no god in the world but Voltaire. It would be a mistake to think that either man was being entirely disingenuous, for Voltaire really did believe that Frederick might prove that rarest of creatures, a monarch with a real taste for literature, philosophy and the arts, while Frederick's admiration of Voltaire was total, and survived the vicissitudes of their relationship until his correspondent's death.

In the 1730s, flattered by effusive letters and presents from Potsdam (a bust of Socrates, Frederick's own portrait, a gold-mounted cane, even a trinket or two for Emilie), Voltaire became increasingly inclined to join the court of this attractive member of the extensive group of European royal families. Emilie, on the other hand, was distraught at the idea. She did not see herself in exile in Potsdam, and from the first moment the plan was broached was determined to prevent Voltaire visiting Frederick.

It has been suggested by almost every writer on the subject that she and Frederick were desperate rivals for Voltaire's attention, the Prince and future King determined to lure him to Prussia as a major ornament at his Court and valuable evidence of his status as a generous, wise and good ruler, while Emilie believed that too close a relationship between Frederick and her lover could only be dangerous both to the latter's reputation and his life. Reading the letters between Voltaire and Frederick, one must also note that the latter's language was almost that of a lover; perhaps because of the fraught relationship between Frederick and his father the emotional importance of the Frenchman's friendship was very strong indeed.

As far as his work was concerned, Voltaire was now to a large extent neglecting poetry and the theatre in order to concentrate more and more on natural philosophy. His admirers could not understand this: science meant nothing to them – what, asked Cideville, could possibly be the advantage of knowing the weight of Saturn? – while his old schoolfellow the Marquis d'Argenson told him very firmly that there were plenty of dullards who could talk about science but that without Voltaire the writer there would shortly be nothing amusing to read. Voltaire shrugged, and continued with Emilie's encouragement to write *Les Eléments de la Philosophie de Newton* which was to become a widely read and popular introduction to Newton's work in French.

Never content to work on one thing at a time, he relaxed by writing another satirical poem, *Défence du Mondain*, contrasting primitive life with that of the civilised world. Positively asking for trouble from the Church, which regarded the Bible as a record of literal truth, he described those respected ancestors of humanity Adam and Eve not as pristine inhabitants of the golden world, but as filthy and unkempt, living on acorns and millet, bored with the prospect of having nothing to do but eat, drink and make love. Who could envy them, he asked? Modern man, on the other hand, could enjoy the sophisticated pleasures of good food and wine in handsome apartments decorated with fine paintings, and when the pleasures of the bedroom palled could go to see the great Camargo dance at the Opéra.

Inevitably, such a delightful piece did not remain private for long: it went rapidly from hand to hand, eventually reaching the study of a bishop – the Bishop of Mirepoix, tutor to the Dauphin – who complained to Cardinal Fleury. The church authorities considered the matter carefully, and concluded that the poem was blasphemous because Voltaire had spoken of Adam and Eve as being so dirty that sex had ceased to be a pleasure and was only '*un besoin honteux*' – 'a shameful need'; moreover, he had suggested that they made love in the Garden of Eden itself, whereas such a libidinous event could only have occurred after the sinning couple had been expelled from that beautiful and unpolluted landscape.[4] An order for the author's arrest was sent off to Cirey but fortunately as usual friends tipped Voltaire off, and on the night of 8/9 December 1736 he and Emilie left the château and plodded through the snow to an inn at Vassy, where at four in the morning Voltaire sat down and wrote to another former school-fellow and friend, the Comte d'Argental, simply because he had to unburden himself to someone other than Emilie.

An almost impossible choice faced him, he said: personally, he would be very happy to leave France for Frederick's Court in Prussia and to live there permanently, but that would mean leaving 'the woman who has done everything for me, who for me left Paris, all her friends and her delightful life, her whom I adore and will always adore . . .'.[5] Could Argental kindly nose around in Paris and find out the degree of severity of the charge against him? Perhaps flight was after all unnecessary.

But he did not stay for an answer. He let it be known that he had decided to go to Prussia, and by 3 January was in Amsterdam. There, for the first time, we hear of crowds gathering in the street simply to see him pass by, while it was said that a special boat-load of admirers crossed the Channel from England for the same purpose. He may really have thought of going on to Prussia, but knew perfectly well that the Prince's father would give him a very dusty welcome, and that Frederick was not sufficiently his own man to disregard the prejudices of Frederick William. Pausing in Holland, he gave out that he was in England, visiting Cambridge University. Meanwhile, Emilie returned to Cirey, whence she sent him by roundabout means message after message counselling extreme caution. She was especially anxious that he was apparently not only cheekily preparing an authorised edition of *Défence du Mondain* for publication, but was determined to publish his book on Newton, to which she was absolutely sure the Church would take exception: there was one chapter on metaphysics which would drive the priests into paroxysms of rage – Voltaire, she feared, would be instantly dispatched to the stake. (It must be remembered that all bishops, and there were over a hundred of them, were appointed by the King, and it was a matter of course that bishoprics were, through him, at the service of titled families. Hence an insult to the Church was also widely regarded as an attack on the nobility, whose antagonism was all too often a passport to the torture chamber and the pyre.)

However, just over two months later the philosopher turned up, unscathed, at Cirey, and there was a delighted and delightful reunion. Life went on placidly for a while, only occasionally disturbed by short, sharp spasms of anger from Voltaire when he heard of some new libel put about in Paris by Desfontaines or Jean-Baptiste Rousseau, who were busily reporting to Cardinal Fleury that Voltaire had been preaching atheism at The Hague, and gossiping about alleged breaches between Voltaire and Emilie. Otherwise, for the most part work was only interrupted by the arrival of long, turgid letters from Frederick which Voltaire insisted on reading to Emilie over breakfast.

Intensely bored by the Prince's courtship of her lover, she was less bored by an emissary who arrived from Potsdam, one Baron Dietrich von Keyserlingkt, described by Frederick as his 'ambassador to the court of Cirey'. The duty of this plump and amiable homosexual (whom Frederick called 'Cesarion') was ostensibly to present Voltaire with a portrait of his friend and master; he was greeted with a display of fireworks which spelt out Frederick's name and the motto: 'TO THE HOPE OF THE HUMAN RACE'. Keyserlingkt became more than a formal visitor. He amused Emilie in particular, whose friendship he elicited with such compliments as 'When she speaks I am in love with her intellect, and when she is silent with her presence'. She managed to overlook the fact that one of the purposes of his visit was clearly to put pressure on Voltaire to visit Potsdam.

Keyserlingkt returned to Frederick with an account of the delights of Cirey and its denizens which made the Prince even more determined to seduce Voltaire into waiting on him at Potsdam. Emilie let it be known that when their friend succeeded to the throne, they would certainly both visit him. Frederick was not comforted: he had no desire to meet Mme de Châtelet, though he sent her a loving message every time he wrote.

Keyserlingkt was indirectly responsible for a minor, benevolent earthquake at Cirey. The lazy and incompetent Michel Linant, now no longer an abbé, had, it will be remembered, been reluctantly engaged by Emilie as tutor to her son. He had proved a disaster, continually proposing himself as a guest to Voltaire's neighbours and staying with them for prolonged periods while he neglected his pupil and bored his hosts – or offended any ladies present by making uncouth advances – gossiping rudely about those guests at Cirey of whom he disapproved, and complaining that his work as tutor prevented him from finishing his masterwork, *Rameses*. When Emilie protested to Voltaire that the man really must be dismissed, she was reminded that nobody else would be remotely interested in offering him a position – and could they send him away to starve to death? Privately, she thought that an admirable solution to the Linant problem, but in the end found herself not only retaining his services, but organising a place in a convent for his mother and giving his sister a position as maid.

After Keyserlingkt had returned to Potsdam, it was found that Linant had asked him to arrange employment with him at the Court there and a little later letters were found written to Frederick's emissary by Linant's sister in which she sniggered at Emilie's life with Voltaire. Despite anything Voltaire could say, both the tutor and his sister were instantly dismissed (Voltaire told Thiériot that he felt like a priest whose penitent had ended up in a brothel).

When the dust had settled after the fracas, Voltaire turned his attention to planning a wedding. His dead sister's eldest daughter Marie-Louise looked dangerously like becoming a permanent spinster: though somewhat plain, she had a certain charm, and was to a degree accomplished (an excellent musician, she had been a pupil of Rameau), but at twenty-six she had shown as yet no signs of an attachment. So when her father died in February 1737 Voltaire conceived the idea of marrying her to the son of a neighbour of his at Cirey, an inoffensive creature whose mother had been a schoolfellow of Emilie and came over from time to time to play backgammon, so frequently indeed that she had her own room at the château. He invited Marie-Louise and her sister Marie Elizabeth to stay at Cirey, and arranged an introduction.

Alas, Louis François Toussaint du Ravet de Champbonin was, despite his splendid name, an insipid nonentity and Marie-Louise would have nothing to do with him. She had in any event already fallen in love with someone else. No sooner was she back in Paris than she married M. Nicolas Charles Denis, a notary with the army. The couple were no doubt pleased with the 30,000 franc dowry Voltaire gave his niece, and seemed to enjoy their honeymoon visit to Cirey. Marie Elizabeth followed her sister's example almost immediately, and received a similar dowry. Voltaire declined to attend either wedding: he hated the noise, the people – all those relatives cracking dubious jokes and paying boring compliments, telling dirty stories which made the bride blush; all those little girls peeping slyly at the grown-ups, too much food, too many slobbering kisses . . . . He continued, however, to pay attention to his nieces' well-being, trying incessantly, though unsuccessfully, to persuade Cardinal de Fleury to offer Denis a position, and giving the couple continual financial assistance. Denis was a hard-working man, indeed in Voltaire's opinion over-work was a major cause of his early death (in April 1744).

In the spring of 1738 Voltaire and Emilie busied themselves with independent entries for a competition set by the Académie des Sciences to define 'The Nature and Diffusion of Fire'.[6] Voltaire made a number of experiments and was able to prove the theory that certain substances actually increased in volume when calcified because of their absorption of elements in the atmosphere. Both papers were read with respect, but the prize went elsewhere (because, the unsuccessful candidates concluded, they were known supporters of Newton, while the judges all admired Descartes).

Meanwhile, there was a great drama centring on the unfortunate Mme de Graffigny, a permanent resident at Cirey. A middle-aged woman, she was entirely without resources, having in a procedure extremely rare in France obtained a separation from her husband, a chamberlain at the court of the Duke of Lorraine, on grounds of cruelty. Mme de Richelieu had persuaded Emilie to offer her the hospitality of Cirey, for which she was extremely grateful. Posterity should also be grateful, for (as we have seen) in letters to friends she left a thorough and apparently faithful record of life there, and of the characters of Voltaire and his mistress.

Though something of a gossip, she was entirely loyal to her host and hostess, and it was a great shock when they burst in upon her and accused her of sending a copy of the latest stanzas of *Pucelle* to Paris, where they were now circulating, enjoyed both by Voltaire's admirers and by his enemies, who saw in them yet another opportunity to persecute him. How could she? Voltaire would not listen to her protestations of innocence, and Emilie actually assaulted the poor woman. After an hour of shouting and screaming, the dust began to settle a little, and Voltaire to suspect that perhaps they had been unjust to their guest. Mme de Graffigny eventually recalled that she had somewhat rashly told her friend François-Antoine Devoux (always known as 'Panpichon', or 'Pan-pan' and a hanger-on at the court of ex-King Stanislas) that she had heard the new stanzas and how witty they were, but without going into any details. Voltaire believed her, asked her pardon, and persuaded Emilie to do the same.

The altercation is not in itself significant other than that it reveals that Voltaire and Emilie were in a very nervous state at the time. This was because they had both been sent a copy of a scurrilous pamphlet put together by the Ábbé Desfontaines and published under the title *La Voltairomanie, ou lettre d'un Jeune Avocat*. The abbé had for years relentlessly attacked and gossiped about Voltaire, and his unpleasantness reached its apogee when he reviewed an edition of *Eleménts de la Philosophie de Newton*. Unfortunately, the copy he received was pirated and badly printed, with innumerable errors for which Voltaire was not responsible. Desfontaines took considerable pleasure in pointing them out and in fixing on the title-page of the book, which bore the legend: '*Mis a portée de tout le monde*' – 'made simple for everyone', translating it as 'shown the door by everyone'. Voltaire, always rashly quick to lose his temper when attacked, lost it with a vengeance and published his own pamphlet, *Le Préservatif*, in which he ridiculed Desfontaines as a careless and inaccurate writer. It is not a publication of which any admirer of Voltaire can be proud: it is inaccurate and unfair. Unsurprisingly, it irritated Desfontaines even more, and he compiled a sort of anthology of the most cutting criticisms and comments made about his enemy and published them as *La Voltairomanie*. It was, alas, much more effective than Voltaire's hasty and rather careless publication. It condemned his plays as blasphemous (the only reason for their success), and his prose as so obscene that he was forced to live in the country lest he be pilloried in Paris. Within a few days it was in every drawing room in the city.

The master and mistress of Cirey each read their own copy, carefully concealing from the other the fact that they had received it. The *débâcle* became ever more complicated: Desfontaines claimed that Thiériot now contradicted Voltaire's statement that he (Thiériot) had told him of an attack the abbé made on him soon after he had rescued him from burning. Emilie wrote to Thiériot insisting that he contradict Desfontaines's allegation. Thiériot unaccountably refused to do so, at first pretending that he did not even know who had written the book. This naturally provoked a wounded letter from Voltaire to the man whom he had supported for so many years, asking whether he did not feel that he had betrayed his old friend, neglected his honour, all in order to support a rascal who had attacked not only Voltaire but Thiériot himself. Surely friendship and truth should triumph over hatred and perfidy? It was all in vain.

The whole affair now seems as complicated as it was surely unimportant, and fortunately Voltaire fairly soon reached the conclusion that it was best to let it drop, despite Emilie's attempts to persuade him to go to law about it. In a way, the brunt of the affair was borne by poor Mme de Graffigny, who was never able to reconcile herself to Emilie, and shortly after the incident left Cirey.[7]

In 1738 Voltaire and Emilie set off on a visit to Belgium, travelling in a leisurely fashion through Valenciennes and Louvain, Voltaire making notes for work in hand – chiefly a new play, *Mahomet* – and Emilie learning algebra from Samuel Koenig, a master recommended by her earlier teacher and lover Pierre Maupertuis. Voltaire, it seems, was of the opinion that a knowledge of algebra would be a comfort to her all her life, and 'make her very agreeable in society'.[8] Arriving in Brussels in May, they found the city the dullest on the face of Europe, illiterate and devoid of wit – when Voltaire made a little joke, giving a fireworks party to introduce Emilie to society and stating on the cards that the invitation was from 'the Envoy of Utopia', it fell completely flat because none of the guests had ever heard of Utopia.

There was a little respite when they were for a while the guests of the Duc d'Arenberg at Enghien, where though there wasn't a book in the house at least the gardens were beautiful, and they were able to mount a production of Molière's *Ecole des femmes* in which Voltaire appeared as Arnolphe and Emilie as Georgette. But it was with relief that they made their way back towards Paris, where they took up residence in August in the midst of public festivity on the occasion of the betrothal of the King's twelve-year-old daughter to the seventeen-year-old son of Philip of Spain. Voltaire found the celebrations tawdry and cheap – a few fireworks and some tired-looking decorations; things had been done better under Louis XIV, when Molière and Lully wrote works for special occasions. Perhaps the King was too interested in his new mistress, Louise-Julie Comtesse de Mailly, to pay the affair proper attention. It was all unnecessary noise and bustle, and the couple were relieved to get away to the peace and quiet of Cirey.

It is now that one begins to hear more substantial rumours of quarrels between Voltaire and his mistress, and there seems little doubt that these were the result of tension arising from the fact that he was, even before her husband's death, sleeping with his niece Marie-Louise, Mme Denis. He had always been fond of her, and at some time, in Paris, fondness was consummated in the bedroom. Technically, they were committing incest, but the Catholic Church did not insist on penalties – indeed, permission to marry one's niece provided a nice source of income (in a later pamphlet Voltaire wrote that 'one can marry one's niece with the Pope's permission; he charges 40,000 *ecu*, I believe, with a bit of petty cash thrown in. I've always heard that M. de Montmartel only paid 80,000 francs, and I know men who have slept with their nieces far more cheaply').[9]

There was clearly a very strong physical attachment between them, stronger on Voltaire's part than on Marie-Louise's; this is quite plain from a number of letters he wrote to her, discovered over thirty years ago by the Voltaire scholar and biographer Theodore Besterman. Such phrases as 'My soul kisses yours. My prick and my heart are in love with you. I kiss your pretty bottom and all your adorable person'[10] leave no room for doubt as to the nature of the relationship. None of Voltaire's friends could understand his infatuation: they saw Marie-Louise as an ill-favoured – nay, downright ugly – pretentious snob, completely unintelligent and hopeless as a housekeeper. She also spent money like water and hated country life, and in particular life at Cirey.

Though in principle Emilie could not object – she had been sleeping around since the very early days of her relationship with Voltaire – their life together could scarcely have been sweetened by the appearance of what was obviously a very potent new female figure in his life, and one she could only have regarded as totally unworthy of him. Perhaps the situation made Emilie restless, but no sooner had they arrived in Cirey than she decided they must return to Brussels, taking Koenig with them. As they bumped along the uneven roads and Voltaire tried to work, the other two endlessly discussed science, in particular, how small an object could become before it effectively vanished. They bitterly differed on the subject and when Koenig appealed to his senior, Maupertuis, the elder took the junior's side, which caused a rift between Maupertuis and Emilie, ostensibly still lovers. Only an appeal from Voltaire ('You were made to love each other') reconciled the mistress of the writer to her mathematics teacher. Then in the summer of 1740 Emilie published a book of her own, *Institutions de Physique*, in which she discussed the philosophy of Leibniz, whereupon Koenig immediately claimed in print that she had merely written up the lessons he had taught her. Naturally she was furious, and the dispute between them rumbled on for months.

Meanwhile on the death of his father on 31 May Frederick, Crown Prince of Prussia had become Frederick, King of Prussia, and started his reign with a number of acts which boded extremely well: disbanding his father's private regiment of 'giants' – terrifyingly huge men who had been happy to do his every bidding; opening the granaries at time of hunger and selling the grain at a reasonable price; finding employment for thousands of idle workers; abolishing torture and censorship; and incidentally inviting Maupertuis to found a Berlin Academy. It was a good start which even Emilie could not criticise. Another of the King's first actions as monarch was to send a loving message to Voltaire, to which the writer replied, addressing His Majesty as '*Votre Humanité*'.

The signs were that the King wished to come to France and stay with the friend he so far knew only as a disembodied correspondent. Though she still mistrusted Frederick, Emilie could not lightly dismiss the honour of acting hostess to royalty, while Voltaire was now almost as eager to meet Frederick as Frederick was to greet him. In the spring of 1739 she, with Voltaire's capital, had bought a house on the Isle Saint-Louis in Paris, the Palais Lambert. They had not made use of it, but now instructions were given to set it in order. All was ready. The King set out, but as he approached Brussels fell ill. He sent for Voltaire but was not, so he said, sufficiently well to meet a woman. Emilie fumed, but they set off and on 11 September 1740 arrived at a castle near Cleves, some 150 miles from Brussels, where Voltaire found Frederick in bed. Obviously the illness was a real one. He prescribed quinine, and soon the invalid was up and about and well enough to listen to a reading of *Mahomet*.

The two men got on quite as well as they might have hoped. Voltaire sat on the end of the royal bed and they chatted like old friends. Meanwhile, Emilie, in a huff, had left Brussels for Fontainebleau, where she busied herself at the Court, eager to prove that while Voltaire was paying court to his new King, she could build up his reputation with an older one.

In April 1741, at Lille, came the first performance of *Mahomet*,[11] an anti-clerical drama which Voltaire cheekily dedicated to Pope Benedict XIV, who accepted the dedication, praising the author's '*bellissima tragedia*'. The play was ecstatically received, and Voltaire had every hope of an equally enthusiastic response from a French audience. Returning to Paris in the autumn of the year, he read his play at as many evening parties as he could contrive to attend, and sent a copy to Fleury. A production was arranged for August of the following year, at the Comédie Française, when the first night proved a brilliant one, with almost every one of the city's celebrities among the audience. The play's reception was quite as enthusiastic as any author could have hoped. On the following morning, however, it was being put about that far from being an attack on the Mahomet of the Koran, it was in fact an attack on Christianity – on Christ Himself. After all, as one eminent intellectual pointed out, Mahomet and Jesus Christ had the same number of syllables in their names! But despite such silliness, the parallel was noted by a number of people, including Lord Chesterfield, who had heard the play read by the author and also attended a performance. He was in no doubt, he said, that Mahomet was meant to be Christ.[12] Voltaire was summoned by the chief of police, and was forced to withdraw the piece after the third night. It had to wait some years for its real success.

Voltaire's next triumph in Paris followed only five months later, when his tragedy *Mérope* was staged on 20 February 1743. Despite the fact that its subject was maternal love, not a topic calculated to engage the enthusiasm of a Parisian audience, it turned out to be the greatest success in the history of the French stage to date.[13] At the end of the first performance the author was summoned from his box to the stage to receive the applause of the audience – the first time this had ever occurred in France. The success was financial as well as artistic, for the author's proportion of the box office receipts broke all records.

The reasons for this were various. First of all, Voltaire had taken unusual care in the writing of the play, reading it again and again to friends whose opinions he valued, continually revising the text over a period of seven years. Then he had taken the same care with the production, attending every rehearsal and personally directing the actors. There is a record of his instructing the leading actress, Mlle Dumesnil, in the role of the mother, to put much more passion into her cry, '*Barbare! – c'est mon fils!*' After several repetitions she protested that she would have to be possessed by the devil to say the line as he required. 'Precisely,' he replied. 'The devil is exactly what must possess you if you are to succeed.'

Four months later, Frederick received, at last, the news that his friend proposed to pay him a visit. While he had no idea that the reason for Voltaire's decision was other than amiable, the truth was that Cardinal Fleury had written to Voltaire suggesting that he might go to Berlin and report back on Frederick's attitude to the swiftly changing state of affairs in Europe – both the Emperor Charles VI and the Empress Anne of Russia had died shortly after Frederick's father, and there was much juggling about the fate of the Empire. Rather than taking offence at being asked to become a virtual spy at the Court of the man supposed to be his friend, Voltaire was flattered that after persecuting him at length through the notorious censorship system his country should now ask him to act as a sort of unofficial ambassador. He agreed to Fleury's proposition and set out for Prussia, arriving on 30 August 1743 and staying for just over five weeks. Frederick was delighted and welcomed him warmly.

We do not know what Voltaire really felt about Frederick's Court. Even relatively distinguished men who attended it – the amiable bisexual Venetian Francesco Algarotti and the pretty marquis de Lugeac, a secretary at the French Embassy – behaved remarkably freely with the King, and the Court was notable for its louche atmosphere. It was one at which Desfontaines would have felt thoroughly at home. The King's factotum, Fretersdorf, when not accompanying his master on the flute, was in charge of the ballet boys and the *Liebpagen* or pages of the wardrobe, and made sure that sufficient velvet was available for the liveries of Frederick's three most intimate young attendants, 'Sidau', 'Canegister' and 'Dinep' (their real names were von Sydow, Canagiser and von Donop). The visitor may or may not have been amused by the continual practical jokes of the adolescent page Carl Friedrich Pirch, or 'Carol', whom both Frederick and Fretersdorf adored (he was killed in battle when only seventeen).

Voltaire's relationship with Frederick, warm enough when conducted at a distance, was not improved by the visit. There was some spirited discussion about money, for instance; the King felt that the list of expenses submitted to him by his guest was excessive. Then, he did not care for what he thought were superfluous corrections to the manuscript of a work of his own. Voltaire was becoming extremely disillusioned with Frederick's character, suspicious, for instance, of his territorial ambitions. He was right. On the death of Charles VI most European powers had recognised his daughter Maria Theresa as his lawful heiress. Frederick was the exception, and without notice invaded Silesia and occupied the whole province (on the basis, he said, of Prussia's inherited right). Voltaire was outraged by this action from a man he had come to regard as something of a protégé. He was also highly irritated when the King declined to discuss European politics with him (necessary if his visitor was to be of any use to Fleury). When he attempted to bring the talk around to the King's intentions, Frederick remarked that to discuss politics with Voltaire would be like offering medicine to a mistress; poetry was a much better subject for discussion.

However, it seems that he was able to send a number of dispatches back to Paris which were of some interest there. A much more intelligent spy than most, where he could not extract positive information from Frederick or his senior ministers he made intelligent assumptions. He also made interesting friends about the Court, the English ambassador among them, wrote incisively to Paris about international finance and the movements of military forces, and managed to secure from the King a message to Fleury assuring him that he would ever be the friend of France. Fleury did not live to see how well his recruit had done: he died on 29 January 1743.

Frederick was distraught when Voltaire announced his imminent return to Paris. He was still intent on capturing the celebrated author as a sort of tame celebrity, offering him any house or apartment he wanted, an allowance which would keep him in luxury, and complete freedom – 'you will always be the master of your fate. I seek to claim you only by friendship and an agreeable life,' he wrote.[14] But Voltaire was unshakable in his determination to return to France.

Whether because of his irritation or simply in an incautious aside, when he left Prussia he wrote a highly indiscreet letter to Maupertuis, whom he had seen installed as head of the Berlin Academy, referring to the King as '*la respectable, singulière et amiable putain*', that 'laudable, singular and amiable whore'.[15] There seems little doubt that Maupertuis showed the King the letter, and there were no more letters from him suggesting that he would 'faint with pleasure' at the sight of the author, or that his company would provoke his host to 'die an agreeable kind of death'.

8

'Very Famous Savant, Paris'

*It is not enough to be exceptionally mad, licentious and
fanatical in order to win a great reputation – it is still
necessary to arrive on the scene at the right time.*

Letter, 1776

When at the death of Cardinal Fleury a chair became available at the Académie Française, Voltaire had some right to hope that after the great popular success of *Mahomet* and *Mérope* he might be elected to the most prestigious academy in France, and possibly in Europe. The Académie had been established over a century earlier by Cardinal Richelieu 'to regulate and maintain the standards of the French language', and its prestige had resulted in authorship becoming a respectable profession – though not, of course, as reputable as the pursuit of arms. Election was an important cachet for any distinguished writer.

Voltaire's election was in question from the start. The Duchesse de Châteauroux, the newly ennobled Marie-Anne, third of the Nesle sisters to become the King's mistress, supported him, but this counted for little when the Académie's President, the political philosopher Charles Louis de Secondat Montesquieu, tutor to the Dauphin, argued against his admission with the words: 'It would be a disgrace to the Académie if Voltaire were a member, and it will one day be his disgrace that he was not one.'[1]

There was also a predictable conspiracy of churchmen: the Bishop of Mirepoix, an old enemy, was a member of the Académie and used his influence with the committee and the King, who was consulted on appointments. The vacant seat went to the entirely undistinguished Bishop of Bayeux.[2] Voltaire, who had already been denied membership of the almost equally prestigious Academy of Sciences, was learning perhaps a little late (he was now fifty), that honours do not come easily to the unregenerate.

He greeted the news with a schoolboy quip. Mirepoix's seat was described as 'the Ancient Bishopric', and when signing himself he abbreviated *ancien* to *anc*. Voltaire let it be known that the Bishop was really signing himself not *l'anc de Mirepoix* but *l'âne de Mirepoix* – the ass of Mirepoix.

When the news of his friend's double rejection reached Frederick, the King was delighted – it offered him an excellent excuse to renew his invitation to Voltaire to enjoy the hospitality of the Prussian Court, where he would be treated as the great man he undoubtedly was. 'Scorn the nation that knows not how to value the writings of a Voltaire, and come to a country where unbigoted people love you,' he wrote.[3]

Voltaire was comforted to receive notice in November of 1743 that he had been elected a member of the Royal Society in London as 'Dr Franciscus Arouet de Voltaire, Parensiensis'. It was an honour which pleased him enormously. Accepting it, he wrote to the President in his unimproved English claiming that 'one of my strongest desires was to be naturaliz'd in England; the royal society, prompted by you vouschafes to honour me with the best letters of naturalization . . . . The tittle of brother you honour me with is the dearest to me of all titles. I want now to cross the sea to return you my hearthy thanks, and to show my gratitude and veneration for the illustrious society of wich you are the chief member.'[4]

During the months between being rejected by one academy and elected to the other, Voltaire did again visit Frederick; he needed to get away from Paris and perhaps from Emilie and Marie-Louise. He made the most of his visit to Berlin by arranging once again to become a secret agent of France. Arriving at Charlottenburg on 30 August, he settled into the routine there, of which this time he left a detailed description.

Frederick, it appears, rose at five in the bedroom in which he slept on a thin mattress (the curtains of the huge bed of state hid a bookcase). After he had been shaved by a footman, a few of his current favourites – young pages or cadets – visited him and took coffee; one was invited to remain behind when the others left. After a decent – or, more probably, indecent – interval, the favoured catamite was dismissed and a valet arrived with state papers. When he had gone through these the King rose and reviewed his guards, then dined, retired to his study and wrote a little poetry or prose until five or six, when a French scholar came to read to him. At seven there was usually a concert at which Frederick himself often played the flute in performances of his own compositions.[5] Supper was taken in a small room where a large specially commissioned painting hung showing an orgy enjoyed simultaneously by animals and humans. The conversation was often highly indecent but very much centred on values of the classical world.[6]

From Charlottenburg Voltaire again sent periodic dispatches to Paris, which unfortunately have not survived. It is difficult to believe that he got anything of importance out of Frederick, who knew perfectly well what he was up to. When Voltaire impertinently handed him a document asking a variety of questions, such as his opinion on Austria's intentions towards Silesia (which proposed invasion), the King turned the queries aside with a joke or a snatch of popular nonsense song, and when Voltaire tried desperately to get him to commit himself to an alliance by sending a special message to King Louis, his friend merely said: 'The only message I can give you for France is to tell her to behave herself better.'[7] He also tried to muddy Voltaire's name in Paris by clandestinely sending there copies of forged verses allegedly written by his visitor, naming Louis XV as the most stupid King in Europe – all part of his plan to make Voltaire's life in his native country so insupportable that he would be glad to remain permanently in Prussia.

The King then invited his guest to accompany him to Bayreuth on a visit to his sister, the Margravine. Voltaire was happy to comply, and made a conquest of the town and especially of Ulricka, Frederick's younger sister, with whom he flirted so disgracefully (and to such excellent effect) that the rumours of an affair got back to Emilie, who was distraught.

His business as a French spy was carried forward with less success; indeed, it made very little progress. The French Ambassador in Bayreuth was violently jealous of him, and put every obstacle in the way of his meeting anyone of importance. Frederick also bitchily sent the Bishop of Mirepoix a number of documents in which Voltaire had been very rude indeed about him. When they parted on 12 October, both were outwardly as passionately devoted to each other as ever, but both had private reservations.

At Brussels in January 1744, Voltaire was reunited with Emilie and they went on together to Paris, where he expected to be greeted enthusiastically and rewarded generously. Neither was the case. His dispatches, he learned, had been considered uninteresting and uninformative. Instead of any tangible reward, he was merely commanded to write a libretto for an opera by Jean-Philippe Rameau to mark the occasion of the wedding of the Dauphin. *La Princesse de Navarre* is not his most distinguished work – a *'farce de la foire'*, 'a fairground farce', he called it – and its birth was difficult. Rameau and Voltaire each had their pride: the first cared little for the verse ('If I sing so quickly the words will be lost,' said one performer. 'So?' Rameau replied) while the second disliked the composer (though it must be said Voltaire behaved angelically during the collaboration).

In April came the news of the death of M. Denis, Marie-Louise's husband. Voltaire wrote her a letter of commiseration from which any eulogy to the deceased was entirely absent. His concern for his niece was, however, generously expressed: 'How I pity you, how greatly I feel for you in all your sorrow, how I fear for your health . . . Go to Paris, where I can expect to embrace you in October. It is one of my misfortunes not to be able to pass all the rest of my days with you, but I want to see you as much as I can.'[8] He may not have shown the letter to Emilie, whom he had recently told that he no longer considered himself to be her lover in the full meaning of the word. She greeted the announcement calmly; for some time they had only rarely had sexual relations, and as long as she was able to enjoy the attentions of other lovers she was ruefully content with an *affaire blanc*.

She had seen the situation coming for a while. In her *Traité de Bonheur* she had written of the happiness love could offer 'two individuals so attracted to each other that their passions would never cool or become surfeited'. But it would, she said, be unrealistic to hope for such a situation, and indeed 'I was happy for ten years in the love of one who had conquered my soul, and those ten years I spent in perfect communion with him . . . . When age and illness had reduced his affection, a long time passed before I noticed it; I loved for two; I spent my whole life with him, and my trusting heart enjoyed the ecstasy of love, and the illusion of believing itself to be loved . . . I have lost this happy state.'[9]

Emilie may have thought that Voltaire's age, continual illness and lack of physical stamina were responsible for his impotence with her; presumably she did not realise that he was eagerly potent with his niece, nor that the truth of the matter was that he had become physically bored with her – and perhaps found even her intellectual company less stimulating than before (though, goodness knows, Mme Denis could not compete in that area). It was not entirely the end of the affair; but the relationship between them was never again what it had been.

There was a second death in February 1745, this time of Voltaire's Jansenist brother Armand, whose animosity survived him. Rather than make Voltaire executor of his will, he appointed a nephew-in-law, who was unlikely to serve the interests of Armand's family as diligently or well as his brother, and to whom he left a large diamond worth 6,000 livres; his brother received only a small life interest in his fortune.

Voltaire's pride may have been hurt, but there was little consequence to his pocket; he was by now financially secure. Apart from his income from the theatre, he had made a mint from a scam organised with the help of his friend d'Argenson, concerned with military supplies, and had also become a money-lender in a very healthy way of business, lending large sums to the city of Paris at 6 per cent, and to a number of distinguished men from the Duc de Richelieu and the Duc de Villars to the Comte d'Estaing and the Marquis de Lezeau. Very few of them ever repaid the principal, but the interest amounted to a staggering sum –

Nicolas de Largillière painted Voltaire in 1718, when the philosopher was twenty-four, as a present for his actress mistress Suzanne de Livry; sixty years later he saw it hanging on the wall of her salon. (RMN)

Voltaire's château at Ferney.
(© Bettmann/Corbis)

On 30 March 1778, the Comédie Française was crowded with admirers as a bust of Voltaire was crowned with a laurel wreath and the abashed philosopher watched from an upper box (top left). (University

Voltaire with Frederick the Great walking down a corridor at Sans Souci.
(Roger-Viollet, Paris/Bridgeman Art Library, London)

Quentin de La Tour's portrait of Voltaire as a young man, holding a copy of his *Henriade*, shows all the keen-eyed liveliness and charm which captivated almost everyone he met. *(RMN)*

One of Voltaire's characteristics was a complete inability ever to stop work; he dictated even when dressing in the morning. *(Photographie François Martin)*

Marie-Louise Denis, Voltaire's niece, was his housekeeper and mistress from 1744 until his death. Coarse and vulgar, she was disliked by almost everyone but himself. *(RMN)*

Émilie, Marquise de Châtelet, writer, philosopher and the love of Voltaire's life. *(Photographie François Martin)*

es Délices, Voltaire's
ome outside Geneva, to
which almost every visitor
o Switzerland felt bound
o make a pilgrimage,
oping to walk with him
n his 'English' garden.
*Photographie François
Martin)*

VUE DES DELICES DE M.^R DE   VOLTAIRE, PRÈS GENÈVE.

(Dédiée à Monseigneur   le Duc de Praslin.
Pair de France, Lieutenant   Général des Armées du Roi
Chevalier de ses Ordres, Chef   du Conseil Royal des Finances
· Ministre et ·   Secretaire d'Etat, &c &c &c.
Se vend chez Daumont au Nouvel hôtel   Par son très humble et très
De Monnoie et chez Dralet Libraire S.t   obéissant Serviteur Daumont
Germain de l'Auxerrois   avec Privilège du Roi

Jean Antoine Houdon's bust is
generally accepted as the most
telling likeness of Voltaire in old
age (he was eighty-three when it
was made), showing eyes which
Madame de Genlis spoke of as
having 'an inexpressible
sweetness'. *(RMN)*

Jean-Baptiste Pigalle surprised Voltaire by insisting on portraying him in the nude; the result was, however, a peculiarly modern portrait of the elderly writer (RMN)

4,000 livres a year from Villars alone. His investments also paid off well: he had put capital into the Cadiz trade, which equipped ships for the West Indies, and enjoyed a return of 25 per cent. And now, though *La Princesse de Navarre* was by no means a riotous success – as so often with celebratory pieces, members of the audience paid more attention to each other than to the piece, and applauded only half-heartedly – the King greeted Voltaire personally after the performance and awarded him a pension of 2,000 livres and the post of historiographer of France. Such an honour for such a silly piece, he thought ruefully, when his really important work had been scorned and attacked![10] He also became, eight months later, a gentleman of the bedchamber (a title he was permitted to sell, and did so for no less than 53,000 francs).

The position of official historian of France was largely honorary, though it did carry with it occupancy of a suite of rooms in the Palace of Versailles, albeit above the public lavatories and a set of kitchens which were in unhappy proximity. Voltaire was forced to write to demand that 'a door be added to the public privies which are at the foot of my staircase, and that if possible the spout of the neighbouring gutter be diverted so as to flush them'.[11] (Privately, he called his suite 'the most stinking shit-hole in Versailles'.)

It should be remembered that while he was extremely interested in money, he was no miser. He made generous gifts to a number of friends, especially young students, and lent freely to others from whom he never demanded repayment. He gave a generous proportion of the income from his plays to the actors who performed them, and when he lost through bankruptcy 40,000 livres loaned to a farmer, he merely remarked that what the Lord had given, He had taken away.

It was perhaps now time to try again for the greater honour. Four chairs at the Académie had fallen vacant since the triumphant production of *Mérope*, and each time Voltaire had been passed over. Now another was available, and things had changed somewhat since his last application for membership. The official historian of France would surely not be treated with quite the same disrespect as the mere upstart playwright. He had also more carefully prepared the ground, having given some friends the difficult but not impossible task of convincing Pope Benedict XIV that he was 'an admirer of virtue' (not necessarily a lie) and a man of piety (rather more questionable). The Pope, who was enlightened and well read, knew all about the *Lettres philosophiques* and *La Pucelle*, and had read and admired *Mahomet*, the dedication of which he had accepted (he was no more a lover of the extreme, fanatical side of the Catholic Church than Voltaire). It may be, however, that the papal tongue was firmly in the papal cheek when he sent the playwright two enormous medals and a portrait of himself 'with the assurance of Our respect for merits which are so outstanding as yours'.[12]

The Pope's blessing having been more or less obtained, Voltaire turned his attention to securing votes. He enlisted the help of his old friend the Comte d'Argental and his wife. He was not, he told them, well enough to run about electioneering, even if he wanted to: 'People have already spoke to V. about who is to succeed Président Bouhier; V. is ill; V. is in no state to exert himself; V. is growing grey-haired and cannot decently go knocking on people's doors even though he counts on the King's support.'[13] On 25 April 1746 he was elected – he claimed by unanimous assent, though tradition insists that one vote was cast against him. His election to the Académie was swiftly followed by admission to a number of other institutions both in France and abroad.

Voltaire was now fifty-two years old and unquestionably the most successful writer in Europe. In France several collected editions of his works (both approved and pirated) had already been published, while there can have been few intelligent readers in the rest of Europe who had not heard his name and probably read him in translation. One letter arrived at his house simply addressed to 'Monsieur de Voltaire, very famous Savant, Paris'.[14] His fame did not prevent some people attacking him. Apart from the usual gaggle of churchmen, inevitably led by Mirepoix and such malcontents as Desfontaines, the most vicious of his enemies was a nonentity called Roi, a bad poet who – probably because his own ambition for election to the Académie had time and again been thwarted – hated Voltaire and published a vicious attack on him at the time of his installation.

Perhaps understandably the irritation of continual sniping eventually led Voltaire, not for the first time, to lose his equanimity.

He began to hit back, indiscriminately and unwisely. A violinist of the Opéra orchestra, one Travenol, had been circulating the pamphlet put out by Roi, and Voltaire insisted that the police arrest him. It was a silly move, especially in view of the fact that a bookseller whose arrest he had also insisted upon had turned out to be a dying man. Travenol was not dying, but was in poor circumstances and had an invalid daughter. The case came to court, and though it was proved, Voltaire had to pay all costs; unfortunately, it also earned him the reputation with the public of a man who persecuted the dying, the poor and the crippled.

In the middle of all the backbiting and tittle-tattle, and such domestic upsets as the desertion of all his and Emilie's servants on the same day (Emilie's because of her unwillingness to pay a decent wage, and Voltaire's in sympathy), the writer was working away at a new play. *Sémiramis* was written at the Château d'Anet and at Fontainebleau, where as a member of the court Voltaire had to fulfil certain social obligations, but got up early every morning and sat at work in his dressing-gown.

He now had a new supporter at court: the King's latest mistress, Jeanne Antoinette Normand d'Étioles. Mme de Châteauroux had died suddenly while in her late twenties, and within a few months Jeanne had taken her place in the royal bed. This extraordinary woman had sprung from the lower middle class. Her father, a M. François Poisson, was a merchant who had at one stage of his life been sentenced to death for financial corruption. Her mother was no better than she should be, enjoying a series of amorous adventures. One of her lovers (he may have been the child's real father) paid for Jeanne's education, and a fine education it was – she learned singing from the great baritone Jélyotte and the art of elocution from the great actor Crébillon; she could play the harpsichord and draw, and by the time she was fifteen her mother was describing her as 'a morsel fit for a king'.

She married a commoner, Charles Guillaume Lenormant d'Étioles, the son of one of Mme Poisson's lovers. He loved and supported her, and she was soon running her own salon, to which Voltaire was invited as an old friend of her mother – he had known Jeanne all her life: 'I saw her born,' he would inaccurately claim.

It was in 1745 that she became the mistress of the King, her husband reluctantly complaisant (he got little from the bargain, merely being given a position as a tax inspector). She was presented at court as 'Madame de Pompadour', though the Dauphin at first referred to her as 'Madame Whore'. The Court was equally unenthusiastic, sneering at what were considered her imperfect manners. But for artists and writers, her ascendancy promised well. She built a library of over three and a half thousand books, and encouraged a number of distinguished authors. She became an avid and knowledgeable collector of works of art; she clearly had 'an eye', and her influence on the development of French art has hitherto barely been acknowledged. Under her auspices a theatre was set up at Versailles where specially commissioned plays were performed by the courtiers themselves with even the Dauphin eventually being persuaded to play opposite her in a Molière comedy. Gradually, she made herself the conduit not only for artists but for those who sought honours or special favours of the King. Moreover, she was prepared to take Voltaire's side in any public controversy – his enemies were hers (she hated the Bishop of Mirepoix almost as much as he). Voltaire had spent some time during 1745 at her house at Étoiles while the King was away at the war with England and Holland, and came to admire her more and more (he seriously irritated Emilie by his praise of her, and especially of her complete lack of interest in gambling, Emilie's major vice).

Their friendship might have seemed to augur well; she introduced Voltaire to court and gave him commissions. But their relationship in fact did Voltaire little good, entirely through his own fault – that vein of blank disregard for the susceptibilities of others which sometimes betrayed him. He failed to recognise how strongly the King disliked any public reference to the fact that he had a mistress, and offended him deeply by studiously deferring to Mme de Pompadour in public exactly as if she were queen, while the Queen herself stood by. Louis, who had a real regard for his wife, took note and though Voltaire was not actually dismissed from court, it was made plain to him that his presence there gave their Majesties no special pleasure. He succeeded in offending the King still further in a poem he wrote to celebrate the success of the French at the battle of Bergen op Zoom, describing His

Majesty as flying from the victory straight into the arms of the Pompadour. True, no doubt, but hardly tactful.

Then there was another major gaffe. One evening in October 1747, Voltaire was looking over Emilie's shoulder while she was playing cards at the Queen's table. She quickly lost the 400 louis with which she had sat down, and another 200 he loaned her. At her request he then sent a footman for 200 more, after losing which she played on giving a note of hand. When she had lost 103,000 livres he lost his temper and remarked clearly, in English, 'Don't you see you're playing with knaves?' There was muttering as those who could speak English translated his remark for those who could not; then an icy silence. Voltaire and Emilie quickly left the room and then the palace. They drove to Sceaux, where they were given refuge by their friend the Duchesse du Maine. There they stayed for some months in secrecy, Voltaire paying for his keep by reading the duchesse his latest work as it came from his pen – a treat which she, an extremely cultivated woman, regarded as generous rent for his apartment at the top of the house, reached by a secret staircase. It all sounds melodramatic; but Voltaire may well have remembered the affair of the Chevalier de Rohan, years before, and acted accordingly.

Among the work he read the duchesse – the 'sublime old personage' as he affectionately called her – at two in the morning, while she lay in bed and he sat at a table by her bedside in nightcap and dressing-gown, were a number of long short stories, among them *Zadig*, his best fiction apart from *Candide*. It is a delightful story, if story is the word, for Voltaire was inventing a new genre, which became known as *conte philosophique*, neither short story nor novella; perhaps 'moral tale' is the best phrase, although that has overtones of tedium these tales certainly do not possess.

Zadig is a young man living in Babylon 'in the reign of King Moabdar', intelligent, well educated, modest and wealthy, and convinced that therefore he can be happy. The incidents of his life sadly teach him otherwise: that no honest man can escape misfortune – that, in fact, happiness may be pursued but will only rarely be captured. Again, this sounds like a dull moral tale but it is lighthearted, witty and ingenious: for instance there is a splendid lesson in deduction when, in the third chapter, Zadig, seeing some tracks in the ground, deduces that they were made by the Queen's 'very small spaniel bitch which has had puppies recently; her left forefoot is lame, and she has very long ears'.

Questioned, he reveals his method: 'The long, shallow furrows printed on the little ridges of sand between the tracks of the paws informed me that the animal was a bitch with pendent dugs, who hence had had puppies recently. Other tracks in a different direction, which seemed all the time to have scraped the surface of the sand beside the forepaws, gave me the idea that the bitch had very long ears; and as I remarked that the sand was always less hollowed by one paw than the three others, I concluded that our August queen's bitch was somewhat lame.'[15] Elementary, one might say.

Overshadowed by *Candide*, *Zadig* really deserves to be better known. In its time it was famous – the King once caused a verse from it to be sung every day to a conceited courtier who had ideas above his station:

> *Que son mérit est extreme!*
> *Que de grâces! Que de grandeur!*
> *Ah! Combien monseigneur*
> *Doit être content de lui-même.*

> [How extremely important he is!
> What graces! What grandeur!
> Ah! How *very* pleased this gentleman is with himself!]

The other stories from this period are almost equally delightful: in *Memnon the Philosopher* a man who succeeds in being wholly reasonable concludes that earth can only be a place to which the inhabitants of other planets consign their lunatics; *The Travels of Scarmentado* foreshadows Candide in its satirical tableaux of cruelty and ignorance; *Micromégas* is more or less science fiction: a visitor from Sirius is appalled when an inhabitant of Saturn reveals that he can only expect to live to be 15,000 years old, and therefore begins to die almost the moment he is born.

Meanwhile, Emilie was working hard to re-establish herself and her companion at court, and by dint of paying all her gambling debts and abasing herself before those whom she had insulted, brought both Voltaire and herself back to Paris, then took him off to Lunéville to visit the court of King Stanislas of Lorraine, where they took over a theatre and mounted several productions, including a highly successful performance of *Mérope*. In the audience was a handsome guards officer, the marquis Jean François de Saint-Lambert, whom Emilie had met some years previously. They now had time to renew what had seemed a promising friendship and by the time she and Voltaire returned to Paris to supervise the extremely successful premiere of *Sémiramis*, they had become more than friends. Once the play had been mounted, Emilie insisted on travelling to Nancy, where Saint-Lambert was stationed with his regiment.

It was not in Voltaire's nature to be jealous of Emilie – he had, now, little right to be so, and recognised the fact; but he insisted on a certain decorum. When, one evening at Commercy, he came upon the couple in a compromising position, he was furious that they should have afforded him the opportunity to do so, and was so violent in his rebuke that Saint-Lambert felt he had no other recourse than to challenge him to a duel. Almost immediately, all three realised that things had got out of hand. Saint-Lambert in particular was really not in love with Emilie, though she was besotted with him; he did not want to kill the foremost author of the age for so trivial a reason.

Emilie went to Voltaire's bedroom in the middle of the night to persuade him that he had not actually seen what he thought he had seen. Voltaire knew perfectly well what he had seen, and Emilie knew that he knew, and Voltaire knew that she knew that he knew; but in the end he saw reason. 'You are in the happy age of love,' he told her; 'enjoy these too brief moments. An old invalid like me is not made for such pleasures.' In the morning Saint-Lambert came, paid his respects and apologised, and on the following evening the three dined amicably together.[16]

But it was a fateful affair, all the same, for in December, when Voltaire and Emilie returned to Cirey, she had to confess that she was pregnant. Aghast, the couple consulted with Saint-Lambert and came up with a solution which they hoped would save all their reputations. Emilie wrote to her husband, at Dijon with his regiment, and invited him warmly to visit her. It was actually rather late for all this: rumours of her condition had already got out, and her more spiteful friends were asking why she suddenly wanted to see the marquis – to which the answer was, 'It's just one of those fancies of a pregnant woman'.

However, the marquis was not privy to the situation, and was delighted on his arrival at Cirey to be welcomed not only to the château, but – most unexpectedly – to the marital bed, to which he had been a stranger for many years. This second honeymoon lasted for three weeks, at the end of which the Marquise de Châtelet announced that she was pregnant. The marquis (for whom one cannot but feel an astonished sympathy) was absolutely delighted. They all drank the health of the coming child, then the marquis and Saint-Lambert rejoined their regiments and Voltaire and Emilie left for Paris.

No one except the marquis was particularly happy. Saint-Lambert cordially wished that he need never see Emilie again, but felt honour bound to support her until the birth; for her part, Emilie was terrified that someone would indiscreetly inform her husband of the true situation; and Voltaire knew that the truth was already being bruited about, and was also frightened because Emilie was far too old for another pregnancy not to be extremely dangerous.

She too must have been aware of the fact, but throughout her pregnancy continued to work steadily at her translation of Newton – from eight or nine o'clock in the morning until three, when she had a coffee break, and then from four until ten, when she would talk with Voltaire for two or three hours before returning to her desk until five. Two or three hours' sleep was quite sufficient, she thought, even for a pregnant woman. In June 1749, the couple travelled to Lunéville, where Emilie had been loaned the Queen's apartments in which to have her child. Saint-Lambert came when he could be spared from his military duties; when he left, she wrote him pathetic letters:

When I am with you, I can bear my condition, often, indeed, I hardly notice it, but when I lose you everything goes blank. I walked to my little summer-house today and my belly is so terribly fallen, I am suffering such pain in my kidneys, I feel so sad this evening that it would not surprise me if I had the baby tonight. I should be miserable, though you, I know, would be pleased. My pains would be easier to bear if you were here in the same house . . . .[17]

The pregnancy had been tiresome; the birth was astonishingly easy. One morning, while seated at her desk, Emilie announced that she 'felt something', and almost immediately gave birth to a little girl, who tradition says was laid on the open pages of a big book. Emilie then put the papers on which she had been working in order, and went to bed. All seemed well. But after a few days, she became feverish, developed palpitations, then seemed to be recovering. Voltaire went one evening to supper, leaving Saint-Lambert at her bedside. A few minutes later she had a short bout of hiccoughs, then simply stopped breathing. Summoned from table, Voltaire acted like a drunken man, staggered to the door, fell down some steps onto a terrace and began beating his head on the flagstones. Saint-Lambert picked him up. He raised his head, looked into the other's eyes, and said gently: 'Ah! Mon ami! C'est vous qui me l'avez tuée.' Then, with a dreadful cry: 'Eh! Mon Dieu! Monsieur, de quoi avisiez-vous de lui faire un enfant?'[18]

His grief was genuine and, for a time, terrible. The fact that he and Emilie had not been passionate lovers for some years did not in the least diminish his mourning for a beloved companion who was in every sense but the legal one, his wife. He felt, as those bereaved after a long partnership do, completely at a loss. Should he retire to a monastery for a period of mourning and reflection? Should he make another visit to England? Immediately after the funeral, he returned to Cirey, and found to his relief that he could bear to be there alone. It was almost as though she was working, as she used to, in a neighbouring room. But he realised that there was no lasting consolation to be found there: he had not lost a mistress, he told d'Argental, but half of himself, and wherever he went he would be but half a man.

The rest of the world did not share his grief. Emilie had done nothing, and cared to do nothing, which would endear her to her critics, and there were no approving or complimentary obituaries. She had been 'different', and that, for a woman in eighteenth-century Europe, was simply not permissible if one wished to be accepted in society. Most people were as critical and dismissive of her in death as they had been in life. 'I have just heard that Madame du Châtelet died yesterday in childbirth,' wrote one critic.[19] 'It is to be hoped that this is the last of the airs she will give herself. To die in childbirth at her age is truly to seek singularity and endeavour to do everything differently from other people.'

There were also cruel jokes, which must have hurt Voltaire when he heard them (as he certainly did; gossips were never still). Someone – King Frederick, it was said, wrote an obituary poem: Emilie had died of giving birth to two children at once, and nobody could tell which killed her; Saint-Lambert said that it was her book on Newton, Voltaire that it was her baby.[20]

Emilie deserved more than this. She may have been pretentious, and certainly did not suffer fools gladly, but was extremely intelligent and devoted to learning. She published three remarkable works: *Institutions de physique* (1740), *Dissertation sur la nature et la propagation du feu* (1744) and *Principes mathématiques de la philosophie naturelle* (1744). During her lifetime as well as after her death, she was accused of deriving much of what she wrote from her teachers, but the major modern student of Voltaire's life, Theodore Besterman, claims that study of her letters clearly shows her capacity for independent thought and scientific methodology.[21] Many of her texts were addressed to the very teachers whose work she was accused of plagiarising, and contained independent and original critical argument which could not have been derived from them. She was generous in her encouragement of those she respected, and her compliments to those she admired and her respect for genuine knowledge cannot be doubted, nor the fact that she had a passionate love of scholarship: 'it is the passion most necessary for our happiness,' she wrote.[22] 'It is a sure safeguard against misfortune, a source of inexhaustible pleasure.' She was one of the most remarkable women of her time.

Though Cirey reminded Voltaire every day of her lively and inspiring presence, it also reminded him of his loss, and he gradually began to pack up his belongings. Within a few months of her death he had moved to Paris, though he hated the thought of living and, more particularly dying in the city where, as a known critic of the Church, he would stand an excellent chance of the kind of burial given to Adrienne Lecouvreur. Longchamps described the first few weeks in the apartment in the Rue Traversière, Voltaire rambling from room to room talking to Emilie, crying her name. But very slowly he began again to take an interest in life, received friends and, at Christmas 1749, took his niece Marie-Louise into his establishment as housekeeper and, though no one seriously suspected it, as his mistress.

The reason why it was not until his letters to her were discovered during the twentieth century that anyone knew of the intimate relationship between M. Voltaire and Mme Denis seems mainly to do with her character. Few who knew this vulgar, salacious, pretentious, greedy, indiscreet gossip seriously entertained the suspicion that Voltaire might share her bed. The fact that she fancied herself as an author cannot have added to her charm as far as he was concerned, and the only possible explanation is that the sexual chemistry between them was considerable – considerable enough to more than satisfy his less than insistent appetite. At all events, she moved in with him, and remained with him until his death.

Voltaire now turned again to the theatre. He wanted to mount his play *Rome sauvée*, and eventually put it on in a little theatre he contrived in the attic of the house in the Rue Traversière. The audience was invited and special tickets were printed for them; and when they arrived they found to their surprise that Voltaire himself was acting the main role, of Nero – a triumph he repeated at the home of the Duchesse du Maine at Sceaux.

Meanwhile, Frederick saw the death of Emilie as removing one of the main obstacles to Voltaire's permanent residence at his Court – and Voltaire at last seemed inclined to accept the invitation. At least, he promised, he would make a visit in summer, when the journey would be a little less dauntingly cold and wet. However, he started making preparations almost immediately, prompted by the suspicion that Frederick was transferring his literary affections to another writer, Baculard d'Arnaud, ironically a previous lover of Marie-Louise –

whom he determined should accompany him to Berlin. Frederick was not at all pleased by the idea; why was Voltaire always so concerned about women? He gave way, reluctantly – he would receive Mme Denis, but insisted that though he was prepared to meet Voltaire's travelling expenses, she must pay her own way. Voltaire's reaction was to ask for 4,000 German crowns, which would pay for his journey and enable him to make Marie-Louise an allowance to keep her while he was away. He would leave for Berlin alone immediately on receipt of the money.

Frederick perhaps thought the sum necessary to relieve himself of the company of his favourite's second mistress well spent, and dispatched the money. Voltaire sent as a receipt a little rhyme in which he rather oddly compared himself to Danaë reclining beneath Jupiter's shower of gold. So the die was cast. But he was still not entirely at ease, and had Louis XV refused him permission to leave France he would probably have been relieved, rather than otherwise. But the King told him coldly that he was free to go wherever he wanted. Of course, his position as official historian of France must be relinquished, together with the salary.

As to the rest of Paris, the general feeling was that while Voltaire had in the past been troublesome and was not altogether to be admired, there was no doubt that he was France's most distinguished author, and it was regrettable that he was leaving the country for a Prussian Court. Indeed, a poster appeared in the streets with a caricature of Voltaire in a bearskin helmet with the caption: 'Voltaire the Prussian – one sou'. But it was too late to turn back, and on 18 June 1750, at the age of fifty-six, he left Paris, not to return for almost thirty years.

9

A Prince's Favour

The dead are indifferent to slander – the living can die of it.

Letter, 1768

Had Emilie lived, it is doubtful whether even the offer of the post of chamberlain and chevalier of the Order of Merit together with free accommodation and a salary of 5,000 *thalers* a year would have tempted Voltaire to leave Paris for Berlin. Had he been so tempted, she would certainly have argued him out of accepting Frederick's proposal. As it was, the freedom to publish his books and perform his plays was as great an inducement as the financial and social ones, and there was also the suggestion (carefully put about by the King himself) that Frederick was about to press his favours on yet another French writer, Elie Fréron (who incidentally had married his own niece). Fréron was not a favourite with Voltaire, of whose work he had lately been one of the severest critics, and the thought that he might be preferred added zest to the idea of accepting Frederick's invitation. He wrote to Berlin announcing his imminent arrival (at the same time pointing out how insignificant a writer Fréron was).

The reception he received when he arrived in Prussia to kiss the hand of his new employer must have reassured him that his decision was the right one. He was set up in handsome apartments at Sans Souci, the summer palace which Frederick had had built at Potsdam only a few years before Voltaire's arrival. It was, and remains, one of the most delightful palaces of Europe: a long, low building at the top of a series of terraces, hanging some 60 feet above magnificent gardens, looking down on the River Havel three-quarters of a mile away, and on a great fountain which sends a jet of water higher than the palace roof. It is said that Frederick decided to be buried on the topmost terrace with his pet dog, for '*Quand je serai là, je serai sans souci*', 'When I am there, I am without care'.

The architect of the palace, G.W. von Knobelsdorf, made it a light, gay building decorated, it was said, in the 'Frederican rococo' style, the rooms well lit, their walls glittering with graceful mirrors, gilded leaves and flowers. Voltaire was given a suite immediately adjacent to that of the King, and was assured that he could make free use of Frederick's coaches and horses and give whatever orders he wished to a corps of at least a dozen servants who were at hand at all hours of the day and night. The members of the court, from the Queen herself to the meanest visiting prince, treated him with deference, and Frederick was the most amiable of hosts. Voltaire wrote to d'Argental in September, 'I find the protection of the King, the conversation of a philosopher, the agreeable qualities of an amiable man, all united in one who for sixteen years has wished to console me for my misfortunes, make me secure against my enemies. . . . Here I am sure of a destiny for ever tranquil. If one can be sure of anything it is of the character of the King of Prussia.'[1]

Frederick indeed treated Voltaire with almost magnificent courtesy. As Carlyle put it, 'Friedrich is loyally glad over his Voltaire; eager in all ways to content him, make him happy; and keep him there, as the Talking Bird, the Singing Tree and the Golden Water of intelligent mankind; the glory of one's court, and the envy of the world'.[2] While the King had lost his taste for metaphysics, he was as interested as ever in French poetry, and regarded Voltaire as the greatest living expert on that subject. He was determined to, as he put it, *posséder* Voltaire – actually to *possess* him – not only as an ornament to his Court but as, still, a tutor who would oversee his own literary efforts.

For his part, Voltaire either did not understand or chose not to understand the fact that Frederick was now a war-monger, and that Potsdam was one huge barracks, five battalions being strictly confined to the city and rarely given permission to leave it. Nor did he comment on the fact that the King seemed to have taken against the whole female race: his court was notable for the almost complete absence of women. There were magnificent banquets, and though Voltaire did not relish the rich food (he said he would die within three months if he had to dine with the King every day), the conversation at table and afterwards was free and marvellously intelligent, the opera and theatre were excellent, and within months of his arrival both his *Mort de César* and *Zaïre* were performed, to great applause. Later, *Mahomet* was equally successful.

He was not, of course, the only guest at Frederick's Court. There was Francesco Algarotti, an Italian count with an interest in science, and the author of a not very good book on Newton; the Chevalier de Chasot, a brilliant flautist who had reputedly saved the King's life at the battle of Molditz (his only defect was his inveterate womanising); Julien Offrray de La Mattrie, a doctor who spent much of his time dissecting bodies in an attempt to prove that they did not contain a soul; and Baron Pollnitz, an eccentric who was a sort of court jester. And there was the Marquis d'Argens, whom Voltaire rather liked, and who was always happy to oblige the company with stories of his adventures – which included an affair with a dancing girl in Turkey, where he narrowly escaped impalement for that impertinence.

But Voltaire was, naturally next to Frederick, at the centre of the life of Sans Souci. He was flattered by the continual attentions paid him by everyone about the Court: the King's brothers seemed positively flattered to be allowed to play him at chess, the royal princes courteously asked permission to call on him, the Queen Mother invited him to dine, and he himself entertained generously – 'Come and have a cut off the royal roast', he would say, sending the account to the King's treasurer. He spent Frederick's money like water – a fact Frederick noted without pleasure.

Voltaire was sufficiently seduced to write almost immediately to Marie-Louise, insisting that she join him in an idyllic life. Frederick, he said, had promised her 4,000 livres a year if she would come and keep house for her uncle. She, however, cannily declined. The friendship of kings, she pointed out, was never entirely to be depended upon, and while Voltaire thought of Frederick as a friend, he might very well soon be reminded that he was also a master. In any case, she was perfectly happy in Paris, where she was enjoying the attention of a circle of lovers, including (Longchamps reported) a large and muscular German bassoonist and an Italian tenor.

In an extraordinary act, Voltaire showed her letter to the King, who sent him a response to it before he went to bed: 'If I could foresee that your removal hither would turn the least in the world to your disadvantage, I should be the first to dissuade you from it . . . I am firmly persuaded that you will be very happy here; that you will be regarded as the father of letters and of people of taste; and that you will find in me all the consolation which a man of your merit can expect from one who esteems him. Good night.'[3]

Voltaire was not too distressed that his housekeeper-mistress had decided not to join him. By the time she had replied to his invitation, he was on familiar terms with a pretty, lively married woman, Charlotte Sophia of Aldenburg, Countess Bentinck. She was in her mid-thirties, twenty-three years Voltaire's junior, and married to a younger son of the Earl of Portland, but she had left her husband after seven years (though she would, she told her friend Catherine the Great of Russia, have been madly in love with him had they not been married) and was happy to become the mistress of so remarkable a man.

But Marie-Louise was, of course, right. The scene almost immediately began to cloud. The Countess was a beautiful woman, but though beautiful boys were more in Frederick's line he was jealous of any woman admired by his friend. His attitude to his guest swiftly cooled, and in order that Voltaire should have plenty to distract him from his new companion, he began to submerge him in a torrent of verses and speeches written in French which he was supposed to approve and/or correct. And while the King deferred to his Chamberlain in the matter of French grammar, he was no happier than any other author to have his work criticised. He was particularly irritated at the extent to which Voltaire found fault with his long, 1,600-line poem *Art de la guerre*; and his irritation was compounded when its readers particularly admired passages which turned out to be among the 300 or so lines contributed entirely by his critic.

Then, with his infallible instinct to foul his own nest, Voltaire involved himself in a shady deal which forced Frederick to dismiss him. Extremely rich, he was never content with the money he had, and though in some ways generous was in others penny-pinching and incorrigibly bent on economy: he would even collect the candle-ends at the close of each evening in order that they could be used the following day. Nor could he ever resist running after a potentially profitable deal. Discovering that in a treaty signed at the end of the recent war with Saxony Frederick had insisted that *Steuerscheine* (revenue certificates issued by the state bank of Saxony) which had fallen to half their original value should be redeemed at full value, in gold, for those Prussians who had bought them, he sensed a seemingly golden opportunity. Some speculators had found that they could buy the certificates in Holland at a very low price, and make an enormous profit by redeeming them at home.

Frederick, in an attempt to foil the scam, had forbidden the importation of *Steuerscheine*, but Voltaire stupidly commissioned a Jewish banker to go to Dresden and buy a large bundle of them at 35 per cent of their face value. Abraham Hirsch set off, but almost immediately Voltaire learned from an acquaintance that his envoy was far from trustworthy, and cancelled the bill of exchange he had given Hirsch. When the bill was refused in Dresden Hirsch was furious. Returning, he demanded compensation. In order to buy his silence, Voltaire arranged to purchase some diamonds from him. They turned out to be paste, and Voltaire unwisely had Hirsch arrested – at which the latter revealed the original deal. Voltaire protested that he had merely commissioned Hirsch to buy furs for him in Dresden, but the story was a thin one.

Frederick was understandably furious. 'I was glad to receive you in my house,' he wrote.[4] 'I esteemed your genius, your talents and acquirements, and I had reason to think that a man of your age, wearied with fencing against authors and exposing himself to the storm, came hither to take refuge as in a safe harbour . . . . You have had the most villainous affair in the world with a Jew. It has made a fearful scandal all over town. And that *Steuerscheine* business is so well known in Saxony that they have made grievous complaints of it to me. For my part, I have preserved peace in my house till your arrival; and I warn you that if you have a passion for intriguing and caballing, you have applied to the wrong hand . . . . If you can resolve to live like a philosopher, I shall be glad to see you; but if you abandon yourself to all the violences of your passions, and get into quarrels with all the world, you will do me no good by coming here.'

Voltaire prostrated himself, but was shown out of his apartments at Sans Souci and put into a small house nearby, where having few visitors he took to spending fifteen or sixteen hours a day in bed, working at a tray placed over his knees. A table at the bedside bore a bag of lentils, some boiled eggs and an endless supply of coffee (he would drink twenty cups in an afternoon). He wrote to his friends in Paris claiming still to be having a wonderful time; but this was far from the truth. There were continual irritants. Someone told Voltaire in a famous but unattributed phrase, that the King had remarked that he needed him (as a tutor in French) only for another year – 'one squeezes an orange and then discards the peel'. For his part, he told Pierre Maupertuis that the King was 'always sending him his dirty linen to wash', a reference to Frederick's literary efforts. He felt increasingly insecure. He was, he told Marie-Louise, like a man falling through the air from the top of a tower: 'I'm all right – so far.' The weather, he said, was turning distinctly chilly; and he was not speaking meteorologically.

In his letters to Paris he always stressed that he was not going to stay in Berlin for ever while at the same time continually making excuses to delay his return. First, there was the prospect of a visit to Italy. Then he promised to return in the autumn, but when autumn came the roads were too muddy. Better to wait until winter, he said, when they would be frozen and hard. But in winter it was too cold to move. Spring would be better for travelling. However, spring found him finishing and correcting his book on the age of Louis XIV. Then the book was published, and he thought it best to wait until he knew how it had been received in France. So, a whole year passed.

It was a dispute with Pierre Maupertuis that brought things to a head. A former lover of Emilie du Châtelet, Maupertuis was now head of the Berlin Academy of Sciences, a post he had held since 1745. Undoubtedly extremely self-satisfied and conceited, he had become something of a thorn in Voltaire's flesh. He was dynamic, intelligent, knowledgeable and not without wit, but sharing a supper-table with him was not something Voltaire particularly enjoyed; there were definitely times when the former conversationally outshone the latter. Voltaire was not used to that, and found it unpalatable. On the other hand, Maupertuis was equally jealous of Voltaire's *bons mots*, at which the attention turned to him. After all, until his rival's appearance, he had been the presiding genius at Frederick's table. Voltaire suspected, and with reason, that Maupertuis had repeated his indiscreet comment on Frederick's 'dirty washing' to the King. The situation was not a recipe for tranquillity.

'My desire is,' said the prophet Job, 'that . . . mine adversary had written a book.'[5] Voltaire's enemy made just that mistake. Maupertuis published his theory of the principle of least action, which contributed to the development of mechanical theory, but which he presented as a reason for believing in the existence of God. Shortly after publication, the Swiss mathematician Koenig published an attack on the originality of the theory, quoting an unpublished letter by Liebniz which seemed to state the identical law. Maupertuis, furious, foolishly accused Koenig of forging the letter, and persuaded his cronies at the Academy to support him.

Voltaire quite properly thought this disreputable, and in an anonymous article told the story with cold, clinical and lethal accuracy.[6] He had underestimated Frederick's regard for Maupertuis and, moreover, for the reputation of the Berlin Academy. Frederick wrote a reply accusing the anonymous author (whom he knew perfectly well to be Voltaire) of being 'malicious, cowardly and infamous', 'a shameless imposter', an 'ugly brigand' and 'a concocter of stupid libels' and had it printed, with no author's name attached, but bearing the royal coat of arms.

Voltaire was not standing for that, and wrote in response a *Diatribe of Dr Akakia, Physician and Ordinary to the Pope*, in which he ridiculed many of Maupertuis's propositions (which were indeed easy to ridicule, among them being the proposal to bore a hole to the centre of the earth to study its composition, and the view that a sufficient dose of opium would enable a man to foretell the future). Frederick saw the pamphlet and was amused, but forbade Voltaire to publish it.

Nevertheless, it was soon being celebrated all over Europe, including Prussia, as a brilliant satire. Maupertuis took to his bed. Frederick was furious: all Europe was being advised that he had chosen a fool to head his Academy. On Christmas Eve 1752, he had a copy of the *Diatribe* burned by the public executioner.

Voltaire wrote to the King asking his forgiveness for 'an old man crushed by sickness and grief',[7] but he saw that his stay in Prussia had run its natural course. On 1 January 1753 he gave formal notice that he wished to leave the court, and returned the gold key which was the symbol of his position as chamberlain. He also, tactlessly and rudely, returned his Cross of Merit with a set of verses:

> *Je les reçus avec tendresse,*
> *Je vous les rends avec doleur*
> *Tel qu'un amant dans sa jalouse ardeur*
> *Rend le portrait de sa maîtresse.*[8]

He later translated it into English:

> With rapture I those gifts receiv'd,
> Now to return them much I'm grieved;
> Such pangs the jealous swain attack
> Who sends his mistress' picture back.

Be that, Frederick must have thought, as it may; to return an order which had been his personal gift was an insult. He made only the very slightest further attempt to persuade Voltaire to stay – he was still, after all, an ornament to the Court; but the die was cast, and on 26 March the philosopher left Frederick's company for good. Maupertuis also left Berlin, to die in Basle never having recovered his reputation.

Voltaire's time in Berlin had not entirely been wasted in argument and recrimination. He had completed his *Le Siècle de Louis XIV* and seen it printed – Berlin being, he felt, the only city in which it could be published free of interference from the censors: 'There is not,' he wrote to Richelieu, 'one little censor of books [in France] who would not have made a merit and duty out of mutilating or suppressing my work.'[9]

The book had taken him almost twenty years to complete, and was the result of the most intensive research and scholarship; he had read, he reckoned, over two hundred books and thousands of manuscripts, and talked to as many people as possible who were old enough to recollect the years of which he was writing. Emilie had helped and advised him and the result was a remarkable examination of a whole epoch of French history, an epoch which he regarded as one of the most civilised in modern history, a period in which taste in art, music, theatre reached an apogee. He also celebrated Louis XIV as a monarch whose personal administration of his country had produced a truly great nation, and whose encouragement and nurturing of the arts and the intellectual life of the State had made France the most civilised country in Europe. The King's grand mode of life also appealed: the elegance of his court and the exemplary courtesy and politeness of every member of it from the King down, had been wholly admirable. Despite certain shortcomings in the administration of law and neglect of what we would now call human rights, a sort of perfection had been achieved during the reign of Louis XIV.

Le Siècle de Louis XIV was and continues to be a remarkable work; it is the first example of the critical examination by an author of a recent period in history rather than of events and personalities of the distant past. Voltaire wonderfully caught the spirit of the age about which he wrote, and though he was not impressive in his attempts to excuse or pass over Louis's military aggression and later defeats, he produced a book which remains an excellent example of modern historical methodology – and one which was astonishingly readable.[10] Sadly, it was at first sparingly read in France, where for years it was only available from beneath the counter of some accommodating bookseller. In itself, it was not considered disreputable; but such praise of a King who was dead could be regarded as criticism of the living, reigning monarch.

Apart from the publication of his history, Voltaire's time at Frederick's Court had one more positive result, though it did not reach fruition for many years. One evening at supper, Frederick suggested that everyone present should collaborate on a book, writing a chapter each on any subject which appealed to him – a person, an event, a work of art . . . . Voltaire obediently went away and wrote an essay on Abraham, portraying the prophet as unintelligent, untrustworthy and implausible. Next day, he found that no one else had taken the King's proposition seriously, and filed his article away. As it turned out, it was the earliest contribution to that remarkable publication, the *Dictionnaire philosophique*.

10

Farce and Raillery

What a fuss about an omelette!
On hearing that one of his books had been burned

Voltaire's escape from Potsdam – for it was to all intents and purposes an escape – was effected in a large coach crammed with belongings: books, manuscripts, furniture, clothing. One of the books was to cause him a great deal of trouble. No sooner had he reached Leipzig than he received a letter from Frederick ordering him to return a volume of the King's poems which he had taken with him. Five hundred copies of *Oeuvres de Pöesie* had been printed, and though most of them had been distributed in and around the Court, the book was certainly not intended for the general public and Frederick was concerned that by way of revenge Voltaire might reprint the poems together with his own critical comments, and publish them in France. He was not exactly afraid to have his poems placed before the public, but he was not at all eager to read, or have other people read, the comments Voltaire was likely to make about them.

Voltaire ignored the message and went on to Gotha, at the end of March to Strasbourg, and on 1 May 1753 to Frankfurt. Waiting for him there was a Baron Franz von Freytag, who had been instructed by Frederick to arrest him (despite the fact that Frankfurt was a free city, and that Freytag had absolutely no right to arrest anyone), confiscate the insignia which had been returned to him, obtain any papers relating to pensions from Frederick, and above all to find the book of poems. Voltaire escaped Freytag's notice for a month, but on the morning of 1 June he and a muscular servant entered the room at the Golden Lion inn where the writer had taken rooms, and confronted him. Voltaire – who, as ever, was in poor health, swooned. Indeed, so frail did he look that Freytag was afraid he would not survive arrest, but nevertheless did his duty.

For eight hours Freytag and his accomplice took Voltaire's rooms to pieces looking for the 'book of poeshy'[1] (he was not a literary man), while his victim protested that he would find nothing – the book in question was in luggage which had been sent on to Hamburg. In the end, Freytag felt so sorry for Voltaire that after he had signed a declaration that the moment the book was recovered from Hamburg he would hand it over, he sent him to a doctor and gave him a cask of excellent wine from his own cellar.

Under house arrest, Voltaire phlegmatically settled down and began to work on a book which he had promised to write for Princess Louisa Dorothea of Meiningen, Duchess of Saxe-Gotha, on the history of Germany since Charlemagne's day.[2] As was always the case when he was imprisoned, a procession of local admirers called upon him, and one or two of the more distinguished were appalled at his illegal arrest. Faced with their intention to rouse Frankfurt city council on Voltaire's behalf, and by the prisoner's declaration that he had written to the Holy Roman Emperor, Francis I, asking that Freytag should be reminded that the arrest of a French citizen in an imperial city was an outrage, the Baron panicked and began writing almost daily to Frederick asking for instructions. His letters were seemingly ignored. In fact they were intercepted by the over-zealous secretary who had ordered Voltaire's arrest – Frederick could have known nothing about it.

Meanwhile Marie-Louise had heard about the situation and arrived at Frankfurt, desperately exhausted by the journey but intent upon rescuing her uncle. She wrote to Frederick at Voltaire's dictation renouncing all rights to any pension from him, and added on her own account an impassioned plea for the prisoner's release. Then at last the box arrived from Hamburg which presumably contained the King's book of poetry but, infuriatingly, Freytag refused to open it until he received definite instructions from Potsdam. Voltaire became hysterical, and seriously feared for his life. He had already told Francis I that he 'had reason to believe that Monsieur Freytag contemplates more violent measures in the hope of gratifying his master' and he was not much comforted by a letter written to Marie-Louise by an acquaintance, Lord Keith, the Prussian minister in Paris, who she had hoped could help. Keith wrote that he was sure that Frederick had no intention of harming Voltaire, but that 'if some big, strong Prussian, upset by something your uncle said, were to hit him on the head, he would certainly flatten him . . . . Prevent your uncle from doing anything foolish; he is as good at that as he is at writing poetry.'[3]

Voltaire decided he must again contrive to escape. He and his secretary, Cosimo Collini (who had entered his service at Sans Souci in place of Longchamps,[4] and proved extremely faithful) sneaked out of the city at night – but Voltaire suddenly discovered that he had lost his purse, insisted on turning back to look for it, and was caught by one of the posses Freytag had dispatched to search for him. He and Collini were taken back to his hotel, and Freytag applied for a second warrant for his arrest. When Voltaire started to burn certain documents he was carrying, Freytag became nervous and offered to take him to his own house. Voltaire refused – if he was going to be arrested, everyone should know about it. He also accused Freytag of accepting a large bribe to allow him to escape, and reneging on the deal. Freytag thrust him into a coach, where the argument continued as they were driven to the house of a Councillor Schmidt. There a company of men began to confiscate the prisoner's money, personal jewellery, even his beloved snuff-box (he protested volubly about this; it was, he said, indispensable). Voltaire made a dash for freedom through an open door, but was easily recaptured, and taken off to a ramshackle inn called the Goat's Horn, where the door of his room was guarded by two sentries with drawn bayonets. Marie-Louise made such a nuisance of herself going round the town complaining about the treatment of Voltaire that Schmidt had her and Collini arrested, and she too was confined at the Goat's Horn.

At last the comedy, rather like a scene from a Donizetti opera, was brought to a close by a letter from Frederick instructing Freytag to set his prisoners free on condition that Voltaire signed a declaration that he would keep no copies of any of His Majesty's poetry. There was some attempt to make him pay for his keep during his imprisonment but he had now learned that Frederick had not in fact been responsible for the fiasco, and the fact that Freytag had over-stepped the mark encouraged him to claim the return of all the money and jewellery stolen from him. Some was given back, but much had vanished – including diamond shoe buckles, rings and a bag of gold *louis*.

With great relief Voltaire and Marie-Louise left Frankfurt on 7 July and made for Mainz where, the news of his approach having preceded him, the writer was welcomed like a conquering hero. He stayed there for three weeks, 'to dry out the clothes soaked in the shipwreck', as he put it, while Marie-Louise went back to Paris, hoping to get permission for him to return. Voltaire went on to Mannheim, where he was greeted with equal enthusiasm and four of his plays were mounted in his honour. He was allowed the run of the Elector's archives (of great value to his researches for his history of Germany), and he began work on a new play, *L'Orphelin de la Chine* (The Chinese Orphan). He hoped to cash in on the passion for all things Chinese which was gripping Europe.

On 16 August he and Collini arrived in Strasbourg. Marie-Louise had returned to Paris; Voltaire sent by her a letter to Mme La Pompadour asking her to intercede with the King on his behalf. It was at Strasbourg that Voltaire completed the history of Germany which he had promised Louisa Dorothea. She was exceptionally grateful, and made him a present of a thousand *écus*, which he refused; he was wealthy enough not to need such a sum, and he did not want ever again, if it could be helped, to be under an obligation to a patron. This same determination persuaded him to decline the invitation of Queen Maria Theresa to join her court at Vienna. No, he told Thiériot, 'Happy is he who lives in his own house with his nieces,[5] his books, his garden, his vines, his horses, his cows, his eagle, his fox, and his rabbits that caress their noses with their paws. I have all that, and the Alps as well, which are an admirable sight. I would sooner grumble at my gardeners than pay court to kings.'[6]

Frederick, in the meantime, ran the whole gamut from rage to sentimental sorrow. At first he circulated wild rumours about his former favourite: Voltaire was going to England as the servant of George II, then to the court of the Queen of Hungary. Hearing that he had been staying with Louisa Dorothy, he wrote to her describing her guest as the greatest knave in creation – many men had been broken on the wheel for causing less trouble than he, who had attacked Maupertuis because he himself had ambitions to be President of the Berlin Academy. But after a month or two he began to miss the philosopher's company, and wrote Voltaire an extra-ordinary letter:

> You wrong me, absolutely, I have forgiven everything, I even want to forget everything. Do you want compliments? I will tell you the truth; I esteem you the greatest genius that centuries have created; I admire your poems; I love your prose, in particular the frivolous parts of your miscellaneous writings. Never before has any writer had such perfect tact [sic], such a certain and refined taste. You are charming in conversation; you know how to instruct and entertain at the same time. You are the most fascinating person I know, able to make yourself loved by anyone you wish. You have such charm in your wit that you can offend and be forgiven at the same time. In short, you would be perfect, if you were not human.[7]

Voltaire himself seems to have been minded to forgive the King: 'It was a lover's quarrel,' he wrote later in his autobiographical notes; 'the bickerings of a Court soon die away; but a laudable passion will long continue . . . . After such a letter I must certainly have been greatly in the wrong.'[8]

Giving up, at least for the time, his ambition to return to Paris, he now sub-let most of his house there, sold some of his belongings and began looking about him for a permanent home at Colmar, 40 miles south of Strasbourg. The tensions of the shipwreck began to subside, and he felt well enough to write consolingly to Marie-Louise, who had sent news that she had a swelling in her thighs: 'What are your legs and mine attempting to convey? If they were together, they would be well . . . . Your thighs were not made to suffer. These lovely thighs so soon to be kissed are shamefully treated!'[9]

It was at Colmar, at Easter, to the astonishment of everyone who heard of the fact, that he made his confession and took communion: the news went around Paris from mouth to mouth – Voltaire has made his first communion! Collini reported that none who saw his master's expression at the moment when the wafer was placed upon his tongue could doubt that he was mocking the pantomime, and the Capuchin friar who had officiated was surprised to receive a gift of a loin of veal and a dozen bottles of wine, perhaps as some sort of apology for what he might have suspected to be a farce. The truth was probably neither that Voltaire was mocking the ceremony nor that he had suffered a conversion. In the first place he was desperate to return to Paris, and had heard that conformity with Christian convention, together with the influence of some powerful friends, might result in permission being given. In the second, he was conscious that certain local Jesuits and other dignitaries in Alsace were eager to be rid of him. This was not something to be ignored; only twelve months previously, the Bishop of Basel, within whose jurisdiction Colmar fell, had ordered the execution of a goldsmith merely for asking that the statutes of his guild should be revised. Not for the first time, Voltaire took on the colour of the country, for convenience and safety. (Years later, his secretary asked him how he would have acted had he lived in Spain under the Inquisition, to which Voltaire replied that he would have worn an enormous rosary, gone to mass every day, kissed all the monks' robes, and done his best to set fire to their monasteries.)

He was now extremely anxious to find a permanent home. He thought for a while of moving to England, then of America: 'If the sea did not make me insupportably sick, I would end my life among the Quakers of Pennsylvania'.[10] He returned briefly, and with some misgivings, to France, spending some time at the Benedictine Abbey of Sénones in Lorraine. Frederick, who always kept in touch with his movements, wrote ironically to enquire about his sudden conversion to Christianity, but Voltaire's preoccupation was with the 12,000 books in the abbey library and with his current work in progress, eventually published as the *Essai sur les Mœurs et l'esprit des nations*.

He had begun making notes for the *Essai* while still at Potsdam, and though the complete work was not to appear in print until 1756, when it was published in seven volumes, portions of the manuscript had found their way into the hands of a printer in The Hague, who had published them, but not without tampering with them in the most disgraceful and (for Voltaire) dangerous fashion. For instance, Voltaire had written that 'historians are like certain tyrants of whom they speak, who sacrifice the well-being of the whole human race to that of a single individual'. The printer substituted the word 'kings' for the word 'historians'. The fragments had been sent to Louis XV, who was not amused. No wonder that Marie-Louise learned from Mme Pompadour that her attempts to persuade him to permit Voltaire to return to Paris had received short shrift.

The offence he gave the Court was paralleled by the offence he continued to give the Church, despite or perhaps because of the pantomime of his attendance at mass. After a brief holiday at Plombières, taking the waters with Marie-Louise, he was the guest for a month at Lyons of his old friend the Duc de Richelieu. At first he was well received in the city, where four of his plays were produced in his honour; but then the Archbishop, Pierre Guérin de Tencin, objected to his presence, and he felt he must leave if he was not to embarrass his host. Late in 1754 he crossed the border into republican Switzerland, and his mind turned towards the possibility of permanent residence in that country. It was not as republican as all that, and was certainly not very democratic. Government was by the representatives of a tiny minority of the inhabitants, and there were strict laws governing even what one might eat or wear, or how one might dress one's hair. Religious strife had come near to wrecking the country intellectually – the University of Basel was almost defunct because of religious extremism, and the rival sects of Catholicism and Calvinism were continually at each other's throats – in some cantons the Catholics forbade any but Catholic worship, while in others the Calvinists permitted none but Protestant services. Only a dozen years before Voltaire's arrival, a man had been tortured and executed for trying to organise independent religious services.

All this does not sound likely to have been very palatable to Voltaire, but on the other hand the lay Swiss authorities were well disposed to him, and when in January 1755 he came across a delightful property on the Lyon road just over 4 miles outside Geneva, he almost immediately thought of buying it. Saint-Jean was a villa which had been built in the neo-classical style some twenty years previously, overlooking the Rhone and with a view of Mont Blanc. It was forbidden for any Roman Catholic to buy property in a Calvinist district, but Voltaire (regarded as a Catholic simply because he was French) contrived through a mixture of charm and bribery to get around the edict, bought the villa for a rather excessive 77,200 francs, renamed it Les Délices, and moved in.

His sudden decision to buy was no doubt prompted by the pleasant aspect of the place, but he may also have been influenced by a letter which came out of the blue from two publishers who had a business in Geneva. Gabriel and Philibert Cramer were brothers, and offered to publish Voltaire with diligence and attention to detail, using fine paper and an elegant and clear type-face. Having met them, he believed that they would fulfil their promise – as indeed they did: the complete edition of his work which they published in 1756 was definitive in its time, and Voltaire was so pleased with it that he refused his share of the profits and even contributed to the cost of publication. The Cramers became friends as well as business associates, and they and their wives happily joined in Voltaire's amateur theatricals.

He and Marie-Louise threw themselves into the refurbishment and redesign of the house and gardens at Les Délices just as enthusiastically as he and Émilie had approached the civilisation of Cirey almost twenty years earlier. It was quite like old times – he and Marie-Louise even argued as he and Émilie had done about decor and furnishings (he knew nothing, she said, if he thought that crimson velvet pile would match damask tapestry). He bought a cow and some chickens, made a vegetable garden and planted currants and gooseberries, flowers, trees, herbs – lavender, thyme, rosemary, mint, basil, rye, saxifrage and hyssop ('to wash us of our sins', he told a friend). Thus he set up a comfortable establishment with a French cook, a valet and two footmen, and a coachman and a postilion to handle the six horses and two carriages, one an elegant little Italian coach gilded and lined with silk. He also acquired a monkey, to remind him, he said, of the nature of mankind. He bought a second, smaller house near Lausanne, in which he spent the winter months when Les Délices was too cold for comfort and a third, larger house in the Rue du Grand Chêne, Lausanne, in which there was room to construct a theatre.

He had found, he believed, just the lifestyle which would suit him – sufficiently far from Paris to put distance between himself and his antagonists, but still close enough to the French border to prevent him from feeling entirely an exile. 'I am so happy that I am ashamed,' he wrote to Thiériot.[11] And importantly for a hypochondriac on so magnificent a scale, he had also found himself an excellent doctor, Théodore Tronchin, who by common consent was excessively disagreeable, but whom Voltaire trusted and who was to attend him for almost sixty years – in fact, until his death. The relationship must surely have been somewhat prickly, for Tronchin, who seems to have been a rather unpleasant man, at one time and another accused his patient of being morally unnatural, too rich and spoiled by too much praise, and steadfastly declined to believe him when he sent messages claiming that he was on his death-bed. However, perhaps this was just the treatment a determined hypochondriac needed, and when Voltaire was really ill (as he often was) Tronchin's care seems to have been exemplary.

He had some difficulty in pacifying his patient when a new scandal threatened to blacken his name with the public. Someone had obtained a copy of that highly amusing but outrageous poem *La Pucelle* and had passed it on to disreputable printers who had added obscenities and blasphemies of their own and issued it under his name. The printers were making a great deal of money from the operation but the public suspected that Voltaire was taking the major share of the income and even his friends, knowing that he was not averse to profit, found it possible that he had sanctioned the highly profitable publication.

He sent Marie-Louise to Paris to look into the matter. She discovered that the manuscript of the poem had been stolen from her house by the Marquis de Ximénès, whom she had taken as a lover while Voltaire was in Berlin. This was embarrassing enough, without having to tell Voltaire that his friends, including d'Argenson, believed him to be behind the poem's publication. She returned to Les Délices and made her confession. Voltaire, enraged, accused her of selling the manuscript to Ximénès, and the domestic atmosphere was soured. In fact, life at the villa was by no means the oasis of calm and delight for which Voltaire had hoped, for now he was in trouble with the local authority.

Soon after moving into Les Délices, he had made the mistake of staging *Zaïre* in the long gallery with a visiting actor in the leading role – Henri Louis Lekain, now one of the most admired performers in France, whom Voltaire himself had 'discovered' years previously and supported while he built a reputation. Private theatrical performances were regarded by the Calvinists as works of the Devil – there was no theatre in Geneva, and none had been permitted for many years – and Voltaire evidently intended that the production of plays should be a regular feature of life at the villa. Mlle Clairon, who had often appeared in the little theatre at Cirey, now came to Les Délices to play the lead in his new play, *L'Orphelin de la Chine*. The fact that the performance was repeated to great acclaim at Versailles did nothing to placate the Calvinists. Worse was to come: Voltaire set about starting an amateur drama group in Geneva and solicited several young men and women to become actors.

The Calvinist element was again outraged. The Grand Conseil, which had earlier happily given him permission 'to live in the republic of Geneva during the good pleasure of their lordships', was importuned to enforce the decrees which forbade all theatrical entertainments, and instructed pastors to order their parishioners to refrain from taking part in any performances at the home of the impertinent Frenchman. A letter was sent informing Voltaire that 'it would be very agreeable to [the city fathers] to see you enter into our views, and to cooperate with all our men of letters, when occasion offers, to dissuade our youth from irreligion, which always leads to libertinism'.[12] He apologised, but went on staging plays in private at his house in Lausanne. He also bought some land at Châtelaine, just over the border in France, and built a theatre there, bringing Lekain once more to open it. The pastors implored their parishioners to resist the temptation to attend, but hundreds poured over the border and filled the place from pit to gallery.[13] Then came more bad news for the burgers of Geneva: copies of *La Pucelle* began circulating in the city and the police confiscated such copies as they could find. It was becoming clear that Switzerland was by no means to be the haven for which Voltaire had taken it.

All these upsetting problems had interfered with his writing, in particular with the life of Peter the Great which an exiled Russian courtier had invited him to write, though amid all the theatricals and despite the various tensions he still managed to research and complete eight chapters within five months. He had also begun to write contributions for the most important literary work of the age, the famous *Encyclopédie*.

This extraordinary work resulted from the proposal to publish in France a translation of Ephraim Chambers' English *Cyclopœdia, or an Universal Dictionary of Arts and Sciences* brought out by Chambers' own firm in 1728. Seventeen years later the French publisher Lebreton made an agreement with the English writer John Mills to translate the work into French, but a number of critics thought the English book unsatisfactory and argued for an original French work. This was eventually put in train by Lebreton, with the financial support of three colleagues. Meanwhile the controversial writer Denis Diderot, then thirty years old and already the author of a book which had the distinction of being condemned and burned by the censors,[14] had been working on the editing and translation of Robert James's six-volume *Dictionnaire de médecine*. In October 1746 he took over the task of editing the larger work – now likely to be very much larger, as its new title suggested: *Encyclopédie, ou Dictionnaire universel des sciences, arts et métiers*. Lebreton reckoned the cost of publication to be not less than 2 million livres, and Diderot was encouraged to write a prospectus which was issued in 1750, announcing eight volumes of text to be published within two years, and offering the set at 280 livres. Eight thousand copies of the prospectus were issued, and the first volume came out as promised in June 1751 in an edition of just over 2,000 copies, dedicated to the Marquis d'Argenson.

Jesuit scholars immediately condemned it for its criticism of their academic standards, for its denigration of kings and saints, and for preaching freedom of speech. The Jansenists, who controlled the *parlement* of Paris, also deplored it, denounced Diderot and demanded his arrest. They were particularly appalled at the inclusion in the encyclopaedia of an article by a young abbé, Jean Martin de Prades, who had presented before the Sorbonne what they regarded as a highly anti-religious thesis, which in addition promoted sensualism. The ass of Mirepoix, Archbishop Boyer, told the King through strangled sobs that if publication was allowed to continue religion would be dead within a few years. Malsherbes, the director of the book trade, was ordered to name three censors to carry out a thorough examination of the work. On 7 February 1752, a few weeks after the publication of the second volume, both were suppressed by order of the royal council, and de Prades was forced to go into exile.

Voltaire offered de Prades sanctuary and from the first was determined to contribute to the success of the encyclopaedia, which he praised in the conclusion of his book on Louis XIV. He suggested to Diderot that the project might be transferred to Berlin, where Frederick, he was sure, would be happy to support it. But with the help of d'Argenson and the support of the cultured Mme de Pompadour, publication was eventually allowed to continue. The third volume came out in 1753, and all three volumes had to be reprinted by February 1754.

There were various stumbling blocks ahead for the *Encyclopédie*, the most notable in 1757, when Damiens' attempt to assassinate the King resulted in the passage of a law prescribing the death penalty or banishment to the galleys for the authors or publishers of 'tendentious and clandestine works'. Then, two years later, the *parlement* violently condemned the project as impious and licentious, forbade further publication, and ordered the publishers to return any subscriptions for further volumes, publication of which would not be allowed. Not a single subscriber took advantage of the offer.

In the meantime work went steadily forward, Voltaire's many contributions – on subjects as diverse as grace, fornication, religion, the identity of the man in the iron mask, tears and the soul – adding to the distinction of the work. He also sprang to its defence in March 1760 after the author Le Franc de Pompignan inveighed against the

Encyclopédie in an acceptance speech at the Académie; in response Voltaire published a series of short, witty pamphlets (*quand?*, *pour?*, *qui?*, *quoi?*, *oui?*, *non?*, *car?* and *ah! ah!*) criticising the critic and supporting the venture.

The *Encyclopédie* was not completed until 1772, when the last of the eleven volumes was published. They contained more than two hundred contributions by Voltaire which are today, on the whole, among his unread works. Yet they are among his wittiest and most succinct. To quote from just three: his article on sects argues that every sect is 'the rallying-point of doubt and error'. 'Sect' and 'error' are indeed synonymous:

> You are Peripatetic and I Platonician; we are therefore both wrong, for you argue against Plato only because you are upset by his fancies, while I am offended by Aristotle because I believe that he doesn't know what he's talking about. If one or other of them had actually proved what he was saying to be the truth, neither would command a sect. To support one or the other is to start a civil war. There are no sects in mathematics or experimental physics – a man who distinguishes between a cone and a sphere isn't supporting Archimedes, and he who understands that the square of the hypotenuse of a right-angled triangle is equal to the square of the other two sides isn't a member of the sect of Pythagoras. When you say that the blood circulates, that the sun has seven coloured rays, you aren't either of the sect of Harvey or Newton – you simply see that they speak the truth, and the rest of the universe will agree with you. You can't argue about it. Any long dispute simply indicates that both sides are wrong.[15]

On 'Laws' he was equally clear: having examined the 'perfect monarchic states' of a chicken-run, a beehive, the democratic state of the ants, the anarchic civilisation of monkeys, he suggests that in human society, to its shame,

> the laws of games are the only ones which everywhere are just, clear, inviolable and executed. Why is the Indian who gave us the

rules of the game of chess willingly obeyed all over the world, and why are the popes' decretals,[16] for example, today an object of horror and scorn? The reason is that the inventor of chess combined everything with precision for the satisfaction of the players, and that the popes, in their decretals, had nothing in view but their own interest. The Indian wished to exercise men's minds equally, and give them pleasure; the popes wished to besot men's minds. I am told there are laws of war. I ask what are these laws of war. I learn that they mean . . . having a prisoner hanged if the enemy has hanged one of yours; that they mean putting to the fire and the sword villages which have not brought their sustenance on the appointed day, according to the orders of the gracious sovereign of the district. It seems to me that most men have received from nature enough common sense to make laws, but that everyone is not just enough to make good laws.[17]

But Voltaire was not above exercising a less ironic sense of humour – on nudity, for instance, asking why on earth a civilised country should want to lock up a man or woman for being naked in a public place when congregations all over the country sat in church looking every Sunday at pictures and statues of a naked or semi-naked Madonna or Christ. Some sects, the Adamites and Abelians, for instance, liked to worship God 'in the state in which He formed them, rather than in the disguise invented by man'. No one need be afraid of provoking improper thoughts, for 'there are so few well-made persons of both sexes that nakedness might inspire chastity, or rather disgust, instead of increasing desire'. Then, making a serious point (and there is always a serious point in Voltaire's most extravagant essays), 'There is no singularity, no superstition, which has not passed through the heads of mankind. Happy the day when these superstitions do not trouble society and make of it a scene of disorder, hatred and fury! It is better without doubt to pray to God stark naked, than to stain His altars and public places with human blood.'[18]

Voltaire's contributions and those of the other Encyclopédists remain remarkable in the force of their arguments for rationality and good sense. Herbert Fisher in his distinguished *History of Europe*, remarks that they 'rendered the incomparable service of attacking all that was cruel, all that was superstitious, all that was obsolete, unequal or unjust, in the constitution of European society and in the fabric of its religious and social beliefs . . .'.[19]

None of the contributors can be seen as great democrats – Voltaire himself was a capitalist who made much of his fortune by money-lending, a determined elitist who despised ignorance and lack of education in others, a decided believer in large rewards for merit and in 'a yoke and a goad' for those who had none. He and his fellow contributors trusted in benevolent dictators such as, they believed, Frederick of Prussia and Catherine of Russia to bring about the ideal society which they craved. These despots bitterly disappointed them. But after all their good sense and moderation, love of truth and tolerance, healthy contempt for nationalism and hatred of war had some effect, and if they were further from the discovery of the secret of life than some of them believed, they nevertheless participated in one of the great intellectual adventures of modern times.

But for Voltaire more distinctive work was on the horizon than the provision of essays for an encyclopaedia. On 1 November 1755 the earth moved, and the Lisbon earthquake provoked a response which resulted in the work for which he is still best known.

11

God and Mankind

If God did not exist, it would be necessary to invent him.

Épîtres, *no.* 96

The earthquake that hit the pious Catholic city of Lisbon at 9.40 on the morning of the feast of All Saints, Sunday 1 November 1755, was one of the great natural calamities of the eighteenth century. In six minutes thirty crowded churches and a thousand houses fell, fifteen thousand people perished and fifteen thousand more were fatally injured.

Great disasters have always provided a taxing riddle for any Church; the eighteenth-century European Churches each responded in their own way. The Italian Jesuit theologian Fr Gabriel Malagrida explained that God had smitten Lisbon because of the sin which prospered there. Lay people however found it difficult to reconcile the disproportion between the few sinners killed and the deaths of a vastly greater number of pious worshippers. The Muslims of Lisbon also suggested that Allah had smitten the ungodly – but He had also destroyed their magnificent mosque of Al-Mansur. Everyone found it curious that while God had permitted the earthquake to demolish the huge Patriarchal Church and the royal palace with its wonderful art works and fine library of seventy thousand books, to say nothing of the houses of most of the city's ordinary people, He had apparently been careful to spare the numerous brothels of Suja Street, together with its population of prostitutes.

The Jansenist Laurent Etienne Rondet wrote a book proving

conclusively that the earthquake was God's commentary on the wickedness of the Inquisition (one of the first buildings to be gutted in the fire which followed the earthquake was the headquarters of that institution). In England, hearing of the disaster, Protestants supposed that God had quite properly punished the Catholics for their abominable papist practices and their worship of the Mother of God, and suggested that the saints had petitioned the Almighty to choose their own special festival day for the demonstration of his wrath. The great and good John Wesley declared that 'sin is the moral cause of earthquakes, whatever their natural causes may be'.[1]

Voltaire, as one might expect, fumed at attempts to suggest that the disaster was the work of a God of any colour and regarded the event as positive proof of the lunacy of Leibniz's suggestion that this was 'the best of all possible worlds'. His mind had been revolving around the problem for some time – ten years previously he had asked a critic, 'Just show me . . . why so many men slit each other's throats in the best of all possible worlds, and I shall be greatly obliged to you'.[2] By the first weeks of 1756 he had completed the poem which became his best known, and is probably his best: *On the Lisbon Disaster, or An Examination of the Axiom 'All is Well'*, with its pealing opening lines

> *O malheureux mortels! O terre déplorable!*
> *O de tous les mortels assemblage effroyable!*

Like all good poetry, the poem is virtually untranslatable; but a verse translation by the English writer Tobias Smollett,[3] though it misses the full force of the original, offers some idea of Voltaire's passion:

> Say, will you then eternal laws maintain
> Which God to cruelties like these constrain?
> Whilst you these facts replete with horror view,
> Will you maintain death to their crimes was due?
> And can you then impute a sinful deed
> To babes who on their mothers' bosoms bleed?
> Was then more vice in fallen Lisbon found
> Than Paris, where voluptuous joys abound?

> Was less debauchery in London known,
> Where opulence luxurious holds her throne?. . .[4]

The conundrum Voltaire posed was, of course, the age-old one of how to reconcile the idea of an all-powerful, all-loving God with the possibility that He was either powerless to combat evil, or was insufficiently loving to save man from it. He recalled in the poem Pope's 'Whatever is, is right', from the *Essay on Man*. In the Foreword to his own poem, Voltaire goes out of his way to say that he loves and admires Pope, but points out that those words

> if understood in a positive sense, and without any hopes of a happy future state, only insult us in our present misery . . . . If, when Lisbon and other cities were swallowed up . . . philosophers had cried out to the wretches, who with difficulty escaped from the ruins, 'all this is productive of general good; the heirs of those who have perished will increase their fortune; masons will earn money by rebuilding the houses, beasts will feed on the carcasses buried under the ruins; it is the necessary effect of necessary causes; your particular misfortune is nothing, it contributes to universal good,' such an harangue would doubtless have been as cruel as the earthquake was fatal.[5]

Voltaire's attitude is now fairly common, but in 1756 it seemed to conventional believers utterly impious. As he must have expected, his poem greatly shocked all but the most thoughtful readers. The first published version ended with the lines:

> *Que faut-il, O mortels? Mortels, it faut souffrir*
> *Se soumettre en silence, adorer, et mourir.*

> [What must we do, we mortals? Mortals, we must suffer,
> Silently submit, adore, and die.]

Realising that most people thought such hopelessness insupportable, he altered the final line to '*Se soumettre, adorer*, espérer, *et mourir*.' But the addition of the word 'hope' seemed to make the poem only slightly less pessimistic, and it continued to attract criticism – indeed it is difficult to think of another eighteenth-century poem which attracted so much interest and analysis.

The critics chiefly inhabited two camps: those who condemned the poem as an irreligious blasphemy, and those followers of Leibniz who denounced it as an unfair criticism of him. The best-known rebuke came from Jean-Jacques Rousseau, who wrote at the behest of a Genevan pastor an idiotic but much admired open letter arguing that all human ills must be the result of human error, and that the people of Lisbon suffered because they lived in tall buildings. Had they lived in the woods and fields, as God intended that people should, they would have escaped the calamity. In any case (he said) it was quite a good thing that a certain number of people should be killed from time to time. Leibniz had been right: man's only hope was to believe that indeed all was for the best. Rousseau's letter, which can best be described as an emotional spasm, was applauded by the unthinking as a complete demolition of Voltaire's poem.

Silly though Rousseau's letter now appears to us, his view of Voltaire was nevertheless one which was widely shared. In his *Confessions*, written towards the end of the 1760s, the former explained his position:

Struck by seeing that poor man, weighed down, so to speak, by fame and prosperity, bitterly complaining, nevertheless, against the wretchedness of this life and finding everything invariably bad, I formed the insane plan of bringing him back to himself and proving to him that all was well. Though Voltaire has always appeared to believe in God, he has really only believed in the Devil, because his so-called God is nothing but a malicious being who, according to his belief, only takes pleasure in doing harm. The absurdity of this doctrine leaps to the eye, and it is particularly revolting in a man loaded with every kind of blessing who, living in the lap of luxury, seeks to disillusion his fellow-men by a frightening and cruel picture of all the calamities from which he is himself exempt.[6]

We may certainly excuse Rousseau for accusing Voltaire of being rich – and of being a pessimist. During the following years the dark cloud of melancholy which hung over him when he considered the world and its ironies gradually became darker and denser, though it neither continually preoccupied him nor disarmed his capacity for enjoying the good things of life, which in his case consisted of work, good conversation and the theatre. Life, in fact, went on much as usual. He and Marie-Louise spent the winter of 1756/7 in the warm comfort of a house at Montriond, near Lausanne, and then in the spring returned to Les Délices. There, he began to play another distant, amusing game with Frederick the Great, exchanging letters with friends and officials at the Potsdam Court which on his side were full of flattering phrases which he knew would reach the ears of the monarch. As he expected, this ploy attracted letters in return in which Frederick renewed his own flattering attentions to his ex-favourite. These eventually culminated in the libretto of an opera written by the King and based on *Mérope*; but Voltaire was unimpressed – it was, he thought, the worst thing Frederick had ever written. His true feelings are suggested by the fact that he called his pet monkey Luc (a nickname he had also given to Frederick), and would show people his caged eagle, whose beak and claws, he said, were as keen as the King's own talons.

Over the next few years, the relationship between the two men continued to swing from positive to negative, influenced by Frederick's fortunes in war, by Voltaire's opinion of the (usually bad) verses the King continued to send him for his opinion, and to some extent by the waxing and waning of Voltaire's desire to return to France. This was an ambition which his relationship with Frederick did not advance, especially when French spies managed to obtain copies of scurrilous verses about Louis XV which Frederick continually dispatched to Les Délices.

Voltaire still entertained some friendly feelings for Frederick. When the King was in serious physical danger as the result of the military defeat of Prussia by the Austrian army, he wrote urgent letters to anyone he thought might be able to persuade Louis XV to negotiate a peace, among them Mme de Pompadour and Richelieu. But the

French firmly favoured Austria, and Voltaire's attempts to explain and advance Frederick's case did him no good, particularly where his own attempts to return to Paris were concerned.

By now, France, Austria, Saxony, Sweden and Russia on the one side and Prussia, Great Britain and Hanover on the other were involved in what was to be known as the Seven Years' War – the result of the Austrian Hapsburgs' ambition to win back Silesia from Frederick, who had annexed it some years previously. In summer 1756, Frederick invaded Saxony and occupied Dresden. Voltaire busied himself in the cause of peace, but had no success: the truth was that he was about the only man in Europe who seemed to want it – the pro-war French whetted the people's antagonism to Frederick by publishing a short book of his *Pensées* which were highly antagonistic to France, and when Voltaire attempted to engage England in the cause of peace Charles James Fox sent a message by his son making it clear that England was not interested.

A bewildering but comic interlude lightened the gloom a little: Mme de Pompadour had begun to notice that the King's devotion to her was on the wane, and was advised that one way of competing with the younger mistresses to whom he was turning would be to brush up on her knowledge of literature and take a more piously devout attitude to Christianity. Perhaps in an attempt to combine the two suggestions, she got a friend to offer to commission from Voltaire a metrical version of the Psalms of David, to be sponsored by herself. As a reward, she said, the Duc de Vallière, who was her go-between, felt almost certain he could secure for the poet a cardinal's hat. When the laughter at Les Délices had died down, Voltaire wrote declining the honour.

In retrospect, by far the most important event of 1756 was the appearance of the seven volumes of *Essai sur l'histoire générale et sur les mœurs et l'esprit des nations*, in which Voltaire attempted nothing less than a comprehensive history of mankind – of 'the nations who live on earth and desolate it', as he says in his preface. The scope of the book is enormous: there are chapters on China, India, Persia, Arabia, the rise of Christianity and the papacy, and the whole range of history from early to modern, including, in remarkable detail, such events as the Norman invasion of England, the rise of Saladin, the scope of science and art in the thirteenth and fourteenth centuries and the English Civil War. It was an olla podrida, but a fascinating one. The author engaged, of course, with many of his usual enemies: religious intolerance ('Blood has flooded scaffolds for five centuries because morality has been sacrificed to dogma'[7]), Presbyterianism, the persecutions by the Inquisition, the excesses and injustices of the law . . . .

He had begun work on the project as long ago as 1739, and it was dedicated to the memory of Mme de Châtelet, whose contempt for contemporary historians had been notable and had inspired Voltaire to make his attempt. The project was so vast that it must fail; readers and critics were all too ready to point out errors of fact in the sweeping panorama of history and of mankind's customs, ideas, beliefs, laws. The Jesuits had a field day exposing what with some justice they saw as bias in the author's concentration on the excesses of some Christian apologists. But again, being highly readable made the book extremely popular, and the sweep of the author's vision, his extraordinary command of extensive research, the ever-present evidence of his humanity and humour far outweigh the work's weaknesses, and apart from its success with the public it laid down a scheme for the writing of popular history which was to be adopted by the best historians of the following two centuries.

It was during 1755–9, first at Les Délices, then at Ferney (which he bought in 1758) and finally while visiting the Elector Palatine at Schwetsingen, that Voltaire worked on the book which was to become his best known, and is still the work for which he is most remembered: *Candide, ou l'optimisme*, a novella of about 42,000 words first published in Geneva in March 1759. Before the end of the month the Grand Council of Geneva had ordered it to be burned, and Voltaire was forced to deny his authorship ('People must have lost their senses,' he said, 'to suspect me of writing such nonsense!'[8]). But no one who read it could have any serious doubts that the book was the work of the only living author anyone thought capable of writing it, and within a very short time it had circulated through France and then Europe, and its career as a classic of ironic humour was firmly established.

God and Mankind

Candide is an extremely funny, extremely pessimistic book, written at a time when Europe was saturated with blood, and in Spain the terrifying, lurid glare of the autos-da-fé once more reddened the skies. Candide, a handsome, innocent bastard has been educated at the Westphalian court of his father, Baron Thunder-ten-tronckh, where he has been taught by his tutor, Dr Pangloss – a teacher of 'metaphysico-theologo-cosmolinigologie' – that he lives in the best of all possible worlds:

> It is proved that things cannot be other than they are, for since everything was made for a purpose, it follows that everything is made for the best purpose. Observe: our noses were made to carry spectacles, so we have spectacles. Legs were clearly intended for breeches, and we wear them . . . . It follows that those who maintain that all is right talk nonsense; they ought to say that *all is for the best*.[9]

Candide falls in love with the Baron's daughter, his half-sister, the beautiful Cunégonde. Thrown out of the castle for this impertinence, he is pressed into the Bulgarian army and when, brutally abused, he absconds he has the flesh flayed from his back by four thousand strokes of the cane. He then becomes involved in a war:

> Those who have never seen two well-trained armies drawn up for battle, can have no idea of the beauty and brilliance of the display. Bugles, fifes, oboes, drums and salvoes of artillery produced such a harmony as Hell itself could not rival. The opening barrage destroyed about six thousand men on each side. Rifle-fire which followed rid this best of worlds of about nine or ten thousand villains who infested its surface. Finally, the bayonet provided 'sufficient reason' for the death of several more. The total casualties amounted to about thirty thousand. Candide trembled like a philosopher . . . .[10]

From that moment on, things go from bad to worse. The castle is attacked and taken, Cunégonde and her brother raped and apparently slaughtered. Candide comes across Pangloss, minus an eye and an ear as the result, he says, of love: 'Love, the comforter of humanity, the preserver of the universe, the soul of all living things; tender love'. But how could that be?

> 'My dear Candide,' replied Pangloss, 'you remember Paquette, that pretty girl who used to wait on our noble lady. In her arms I tasted the delights of Paradise, and they produced these hellish torments by which you see me devoured. She was infected . . . given this present by a learned Franciscan, who had traced it back to its source. He had it from an old countess, who had it from a cavalry officer, who was indebted for it to a marchioness. She took it from her page, and he had received it from a Jesuit who, while still a novice, had had it in direct line from one of the companions of Christopher Columbus. As for me, I shall not give it to anyone, for I am a dying man.'[11]

But how did his predicament accord with the proposition that we lived in the best of all possible worlds? Ah, says Pangloss, had Columbus not visited the West Indies, where he caught the disease, we would have neither chocolate nor cochineal.

Candide's education in the way of the world continues: he and Pangloss are shipwrecked on the Portuguese coast and witness the Lisbon earthquake, then are arrested by the Inquisition. Pangloss is hanged; Candide escapes with the help of Cunégonde, who turns out to have survived her ordeal and been sold by a Jew to a member of the Inquisition. They are helped to escape by an old woman one of whose buttocks has been eaten by starving Turks during a siege (be thankful, she tells them, that you can sit on two buttocks).

Candide and Cunégonde sail to Buenos Aires, where they are parted after Candide has killed her brother (who suddenly reappears and attacks him again for daring to think of marrying out of his station). He finds the land of El Dorado, where gold and jewels lie around like stones, where there are no prisons, no lawyers, no priests, where the happy citizens live for 200 years and have no formal religion except the worship of a single god. (When Candide asks what religion the country follows, an inhabitant answers, 'Can there be two religions? . . . there is only one God, not two, three or four. What odd questions you foreigners ask.') Leaving with eighty sheep laden with gold and jewels, Candide loses all but one on his journey back to Europe. By-passing England, he goes on to Italy, then to Constantinople, where he again discovers Cunégonde, now grown old and ugly; he marries her, and they settle down with Pangloss (whose hanging was inefficient) and Paquette, the one-buttocked woman and some other friends, to make a living from the land. They are not perhaps happy, but they are reasonably content. As Pangloss always says,

> 'There is a chain of events in this best of all possible worlds; for if you had not been turned out of a beautiful mansion at the point of a jackboot for the love of Lady Cunégonde, and if you had not been involved in the Inquisition, and had not wandered over America on foot, and had not struck the Baron with your sword, and lost all those sheep you brought from El Dorado, you would not be here eating candied fruit and pistachio nuts.'

'That's true enough,' replied Candide; 'but we must go and work in the garden.'[12]

'*Il faut cultiver notre jardin.*' The phrase almost instantaneously became famous, and there can be no dictionary of quotations from the past century or more that does not contain it.

A single quotation does not make a great book; but the fact that in one short work Voltaire sent telling bolts of wit against so many targets – war, degenerate priests, avaricious lawyers, class prejudice, the barbarity of the prison system, the abuse of religion by members of the Church, the injustice of slavery, political degeneracy, the optimism of Leibniz, Rousseau and Pope – and shot those bolts with such deadly, light-hearted wit has ensured that this slim work – short, but as Flaubert said, '*le résumé de toutes ses œuvres*'[13] (the summary of all Voltaire's works) is very possibly as often read and taken to heart today as it was during the years immediately after its publication. The spare elegance and gaiety of its style are a delight even in the most bungled and clumsy translation, and the mixture of farce and the most mordant pessimism has a bite and bitter tang which makes it as memorable as any book of its time, and more memorable than most.

Candide was greeted with as much delight by Voltaire's friends and admirers as it was reviled by his enemies. He was now, by the standards of the time, an old man – sixty-five in the year it was published; but clearly he was no less ready and able to engage his enemies or interest himself in cases of injustice than he had ever been. Three years before the publication of *Candide*, in 1756, the British admiral John Byng was accused of cowardice after failing to relieve the siege of Minorca by very considerably superior French forces led by the Duc de Richelieu. The British Prime Minister, the Duke of Newcastle, seized the opportunity to use Byng to distract attention from the failings of his government, and ordered his court-martial with the words 'He shall be tried immediately; he shall be hanged directly.' Byng was executed by firing-squad on the quarter-deck of his own ship, in Portsmouth harbour.

Voltaire had been introduced to Byng in England, and hearing of his predicament obtained from Richelieu a letter suggesting that any commander might have taken the course followed by Byng, and forwarded it to the Admiral hoping that it would help him. It did not save him, but Voltaire subsequently immortalised him in the familiar line in Candide when, on his way to Italy, the boy sees an admiral being shot for no other reason than 'to encourage the others' ('*pour encourager les autres*').

Voltaire was now one of the sights of Europe, and it became as obligatory to call on him as to contemplate Mont Blanc, be sculled along the Grand Canal in Venice or climb to the top of the dome of St Peter's in Rome and inscribe one's name there. A string of friends and strangers turned up at Les Délices every day. Fortunately, he on the whole enjoyed his fame – though he took great care not to submit himself altogether to strangers, even to those armed with an introduction. If they were boring, he was quite capable of retiring to bed until they had gone; and if he suspected that they might bore him, he would simply fail to make an appearance. Visitors took these avoiding tactics as part of the eccentricity of genius; they were really part of the carapace which Voltaire drew around himself whenever he needed to work, or simply be at peace.

Theatrical performances continued to be a major part of life: Marie-Louise now presented herself as an actress, and according to most accounts as an exceptionally bad one, though the fact that Voltaire tolerated her suggests she was at least competent – he was too eager for his plays to be well presented to put up with positively bad performances. Professional actors and actresses from Paris came and went, mingling freely with local amateurs who were prepared to run the gauntlet of the antagonism of the Geneva authorities. All three of Voltaire's houses were crammed at one time and another with players and playgoers – it has been estimated[14] that on occasion almost two hundred people were housed under his three roofs, sleeping at least four to a bedroom.

The continual drip of criticism and interference from the authorities meant that Voltaire's own situation in Geneva became not so much dangerous, though it was to some extent that, as thoroughly tedious, and in 1758 he decided it was time to leave. He bought an estate in Lorraine called Ferney, and the nearby manor of Tourney (which brought with it the honorary title of count, to which he was introduced in a handsome, outdated but enjoyable ceremony). He now owned four houses, though the one at Tourney was virtually derelict. He told Thiériot, 'I have four legs instead of two: one foot in Lausanne in a fine winter residence, one in Les Délices near Geneva, where I am visited by society. So much for the front feet. The two hind ones are in Ferney and the Comte of Tourney.'[15]

At Ferney he immediately set about improving his property and alleviating, where he could, the situation of the peasants on his estate. Here, as elsewhere, the complete control exercised by the Catholic Church perpetuated injustices which infuriated him. His neighbours, the canons of Saint-Cloude, still owned serfs and their insistence on a proper distance being maintained between Catholic and non-Catholic families had further impoverished an already poor district. He set in train a number of projects which would improve the lot of the local people. He repaired roads and restored vineyards, improved the methods of wine production, decided to run a stud farm, and brought expert watch and clock-makers – Protestant as well as Catholic – into the district, encouraging them to work together. In many of the numerous letters he wrote to wealthy people all over Europe he mentioned the watches of Ferney, with the result that a startlingly profitable trade in them was soon established. He encouraged lace-making and started a silk factory; after the Duchesse de Choiseul accepted the gift of the first pair of stockings from Ferney, quantities of them were ordered by ladies of the Court. And he negotiated a fair taxation system for the workers. When the local tax authority accepted his proposal, he put his head out of the window of their offices and shouted 'Vive la liberté!' His tenants, who had accompanied him and were crowded below, shouted back: 'Vive le Roi! Vive M. de Voltaire!'

His activities at Ferney and Tourney (where one of his first actions was, of course, to build a theatre) kept him busy through 1759 – while he was still 'improving' Les Délices, despite his decision to leave the house. He was also, of course, writing. Among other things, he produced verse transcriptions of Ecclesiastes and the Song of Solomon, both burned by the authorities despite the fact that they are simple, straightforward versions of the Biblical texts. (The idea may have originated with La Pompadour's earlier request, but the versions were produced because of Voltaire's admiration for the language of the originals, rather than from a desire to court her influence, much less from religious devotion. They are none the worse for that.) He was also once more regularly and argumentatively exchanging letters with Frederick the Great. But the mild courtesies with which the correspondence was resumed did not last long. The King accused Voltaire of intolerable impertinence. Voltaire told Frederick that he might have been quite an agreeable man were he not seated on a throne; Frederick retorted that the philosopher should learn 'in what manner it is fitting for you to write to me'. Finally, Voltaire had had enough:

You have embroiled me with the King of France, you have made me lose my posts and my annuities, you ill-treated me at Frankfurt, me and an innocent woman, a respected woman who was dragged in the mud and thrown into prison, and then, in honouring me with your letter, you poison the sweetness of this consolation by bitter reproaches.[16]

For a time, the correspondence once more ceased.

It was during the bitter winter of 1759/60 that Voltaire ordered the building of a church at Ferney. One already existed there, but was tumbledown and blocked the road to his château, so he had it demolished and at the same time annexed, without permission, some yards of the adjacent cemetery, and ordered the removal of a large cross which stood in the middle of the churchyard. Unfortunately, some local people heard his peremptory phrase 'Take down that gibbet!' and the *curé* of the neighbouring parish, Moens, descended on the church to rescue the Sacred Host just as dust and plaster descended from the tottering walls. He complained to the Bishop of Annecy. Threatened with imprisonment for blasphemy Voltaire first denied that he had called the cross a gibbet and then explained that in any case 'gibbet' was simply another word for 'cross'.

There was consternation in the surrounding countryside, though not at Ferney itself – the people there were happy with Voltaire's interest in improving their lot. In any case, he was careful to draw some of the fire by instructing them to attend mass in a nearby church, and by preserving the altar, font and church bell from the demolished building. These were replaced in the new building, over the door of which he set the inscription 'DEO EREXIT VOLTAIRE' – (built for God by Voltaire). This was well calculated further to enrage the *curé* and the bishop – a church built simply for God, indeed; everyone knew that the proper course was to dedicate such a building to a carefully chosen saint, an intermediary with the Almighty.

The church completed, he set about demolishing the château and rebuilding it and planned a 'model village' to replace the present sprawling mess of buildings. All this while dealing with the extraordinary activities of the curé, who irritatingly now went to law with the support of the Bishop of Annecy against some of Voltaire's tenants for the payment of some tithes, and won the case. Voltaire paid the curé several million francs out of his own pocket – his tenants were too poor to be able to gather even a tiny proportion of the money demanded.

The tenants took an early opportunity of revenge, and a number of local lads paid a visit to a widow with whom the curé was either having an affair or hoped to do so. The would-be lover, mad with jealousy, set some bullies on the lads, had them violently beaten, and shot the dog of one of them, threatening that he would do the same to them all. Voltaire tried to persuade the father of the most severely injured boy to sue the curé, but he was too frightened to do so. ('They will kill me!' he said, to which Voltaire replied, 'All to the good – it'll make your case all the stronger.')

In the middle of all this brouhaha, he completed a new play, *Tancrède*, which was first performed in the little theatre at Tourney on 3 September 1760, carefully revised and rewritten in light of that production, and subsequently mounted at the Comédie Française, where it seemed at first only a qualified success, running for a mere thirteen performances. However, word of mouth underlined the fact that it was a seriously good piece – it has been suggested that the politics of the theatre had something to do with its limited run.[17] The author and savant Denis Diderot claimed that the third act, in particular, was as good as anything in Corneille or Racine, and other knowledgeable theatre-goers celebrated it as Voltaire's best work since *Zaïre*. Years later, Byron praised it: 'Voltaire has been termed a "shallow fellow" by some of the same school who called Dryden's *Ode* "a drunken song"; – a *school* (as it is called, I presume, from their education being still incomplete) the whole of whose filthy trash of Epics, Excursions, &c, &c, &c, is not worth a single speech in *Tancred*.'[18]

In the following year, a single event in which Voltaire interested himself was to provoke him to a greater degree of indignation and to stronger protest and action than anything since the death and scandalous burial of Adrienne Lecouvreur. His intervention in what became known as the Calas affair still reverberates as one of the noblest actions of his life.

12

Persecution and Tolerance

*It is better to risk saving a guilty man than
to condemn an innocent one.*

Zadig, 1747

While by 1761 Voltaire was celebrated throughout Europe as a philosopher, playwright, pamphleteer, poet, and scientist manqué, it was the Calas affair that made his name a byword even among those who had never read anything he had written.

Jean Calas was a linen-merchant who lived with his wife and three of his five children above the draper's shop at 16 Grand'Rue des Filatiers in Toulouse where for 40 years he had sold soft furnishings and materials for women's clothing. He was a Huguenot; the term, of which the origin is obscure, was used to describe French Protestants originally influenced by the Reformation in Germany in the first years of the sixteenth century. Catholic France had quickly and violently responded to Protestantism, burning the first martyr, Jean Vallière, in 1532. In 1560 the plot laid by Huguenots to capture the boy-king Francis II attracted the intense hatred of many French people, and there were few protests when, for instance, a number of Protestants at prayer in a barn at Vassy were massacred by Roman Catholic soldiers.

The Wars of Religion which followed lasted until almost the end of the century and included the infamous 1572 St Bartholomew's Day massacre in which almost all the leading Huguenots in Paris were slain. Similar massacres followed throughout France, and the internecine struggle went on until 1629, when the Peace of Alès allowed the defeated Huguenots freedom of conscience. This was a mere gesture; the French Roman Catholic clergy had no intention of permitting freedom of worship, and the French State made life as difficult as possible for Huguenots like Calas – as Voltaire was to remark, life in the France of the 1760s was bad enough for Roman Catholics; for Huguenots it was next to intolerable. Religious intolerance debarred them from public office and from certain professions – a young Huguenot could not for instance be ambitious for a career in the law, medicine or as an apothecary; he could not become a goldsmith, or even a grocer or bookseller. Because Calas and his wife had not been married by a Catholic priest, they were regarded as living together in sin, their children officially illegitimate. They took their lives in their hands every time they attended a Protestant religious service, for any man discovered at such a service could be sent to the galleys for the rest of his life, while his wife was in danger of life imprisonment; any unfortunate man found to be conducting such a service would almost certainly be executed.

An additional misfortune for the Calas family was that they lived in the south of France. In Paris there was a certain leniency towards Protestants. Not so in the south, where long memories preserved old prejudices. In Toulouse, for instance, there were annual religious services commemorating the blessed occasion in 1562 when three thousand Huguenots had been tortured and killed there by Catholics, the most prominent citizens of the city joining the clergy in ceremonial processions to church, walking behind priests bearing bones alleged to be those of some of the children slaughtered by King Herod, to remind the population of its duty to hate and despise any non-Catholic. Such reminders were superfluous. The people of Toulouse were still, in the middle of the eighteenth century, rigorous in their persecution of Protestants. In March 1761 a Pastor Rochette was condemned to death for holding a Protestant service, and three friends who attempted to rescue him joined him on the scaffold.

If one had no very strong religious convictions one could always convert to Rome. The temptation to do so was strong for Calas's eldest son, 28-year-old Marc Antoine, who wanted to practise law, but could not do so unless he could secure a 'certificate of Catholicity'. At first this seemed not impossible – his friend Gaubert La Vaysse had managed to procure one, though remaining strong in his Protestant convictions. It was only a matter of knowing a priest avaricious enough to accept a bribe, or sympathetic enough to sign the certificate without one. Unfortunately the only priest with whom Marc Antoine was familiar, the *curé* of St Stephen's Church, refused to do so without a written assertion that the young man had actually been converted. Marc Antoine's conscience would not allow him to sign a false declaration.

His younger brother Louis was already a convert, living outside the family. His father had disapproved of his conversion but had recognised it as genuine, and had readily continued the young man's allowance without the compulsion of the law, which insisted that a convert should receive financial aid from his family even if they objected to his religious convictions. Marc Antoine's convictions were as strong as Louis's, but unfortunately in the wrong direction: he hated Catholics. The seeming impossibility of his obtaining the certificate which would allow him to follow his chosen profession naturally rankled. He told his friends that his life was in ruins.

Reluctantly he resigned himself to a career in business, but was unable to take up a proffered partnership for lack of capital. His father sympathised with his predicament, but declined to give him the necessary sum, and was even reluctant to take him into partnership. The truth was that his son's lifestyle disturbed him: Marc Antoine was in his view far too fond of new clothes, old wine, and the company of disreputable friends. And then he was keen on the theatre – anathema to any devout Protestant – and was given to memorising speeches from plays and reciting them in public. Moreover, there was the matter of the evenings he spent gambling at the Four Billiard Tables, a shady hostelry. True, he occasionally visited churches, but ironically Catholic churches, and not for the sermons but for the music.

Two more sons, two daughters and one other person completed the family. Donat, the youngest son, was an apprentice living at Nimes; Pierre still lived at home with his sisters, who were under the care of a Mlle Jeanne Vignière, who was, surprisingly enough, a Catholic. She had been a member of the family for 30 years, governess to all the children in turn. It had been she who had encouraged Louis's conversion, but this had not resulted in her dismissal; she was a friend as much as a servant, and the family was devoted to her, although Marc Antoine may have found it difficult to endure the presence of a Catholic in the house when it was the rigour of Catholic prejudice which had destroyed his ambitions.

On the evening of 13 October 1761 the family was entertaining La Vaysse, who had come home unexpectedly from Bordeaux to find his own family away. When they had eaten and were sitting talking in the living room above the shop, Marc Antoine said that he felt hot, and excused himself to go downstairs and take a little air in the street. When after some time he failed to return, his father, La Vaysse and young Pierre went to find him. He was hanging by the neck from a bar placed across the top of the folding doors between the shop and a storeroom. They cut him down and though he was clearly dead, sent for a doctor.

Calas and his wife were distraught. The body of a suicide was treated with the utmost contempt, first placed face downward on the floor of a court-room and tried for the crime of self-murder, then stripped naked and dragged to the main square of the city, where it was pelted with stones, mud and the detritus of the streets before being hanged until it putrefied and fell to pieces. What loving parents could contemplate such a fate for the body of a son? M. and Mme Calas decided to report the death as a natural one. But the opportunity to do so never presented itself: neighbours had heard the uproar when the body was discovered, and a police officer, arriving even before the doctor, saw the rope with which Marc Antoine had hanged himself, and the mark it had made around his neck. One might have thought the situation was clear enough, but already the rumour was circulating that Marc Antoine had been killed by his family because he wanted to convert to Catholicism.

The speculation was not entirely ridiculous where Catholic extremists were concerned. Calvin, after all, had written that 'God commands those who disobey their father to be put to death',[1] and it was the general view that a Protestant father, as the law-giver in a family, believed that he had the authority to kill a son. To Calas, of course, the idea was obscene; but his neighbours were ready to believe it; perhaps they thought he had been driven to the crime by fury at having been forced to support a son who had converted to Catholicism.

David de Beaudrige, a fanatical member of the *Capitouls* or investigating magistrates of Toulouse, was quick to hear and believe the rumours. Without wasting time by making any inquiry, he had the entire Calas family, together with La Vaysse and the governess, arrested and imprisoned in the cells of the Hôtel de Ville. As they were led out of their house Pierre wanted to place a lighted candle in the window against their return. 'Don't trouble yourself,' said de Beaudrige; 'you won't be home as quickly as all that.'

Meanwhile, public opinion in the city burst into flames, fanned by the White Penitents, the most important of the many penitential congregations of the Roman Church, whose main duties were to care for the sick and bury the dead. It was the latter task which now exercised them in the case of Marc Antoine, who had been killed, it appeared, because he wanted to become a Catholic and so merited particular attention. The monks staged a theatrical *scena* in their chapel with the coffin surmounted by a skeleton bearing in one hand a placard on which was written 'Abjuration of Heresy' and in the other the palm of martyrdom. After the body had been exposed and revered for three weeks, there was an impressive Catholic funeral, presided over by the curé of St Stephens – the one man who above all others knew perfectly well that Marc Antoine had died a stalwart Protestant. Forty priests surrounded the coffin, which was led into the church by a procession of Carmelite monks. This was the clearest assertion by the Church that the dead boy had not killed himself, though no attempt whatsoever had been made by anyone to discover whether this was or was not the case.

De Beaudrige was immovable in his determination to secure the conviction of the whole Calas family. First, he issued a Monitory to be read from the pulpits of all the churches in the city demanding that anyone with information should come forward; although the law decreed that the document should be impartial, on the contrary it insisted that the boy had been murdered. Then a Fulmination was issued, threatening anyone who withheld information about the murder with instant excommunication.

Some of de Beaudrige's fellow magistrates were critical of his methods, but not sufficiently courageous to criticise him openly. One colleague who suggested that he was proceeding without due respect for the law was frightened off by the reminder that the case was being brought in the cause of 'true religion' (as though any suggestion that the death might indeed have been suicide was an aspersion on Catholic law). De Beaudrige also succeeded in frightening off the lawyer who had been appointed to defend the family. On a specious pretext, he had the counsel suspended for three months and forced to make a public act of repentance simply for agreeing to conduct the defence in the case.

When the trial began a deposition was read from the Catholic convert Louis Calas (made under who knows what pressure) stating that his dead brother had told him he wanted to join the Carmelite order. This was later retracted, but the damage had been done. A number of witnesses appeared, one asserting that he had heard the dead man cry out, clearly, 'Ah! My God! they are strangling me!', which struck no one as absurd. Other neighbours alleged that they had heard similar cries. Calas, Mme Calas, young Pierre and La Vaysse then underwent the first degree of torture.[2] This had no effect. Nor did torture succeed in persuading the Calas's maid to give evidence against any of the accused (it is a mark of the fervour of the prosecution that though she was a convinced Catholic, a regular attendant at mass, and one of those who had encouraged Louis to convert, she was still accused and tortured).

On 10 November the court found Jean Calas, his wife and Pierre guilty of murdering the dead boy, and sentenced them to death by hanging. La Vaysse,[3] charged with complicity, was condemned to the galleys, but the governess Jeanne Vignière, who had sworn that her employers were innocent, was sentenced to a mere five years' imprisonment, the court showing leniency to a Catholic.

An automatic appeal to the *parlement* of Toulouse resulted in a survey of the case which lasted three months. Most members of the *parlement* seemed as determined to convict as Beaudrige. Only one had doubts, and when he voiced them he was told that he was behaving just like the accused – to which he replied that his accusers were behaving just like the mob which gathered outside the *parlement* building all day, shouting 'Calas, *assassin!*' sufficiently loudly to be heard in the room in which the case was being considered.

Over sixty new witnesses were called, not one able to provide any hard evidence against the family. The result was the acquittal of Mme Calas, her son, La Vaysse and the governess. Calas himself was, however, again found guilty, and condemned to be executed, but not before being tortured once more, in order to secure a confession which would justify his death.

On 10 March 1762 the 64-year-old was stretched upon the rack until his joints were dislocated, but continued to assert that his son had committed suicide. He was allowed to rest before undergoing the water torture, when fifteen pints of water was poured down his throat, his penis first having been tied to prevent him urinating. When this had no effect, fifteen more were added. When the presiding priest, a Fr Bourgès, implored him to confess, he merely asked whether a priest could seriously believe a father capable of killing his own son. Invited to condemn his accomplices, he said that since there had been no crime, there could be no accomplices.

He was allowed to relieve himself before being driven on a cart to the door of St Stephen's Church, where he was bound face upwards to a wheel and an executioner broke each of his arms and legs in two places while the priest warned him that unless he confessed he would spend eternity in torment. Calas continued to cry out his innocence for two hours, after which he was charitably strangled before his body was tied upright to a stake and burned and the ashes scattered.

De Beaudrige dutifully wrote to Paris reporting the case and its outcome – the execution of Calas and the sentences on the other members of the family. The result of the trial, he said, had surprised no one in Toulouse, though there had been some public disquiet at the leniency shown to Pierre, Mme Calas and Mlle Vignière. He expected to be congratulated on his efficiency.[4]

Voltaire first heard of the case from a M. Audibert, a Marseilles merchant who happened to be in Toulouse during the trial and execution, had suspected a cruel injustice, and brought events to the philosopher's attention, convincing Voltaire that he should look into the matter. Mme Calas and Pierre had, unsurprisingly, vanished; as soon as they were released, they went into hiding in Montauban. Nor could Mlle Vignière be found, while the two daughters had been placed in separate convents. Donat, the son who was in apprenticeship in Nimes, also fled. Happily he had come to Geneva, where Voltaire was able to find him and invite him to Les Délices. There, he was closely questioned. Were his parents ever violent towards him? Had M. Calas ever shown more than impatience to Marc Antoine? Donat was able to confirm that his father was a patient, kindly man who had treated all his children, even the renegade Louis, with the greatest indulgence, and who though worried about Marc Antoine's somewhat rackety lifestyle, loved him as much as the others.

Not content to rest his case on the evidence of a son, Voltaire wrote to two merchants who had lodged with the family. They confirmed that their host was a mild and quiet-mannered man. Voltaire wrote to Cardinal Bernis, pointing out that everyone to whom he had spoken believed there had been a miscarriage of justice. The Cardinal did not reply. He then wrote to Richelieu, marshal of France, who made some enquiries before advising Voltaire to drop the matter: there was nothing further to be said or done. By now Voltaire had received a letter from Mme Calas, with whom Donat had put him in touch, and her narration seemed to him to be so patently honest and sincere that there could be no doubt left in the matter.

Once convinced, he worried at the case like a terrier. He wrote to Etienne Damilavile, Chief Inspector of Taxes and an old friend, and to the Duc de Villars and the Duchesse d'Enville, and despite Richelieu's attitude implored him to persuade the King's ministers to order an inquiry into the conduct of the trial. Lodging Donat permanently with himself, he took down the young man's narration of the events leading up to Marc Antoine's death, and re-composed them in an affecting statement which was copied, published in France, and sent to London, Vienna, Amsterdam and various cities in Germany in the hope that international interest and pressure might persuade the French authorities to act. He sent for Pierre in order to set down every memory he had of the finding of the body, and what had happened immediately afterwards. The boy, like the other members of the family, was, he thought, transparently honest.

As a notable pamphleteer, Voltaire naturally issued a summary of the evidence he had been able to collect, *Original Documents Concerning the Death of Sieur Calas*,[5] following it up with several shorter persuasive leaflets. He unhesitatingly poured his own money into the campaign, but also persuaded the Queen of England, the Empress of Russia and the King of Poland to subscribe, publicly, to the Calas fund. When this became known, more money flooded in from all parts of Europe.[6]

Next, Voltaire invited an advocate of the King's Council, Maître Mariette, to place an appeal before the Council. Mariette insisted he could only act if he was in possession of all the papers relating to the affair. This gave de Beaudrige and the Toulouse authorities the opportunity to delay matters by refusing to hand over the documents. However, Maître Elie de Beaumont, another very well-known Parisian lawyer, was persuaded to write four papers arguing the illegality of the trials, and fifteen of his most distinguished colleagues added their signatures to his.

Voltaire was beginning to be confident that a review of the case was imminent, and arranged for Calas's two daughters to join their mother in Paris, convenient for their attendance in court if that was necessary. Richelieu now found himself forced by mounting public opinion – and the fact the Mme de Pompadour had expressed her sympathy with Mme Calas – to take a serious interest. She had told Voltaire that the King himself had not only heard of the case, but believed with her that something must be done to make it clear that the executed man could not have committed the crime of which he had been accused.

Richelieu himself now called on Voltaire and interviewed Donat, whose simple narrative convinced him that action should be taken. Eventually, on 7 March 1763, not quite a year after Calas' execution, the widow and her daughters were summoned to appeal before the King's Council of Ministers. Voltaire was confident of the result. 'I have neglected nothing to come at the truth,' he wrote; 'I am as sure of the family's innocence as I am of my own existence.'[7]

Eighty-three members of the Council, including not only law lords but the Duc de Choiseul, the Duc de Praslin, three ministers of State and three bishops attended the meeting which considered the case; an unprecedented congregation which unanimously ordered an examination of all the papers relevant to the trial. De Beaudrige was now in a state of panic, as were those who had so energetically supported him. They got together and informed Voltaire that it would cost the huge sum of 1,500 livres to have the necessary documents copied. Voltaire blandly replied that such a sum was readily available.

On other pretexts, de Beaudrige contrived to stall the inquiry for almost two more years; but eventually the necessary documents reached Paris, and examining them even the meanest intelligence on the Council could not but be convinced that Jean Calas had been innocent. It was decided that the case against him should be annulled. Some of the judges from Toulouse who had been present at the original trial were summoned to attend the Council's final meeting. One of them excused himself to the Duc d'Ayen: 'My lord Duke, even the best horse sometimes stumbles.' 'Possibly,' replied the Duke; 'but a whole stable?'

Voltaire described the effect the decision had on the ordinary folk who had been following the case:

The whole of Paris erupted with joy; people gathered together in the squares, on the promenades; they flocked to see this family once heaped with misery and now so triumphantly vindicated; they applauded the judges as they passed, overwhelming them with gratitude. The spectacle was made all the more touching by the fact that this was the very day, the 9th of March, when Calas had been so cruelly put to death three years before.[8]

Calas's widow was awarded 30,000 livres by way of compensation, and received at court. As she was led towards the King, his attention was – perhaps unintentionally – distracted, and he never met the woman whose case had exemplified the State justice system at its most implacably severe. She was, however, introduced to the Queen.[9]

Persecution and Tolerance

As if the Calas case had not sufficiently exercised Voltaire, he found himself at the same time embroiled in a similar one. On 19 March 1764, while the Calas appeal was still dragging on with painful slowness, a court in Mazamet, some 50 kilometres north-east of Carcassone, ordered a man and his wife to be hanged in the presence of their two daughters. They had, it was alleged, murdered a third daughter, Elizabeth, rather than see her convert to Catholicism.

Pierre Paul Sirven had the misfortune to live at Castres, 65 kilometres from Toulouse, and thus in the middle of the virulently anti-Protestant area in which Calas had been condemned. On 6 March 1760 his younger daughter Elizabeth suddenly disappeared. The parents were distraught, and were relieved when the Bishop of Castres had the girl returned to them. They were told that Elizabeth had gone to him and claimed that she wanted to become a Catholic. He had quite properly ordered her to be placed in a convent – it was perfectly legal for the Catholic authorities to remove from their parents or guardians any young person over the age of seven who expressed the desire to be converted. Unfortunately, the case had turned out not to be as straightforward as the Bishop at first thought.

Once in the convent, Elizabeth began to hold long conversations with angels. The nuns might have regarded this as, at worst, impertinent; but when she insisted on stripping herself naked and begged to be flogged, they began to wonder whether her vocation was well founded. Eventually, she had to be put in a straitjacket, and the Bishop, informed of her eccentricity, ordered her to be restored to her family. Her parents found it difficult to control her, and her father unwisely accused the nuns of having driven her mad. The nuns counter-attacked by accusing him of cruelty to her because she wanted to convert. Life in Castres became uncomfortable for the family, and in July 1761 the Sirvens moved 80 kilometres to Saint-Abby. Five months later, Elizabeth got up in the middle of the night, claimed it was midday, and went out to gather wood for the fire. Her father was away from home, and her mother, worn out and ill, had not the energy to detain her. When the local curé heard of her disappearance, he said that wherever she was she would be better off than at home – clearly believing that she had taken herself back to a convent. The girl was mad, but would be safe in the arms of Mother Church. A few days later, some children found her body in a well near her home.

There was an inquest at which no fewer than forty-five witnesses expressed the opinion that the girl was emotionally unstable, and had either committed suicide or accidentally fallen to her death. But while the local people on the whole believed in the family's innocence, there were others determined to see the Protestant scum prosecuted. The local prosecutor, one M. Trinquier, sent a report to the Prosecutor General in Toulouse, which resulted in an instruction to accuse Sirven of the murder of his daughter. There was reliable evidence that he had been away from the house on the day of Elizabeth's disappearance, but this was no obstacle to a determined lawyer, who said that if Sirven had not done the deed doubtless his wife was guilty; and if she was innocent, one of the other daughters had no doubt committed the murder. In any case, Sirven was responsible.

Sirven had heard of the trial, torture and execution of Calas, and was not inclined to trust himself to the courts. He, his wife and daughters, one of whom was pregnant, left Saint-Abby late at night and made their terrified, shivering way over the Cévennes, Sirven to Lausanne and his wife and daughters to Nimes. In their absence, the husband and wife were condemned to death – to be hanged while their daughters looked on. Since a satisfactory execution could not take place in the absence of the guilty parties, M. and Mme Sirven were burned in effigy in the Place du Plô at Mazamet.

Voltaire was outraged when he heard of the affair: it was as though, he said, four sheep had been accused of eating a lamb. A sympathetic friend introduced Sirven to him, and though it was unfortunate (he said ironically) that no one had actually been broken on the wheel in this case, for that concentrated people's minds, it would surely be possible to do something to set things straight. Though at first he was reluctant to take on the case – he was much caught up with the Calas arguments, and after all Sirven and his family were in no immediate danger – he saw to it that they had accommodation and food, and when the Toulouse authorities continued to place obstacles in the way of obtaining the papers in the Calas affair, he decided to take up arms in this second notable case of miscarriage of justice. He sent the details of Sirven's predicament (apart from having had to flee from France, the man had had all his property confiscated) to Frederick, Christian VII of Denmark, and once more to Catherine of Russia and Stanislas of Poland. Some of his friends were a little impatient: was it really necessary for him to become some sort of professional apologist for everyone who thought themselves victims of injustice?

'I am involved in too many murder cases', he admitted to d'Argental. 'But by everything angelic, whose fault is that?' The court at Mazamet, under the jurisdiction of which proceedings against Sirven had been brought, followed the example of the Toulouse court and refused to send him the papers in the case. Once again he had to engage in a long legal battle during which Mme Sirven died without being pardoned. The case remained unresolved until 1771, when the *parlement* of Toulouse pronounced Sirven innocent and restored his property. As Voltaire said, 'it took two hours to condemn him, and nine years to recognise his innocence'.[10]

The result of all this was that he now received appeals for help in almost every post. Occasionally he could and did help – he argued successfully for the release, for instance, of a Protestant condemned to the galleys for preaching. Many of his efforts were on behalf of Calvinists and others whose religious beliefs were anathema to him; his interest was in the reform of the justice system rather than in the views and attitudes of those who suffered as a result of its administration by religious and other bigots.

Naturally, he was attacked for this; and the authorities were delighted when the opportunity arose to involve him in a case which might damage his reputation. One night in August 1765 a wooden crucifix which stood on the Pont-Neuf over the river Somme at Abbeville was hacked and damaged, and in the nearby cemetery of Saint-Catherine excreta was smeared over another crucifix. The local people were aghast at such blasphemy, and the Bishop of Amiens led a procession of penitents to the church to ask forgiveness. A Monitory was read, and as a result seventy-seven witnesses came forward with a farrago of anecdotes: one young man had been seen failing to remove his hat as a religious procession passed him in the street, another had been heard singing profane songs, and there were stories of anti-religious tracts being passed from hand to hand.

Eventually, with all the confidence of prejudice, warrants were signed by a magistrate ordering the arrest of three young men: Gaillard d'Étallonde, Chevalier Jean François LeFebre de La Barre, and a ne'er-do-well called Moisnel. D'Étallonde left town before he could be arrested, but the other two were taken, and almost immediately the terrified 17-year-old Moisnel accused La Barre of smearing ordure on the crucifix in the cemetery and damaging the cross, spitting on the picture of a saint and singing an obscene song ('La Madeleine'). Moreover, La Barre had loaned Moisnel two books by the well-known anti-Christ Voltaire: the *Dictionnaire philosophique* and the *Épître à Uranie*.

La Barre was the son of an army officer and had been placed in the care of his aunt, the Abbess de Willancourt. She had an indifferent reputation, and was celebrated locally more for the promiscuous parties she gave than for her care for her religious duties. She had always been happy to welcome her twenty-year-old nephew to her carouses, and was probably the source of the books he had unwisely been reading.

A rather remarkable young man, when questioned La Barre courageously admitted everything. He had, he said, often heard his elders – even members of the cloth – question religious beliefs; why should he not have reached his own conclusions about the matter? Warming to his theme, he admitted that he had enjoyed quoting from Voltaire's *La Pucelle* and *L'Épître*, and rashly blurted out the fact that religion seemed to him to be monumental nonsense – what could be more ridiculous than adoring the host, which was simply a piece of bread? He had been accused of 'uttering blasphemies against God, the Holy Eucharist, the Holy Virgin, the religion and commandments of God and of the Church', of 'singing two songs filled with excremental and abominable blasphemies . . . rendering marks of adoration and respect to infamous books; profaning the sign of the cross, the mystery of the consecration of the wine, and the benedictions in use in Churches among Christians',[11] and on his own evidence there could be no question of his guilt. The sentence proper to such enormities was passed.

La Barre was to be tortured to make him reveal the names of his accomplices (despite the fact that their names were already known); then after he had done penance outside St Wolfran's Church his tongue was to be torn out before he was driven to the main square of the town, where he would be beheaded and his body burned. Voltaire's books were to be thrown on to the fire with the body. When the young man appealed to the *parlement* of Paris, Councillor Pasquier admitted that the real criminal was Voltaire, but declined to pardon La Barre. The other members of the *parlement*, save two, agreed with him, though they charitably excused the condemned youth from having his tongue torn out.

Having declined to name any of his friends as sharing his humanist views, the victim was prepared for execution on 1 July 1766. As his hair was being cut to bare his neck for the axe, he retained his composure, asking whether they were trying to make a choirboy of him. The windows of the houses along the route to the square were crowded with onlookers, among whom La Barre recognised many of his friends and drinking companions, and nodded his head to them. The crowd in the square broke into spontaneous applause as that head fell into the basket.[12]

Meanwhile the Bishop of Annecy wrote to the King demanding that Voltaire be burned at the stake for his part in corrupting La Barre – hearing of it, the philosopher told his friends that he was laying in a supply of holy water with which to extinguish the flames.

The Calas and Sirven affairs, and now the execution of La Barre, had concentrated Voltaire's mind on the unjust persecution visited by the Church on anyone who questioned conventional religious beliefs. Not all his friends subscribed to his outrage. Frederick, for instance, told him that while the beheading of La Barre was no doubt unfortunate for the boy, he had after all brought it on himself. Rash attacks on the accepted beliefs of the majority were to say the least unwise, and after all 'should we directly attack the prejudices that time has consecrated in the mind of nations? And if we wish to enjoy liberty of thought, must we insult established belief? A man who does not wish to make a disturbance is rarely persecuted.'[13] Moreover, he asserted that if a government of philosophers agreed to abolish religion, within a century men and women would be worshipping the sun, or little wooden idols. It was fruitless to try to educate the idiot people.

Needless to say, Voltaire did not agree. He wrote to Louis XV asking the King to issue a posthumous pardon of La Barre, and later sent his successor, Louis XVI, a pamphlet entitled *The Cry of Innocent Blood*. He published, anonymously, an account of La Barre's trial and execution, continued to take an interest in specific cases of religious intolerance and persecution, and to inveigh against them. He published his first direct attack on Christianity, *Sermon des cinquantes*, which had actually been written a decade earlier, while he was at Potsdam with Frederick. In it he condemned the God of the Old Testament as a being no sane man could worship – a pompous, jealous, angry, cruel, malevolent and murderous deity. The other personalities of the Old Testament were equally abhorrent: take David, for instance – a lecherous, bloodthirsty blackguard. And the Old Testament, which merited burning much more than many contemporary books condemned by the law, was the Word of God? The idea was absurd.

His campaign against Christianity was to occupy much of his time during the remainder of his life, and was if anything to increase in virulence. But the strain of all his work in the Calas and Sirven cases had drained his energy, and while he seemed to ride the attacks of those who hoped to be able to convict him for those works which had been the chief basis of the case against La Barre, this too had had an effect on his health. His friends became seriously concerned. Théodore Tronchin pointed out that his fears were groundless: no one in Europe could afford to prosecute so celebrated a writer and philosopher. Why was he giving way to these irrational fears? To his embarrassed surprise, Voltaire admitted that he was being foolish: '*Je suis fou!*' he muttered, and burst into tears.

13

Friends and Enemies

*Madness is to think of too many things in
succession or of one thing too exclusively.*

Letter, 1746

Voltaire was always pleased to discuss the shortcomings of French justice with the many visitors who sought him out, and the details of his intervention in the Calas affair, and news of the other instances of religious persecution in which he took an interest, spread throughout Europe as much by word of mouth as by anything he published. As far as publication was concerned, it was the *Traité sur la Tolérance* (Treatise on Tolerance) which, taking Calas's trial and execution as its starting-point, rang out as one of the strongest arguments he ever put forward in favour of the State allowing freedom of religious belief. Indeed, it advocated freedom of belief in general, for in it he asserted that the quiet possession of a personal conviction did no harm as long as society was not disturbed by actions resulting from it; only when belief was fanatically asserted should the State take action – and perhaps not even then.

He wrote the book while the Calas case was still in progress, but deferred publication until it had been resolved. It was in 1764 that the treatise was brought out anonymously in Geneva. It found its way in great numbers into France, and translations were almost immediately published in Holland and England. The French censors instantly condemned it as a dangerous attack on the State, and those copies which came into private hands (and many were confiscated and destroyed when they were discovered in the post) were carefully hidden by those who had managed to come by them.

No one, least of all those about the Court (many of whom were among its earliest readers[1]) was in any doubt who had written the book. It bears throughout its length the mark of Voltaire's witty, iconoclastic style. His historical survey of religious persecution, with the insistence that Christians had been among the worst religious terrorists, is selective but telling, his attack on reverence (for whatever idol or belief) and his suggestion that many of the Christian saints were fictional characters were typically startling to his contemporaries. His demand that society should tolerate those of its members who chose not to follow in the tracks of the majority was insistent.

'I do not say,' he wrote, 'that all those who profess a different religion from that of the reigning prince should share in the places and honours available to those who are of the prevailing religion. In England, Roman Catholics are considered as belonging to the party of the Pretender, and are therefore denied office; they even pay double tax; yet they still enjoy all other privileges of the citizen.'[2] It followed that everyone should be allowed to believe 'whatever his reason tells him, to think only what his reason, be it enlightened or misguided, may dictate . . . provided always that he threatens no disturbance to public order. For a man is under no obligation to believe or not to believe. His duties are to respect the laws and customs of his country, and if you claim that it is a crime not to believe in the prevailing religion, you are pointing the finger of accusation against our ancestors, the first Christians, and you are justifying the actions of those you previously blamed for putting them to death.'[3] If members of a particular sect did no harm, it was patently wrong to persecute them: 'The right to persecute is . . . absurd and barbaric; it is the law of the jungle. Nay, it is yet worse, for wild animals kill only to eat, whereas we have exterminated one another over a parcel of words.'[4]

In a lighter vein he published his *Dictionnaire philosophique portatif*, a collection of the many articles he had contributed to the larger *Dictionnaire*, which was remarkable for its wit and pertinacity, and for a number of declarations which have found their way into most dictionaries of quotations: from the entry for *Miracles*, for instance, comes the famous injunction, 'Define your terms!' The authorities in Geneva burned every copy they could find, and Voltaire had to assure them that he had absolutely no idea who could be the author of such a scurrilous collection of outrageous thoughts – probably a number of disreputable writers, he thought. Nevertheless the book remained in print for the rest of his life, and he regularly added articles to it.

In his seventies, despite the illnesses both real and imaginary that continually plagued him, Voltaire retained the energy of ten men of his age. When so ill that he thought he was dying, he said he would remember those three or four princes who would by his death be relieved of the necessity to pay his annuities, and 'take courage from pure malice, and conspire against them with rhubarb and sobriety'.[5]

Though much of his time was taken up by the Calas and La Barre cases, and by the many others to which he gave at least passing attention, his literary work continued. Apart from his more important writing, he had turned reviewer for the *Gazette littéraire*, for which he reviewed English as well as French books, among them the letters of Lady Mary Wortley Montagu (whose introduction into England of the practice of inoculation against smallpox he had much admired) and David Hume's *History of England*. His fame, not only in France but throughout Europe, continued to attract a procession of distinguished men to Ferney. A number of British travellers visited him in 1763–4, and left written sketches which bring him to life for us.

Thomas Pennant, the naturalist, traveller and author of *British Zoology*, was received at Ferney by the 'sedate, worthy-looking' Mme Denis, and was startled by Voltaire's frail appearance – he was 'as meagre and arid a figure as ever I saw,' he wrote in his journal.[6] By now, the writer was suffering from sciatica, and in the winter his sight was badly affected by snow-blindness. However as soon as he had got into conversation Voltaire quickly cheered up and his dark eyes 'which were the most brilliant I ever saw' sparkled with pleasure. He took his visitor for a walk in his garden, which seemed to Pennant to be extremely ill-kempt, talking all the while in English, though an English which 'he seemed to have forgotten except our imprecations'. He was enthusiastic in his regard for Pennant's nationality: he loved the English: "'By G— I do lov de Ingles G— dammee, if I don't lov them better dan de French by G—.'"[7]

Better known than Pennant was 26-year-old Edward Gibbon, already a published author,[8] and until recently a captain in the Hampshire militia. *En route* to Italy on a European tour (during which he conceived his scheme for a massive examination of the decline and fall of the Roman Empire), he looked in on the great Frenchman whose reputation was almost as distinguished in England as in France. He had met him on a previous occasion, and found him now in altered, less grand circumstances, in a 'pretty tho' small house', and remarked that 'after a life passed in courts and Capitals, the Great Voltaire is now become a meer country Gentleman . . .'. 'He says he never enjoyed so much happiness', Gibbon told his stepmother.[9] 'He has got rid of most of his infirmities and tho' very old and lean, enjoys a much better state of health than he did twenty years ago.'

Gibbon was invited to a special performance of Voltaire's *L'Orphelin de la Chine* in which the author acted the part of Genghis and his mistress that of Idamé. When he last saw him act he had been rather impressed; now, however, he found the spectacle of a seventy-year-old man 'acting a Tartar Conqueror with a hollow broken Voice, and making love to a very ugly niece of about fifty' ludicrous. However, the evening was a rather remarkable one, for after the end of the performance the whole audience of a hundred sat down to a supper the last dish of which was served at 2 a.m. Then the company danced until four, 'when we broke up, got into our coaches and came back to Geneva just as the Gates were opened. Show me in history or fable [Gibbon concluded] a famous poet of Seventy who has acted in his own plays, and has closed the scene with a supper and ball for a hundred people. I think the last is the more extraordinary of the two.'

A little later, a 23-year-old Scots author on the Grand Tour, who always had an eye for a Great Man, determined to make the acquaintance of two of Europe's most famous personalities, Rousseau and Voltaire. Having succeeded in his first ambition, on Christmas Eve of 1763 James Boswell took a coach for an hour through the snow from Geneva to Ferney, carrying a letter of introduction to Voltaire from a Colonel Constant d'Hermenches, one of the Frenchman's numerous correspondents, who had been an actor in his amateur theatre. Received by three elegant footmen, Boswell sent the letter in, and after he had waited for a while – Voltaire was still abed – the philosopher made his appearance dressed in a slate-blue dressing-gown, and having greeted his guest with 'that air of the world which a Frenchman acquires in such perfection', sat himself bolt upright on a high-backed chair and talked.

The conversation was not at first particularly intellectual.[10] They conversed in French, which Boswell spoke reasonably well. He asked Voltaire if he spoke English. 'No,' said the philosopher; 'to speak English one must place the tongue between the teeth, and I have lost my teeth.'

Voltaire cordially invited his guest to stay for dinner, but did not dine with him. Mme Denis was left to entertain the susceptible Boswell, who with his eye for the ladies enjoyed her company despite her age and *embonpoint*. He noted that he himself became more and more 'lively and agreeable' as the meal progressed. Back in Geneva, he sat down on Christmas Day and wrote a letter to his hostess thanking her for her hospitality (particularly, for a double helping of a sweet dessert *tarte*) and asking if he might spend a night at Ferney. He intended to visit them again, he said, during the coming week, and since the gates of Geneva shut at an early hour (before five o'clock in the afternoon), it would be most convenient if he could stay overnight at the château. He was 'a hardy & vigorous Scot', he said, and 'you may mount me to the highest and coldest Garret. I shall not even refuse to sleep upon two chairs in the Bedchamber of your Maid' (he had particularly noticed one maid who had passed through the rooms, and implied that accommodation in her room might be particularly agreeable).

The letter really is an extraordinary piece of impertinent wheedling, even for Boswell.[11] He would bring his own night-cap, he said, because he 'would not presume to think of having my head honoured with a nightcap of M. de Voltaire', though this 'would immediately convey the qualitys of it's master [*sic*]; and I own to you Madam, my head is not strong enough to bear them.' Finally, he promised (threatened?) a reading of his own poems: 'All I can offer for the favour which I ask is many many thanks; or if M. de Voltaire's delicate French ear would not be offended, I might perhaps offer him a few good rough english verses.'

Voltaire himself wrote a reply, in English, in the person of his niece: 'We have few beds, but you will not sleep on two chairs. My uncle, tho very sick, hath guess'd at yr merit. J know it more, because j have seen you longer.'

Delighted, Boswell returned to Ferney on 27 December, where he found only a few other visitors. Voltaire made a brief appearance, then left his guests to amuse themselves at shuttlecock, or by playing the guitar, singing, and chatting among themselves. Boswell was extremely bored: it was just like an evening in any dull English house. He did have a brief, interesting conversation with Père Adam, an unfrocked Jesuit priest who lived permanently at the château, who described Voltaire's hospitable lifestyle: there were rarely fewer than fifty people in the house, he said, including travellers – both friends and strangers.

Then they were summoned to the drawing-room and Boswell managed an hour's tête-à-tête with the great man, persuading him to speak English which, despite his toothless state, he did with great facility, using a number of colloquial curses. He had some Dryden by heart, but when they talked of Shakespeare Voltaire described him as 'a buffoon', and accused Boswell of lack of taste for admiring his work.

Boswell was determined to sound him out on the subject of religion, and eventually managed to drag the conversation around to the subject – 'then did he rage'.[12] Dr Johnson was 'a superstitious dog' for being an orthodox Christian; the Pope was 'a bigot, a poor being' whose son was a drunken rapist. The subject aroused considerable emotion: while 'raging', Voltaire's head swam and he almost fainted. Boswell changed the subject. They got round to politics:

VOLTAIRE: You have the better government. If it gets bad, heave it into the ocean; that's why you have the ocean all about you. You are the slaves of laws. The French are the slaves of men. In France every man is either an anvil or a hammer; he is a beater or must be beaten.

BOSWELL: Yet it is a light, a genteel hammer.

VOLTAIRE: Yes, a pocket hammer. We are too mean for our governors to cut off our heads. We are on the earth; they trample us.

By the end of the conversation they had returned to religion, and Boswell had persuaded Voltaire to express 'his veneration – his love – of the Supreme Being, and his entire resignation to the will of Him who is All-wise. He expressed his desire to resemble the Author of Goodness by being good himself. His sentiments go no further. He does not inflame his mind with grand hopes of the immortality of the soul. He says it may be, but knows nothing of it. And his mind is in perfect tranquillity. "I suffer much. But I suffer with patience and resignation; not as a Christian – but as a man."'

The furthest Voltaire would go was to suggest that men should meet four times a year in a temple where they could listen to great music and 'thank God for all his gifts. There is one sun. There is one God. Let us have one religion. Then all mankind will be brethren.'

Voltaire retired, and after enjoying a meal with the other guests, Boswell was shown to a room with a marble fireplace and a bed hung with purple cloth lined with white quilted satin, a room quite as handsome as any in Edinburgh, he concluded. Waking early, he decided to stay longer than he had intended, and sent a servant to Geneva with a message to stop his coach from coming to fetch him until the following day. After a short walk in the garden, he occupied himself by making a fair copy of one of his own poems and inscribing it:

Most humbly presented to Monsieur de Voltaire, the glory of France, the admiration of Europe, by Mr Boswell, who has had the honour of regarding and loving him in private life at his Château de Ferney.[13]

Voltaire was having one of his bad days, and did not come down for dinner. Boswell went to the library and read *Mahomet*. When Voltaire did appear he was in low spirits, and the conversation was disappointing. Next morning Boswell was shown his host's private theatre and library, but Voltaire did not leave his room, and Boswell went to him to say goodbye. He told the philosopher (somewhat impertinently – but that was Boswell) that before he met him, he thought him a very great but a very bad man; encountering him personally had made him feel that that was not the case – though he must continue to quarrel with his host's questioning of the immortality of the soul. After all, the wish for immortality was a noble one. Ah, said Voltaire, but after all his guest might have a noble desire to be King of England, but the fulfilment of that desire was not probable. At which Boswell took his leave.

In mid-January he wrote to Ferney from Turin reminding Voltaire how much he had liked meeting his Scottish guest – whose conversation had, after all, been 'singular and agreeable', had it not? – and returning to the subject of the immortality of the soul. Voltaire would have nothing of it: 'You seem sollicitous about that pretty thing call'd soul', he wrote in his uncertain English. 'J do protest you j know nothing of it. Nor wether it is, nor what it is, not what it shall be. young scolars, and priests know all that perfectly. for my part j am but a very ignorant fellow.'[14] After which the correspondence failed to flourish. But Boswell was pleased, ever afterwards, to repeat his memories of the philosopher and to quote his bons mots, and whenever questioned on the subject always said that Voltaire was the most brilliant conversationalist he had ever heard.

Among the people staying at Ferney when Pennant visited was a descendant of the dramatist Pierre Corneille, who proudly displayed to the visitors the edition of his plays which Voltaire had edited. Its history illustrates Voltaire's generosity of spirit. In 1760 an acquaintance had told him of the sad straits in which a young female relative of the playwright found herself. She was, it seemed, living in abject poverty. Voltaire immediately suggested that the girl be sent to him; he and Mme Denis would be happy to see to her education: 'We shall bring a master here who will be highly honoured to be teaching the Great Corneille's granddaughter, though not nearly so highly as I shall be to see her living under my roof.'[15] He organised her journey from Paris to Ferney, carefully arranging for her to be escorted when she changed coaches, to be met at Lyons and then conveyed onwards to Ferney.

Friends and Enemies

Marie-Françoise was a descendant of the dramatist's uncle, and turned out to be a pretty and enchanting young girl, 'gay, natural and unaffected . . . she has a little pug face, the most beautiful eyes, lovely skin, and a wide, rather tempting mouth with two rows of pearls,' Voltaire wrote.[16] It is a little surprising perhaps that Marie Louise Denis showed no signs of jealousy. Voltaire immediately christened the girl Rodogune (after a character in one of Corneille's plays) and treated her with great generosity, seeing to it that she was not only well educated (she had to write him a letter every day, which he corrected and returned to her) but beautifully dressed, and introduced to visitors as part of the family. She soon became a real asset, receiving and entertaining visitors with considerably more charm than Marie-Louise herself. Her future was a matter of concern, and Voltaire had the happy idea of producing a complete edition of the works of her 'uncle', the profits from which would provide a dowry against the time of her marriage.

He set about raising money for the project, and his familiar sources of encouragement – the King of France, the Empress of Russia, and Frederick (with whom he still maintained a prickly and volatile correspondence) – subscribed. He also wrote to other friends and acquaintances all over Europe, sometimes referring to the dramatist's 'niece', sometimes, as in a letter to Lord Chesterfield, to his 'gran daughter' ('If there was a grand daughter of Shakespear j would subscribe for her').[17] In 1764, the edition of Corneille appeared in a dozen volumes and brought in almost 100,000 francs for Marie-Françoise.[18] It is a work of the greatest scholarship, almost every line of every play annotated and glossed. Considering that Voltaire found Corneille's plays extremely dull, the time and energy he expended on the work was a remarkably generous gesture, and all undertaken while he was working on the *Dictionnaire philosophique*.

Life at Ferney, meanwhile, went on much as usual. Voltaire was as prolific as ever in his output, but it was difficult for him to settle quietly to work for any period of time: he was relentlessly pursued not only by visitors – sometimes welcome, more often impudent – but also by the censors, by jealous rivals, by petty local officials he had upset by his views or actions. Perhaps unexpectedly, a fellow author was a major irritant. Jean-Jacques Rousseau never ceased to pursue him.

Rousseau had been born in Geneva 1712, and was therefore Voltaire's junior by some eighteen years. Initially, his relationship with Voltaire had been cordial; when in 1745 Cardinal Richelieu asked Rousseau to edit Voltaire's *La Fête de Ramire*, an unfinished poem, to be set to music by Rameau as a court entertainment, they had had a pleasant exchange of compliments. But in 1762, when Rousseau's novel *Emile* was publicly burned in his native city of Geneva and he was exiled, he irrationally concluded that Voltaire had worked against him. On the contrary, not only did Voltaire sympathise, as someone who had himself been in much the same situation, but he actually offered Rousseau sanctuary: 'Let him come to Ferney – all I have is his.' Rousseau's response was that he would die rather than accept his enemy's hospitality, and he spoke of Voltaire as showing 'the blackest ingratitude and wickedness'. Two years later he published a book[19] in which he alleged that Voltaire had positively boasted of his attacks on religion.

The relentless drip of Rousseau's antagonism eventually provoked Voltaire to retaliate, describing his antagonist as the enemy of literature, puffed up with 'ridiculous pride' and displaying 'ridiculous behaviour'. Rousseau's novel *Julie: ou, la Nouvelle Héloise*, which enjoyed enormous success in 1767, nauseated him. He could not understand what anyone saw in it. It was carelessly written, and the characters were ludicrous: a whore who preached morality and a seducer who pretended to be a philosopher! What could be more ridiculous? While publicly ignoring the book, he employed Thiériot to distribute letters denigrating it, none of them signed with his own name. His authorship of them did not long remain a secret. In response, Rousseau looked out an old and unsuccessful anti-biblical play of his enemy's, *Saül*, and denounced it as irreligious and blasphemous. In response, Voltaire published an anonymous polemic in which he denounced Rousseau for attacking religion, writing unhealthy novels and insulting the pastors of Geneva, descending to the most virulent personal abuse. He did it very well:

We confess with pain and shame that he is one who still bears the baleful marks of his debaucheries, and who goes like a mountebank from village to village and mountain to mountain, dragging with him the unfortunate woman whose mother he killed and whose children he abandoned on the steps of an orphanage, rejecting a charitable person's offer to look after them and thus abjuring all the sentiments of nature just as he casts aside those of men and of religion.[20]

Things could not very well get worse, and indeed had reached their nadir. Neither man was now capable of rational behaviour where the other was concerned. The situation was exacerbated by the friends of both parties, who mischievously repeated gossip, made up false anecdotes and did their best (what a pleasure mischief-making was!) to make the quarrel worse. A king-pin of the malevolent gossips was Voltaire's doctor, Théodore Tronchin, who thoroughly enjoyed himself repeating to each man the libels of the other. They became almost manic in their mutual mistrust: any letter from a lunatic – and a successful writer receives plenty of those – was ascribed at once to the 'Great Enemy'. Rousseau and Voltaire remained the most steadfast enemies until they died, within two months of each other. Their relationship throws an unattractive light on both. Friendship between them was probably impossible; we can only regret that the two great philosophers of the eighteenth century should have been such implacable antagonists.

14

The Universal Man

*Superstition sets the whole world in flames –
philosophy quenches them.*

Dictionnaire philosophique ('Superstition')

Despite his work on behalf of the persecuted, his continual feuds with the Geneva authorities, the constant bickering with Rousseau and the interminable stream of visitors to Ferney (some of them welcome, like the beautiful actress Mlle Clairon,[1] who had been his friend and correspondent for twenty years), Voltaire continued to sit at his desk every day, and to turn out a quantity of work almost incredible in its volume and range.

He had begun in the early 1760s the chore of producing an authorised collected edition of his works, which needed bringing up to date almost monthly, as he published new volumes and pamphlets. He wrote a short book questioning the idea of miracles,[2] another pointing out the impossibility of answering unanswerable questions,[3] a commentary on crime and punishment.[4] However, his most notable book of the 1760s was his *Philosophie de l'histoire* (1764), which ranged over a huge number of subjects from geology to religious history, and protested with even greater vigour that detestation of Christianity which by now might be called a one-man crusade led by a banner bearing the words 'Down with villainy!'[5] There was no doubt at what 'villainy' he was aiming his polemic – at the concept that biblical authority should be regarded as the end of all religious discussion. 'Every impious law-maker who dares to pretend that his laws have been ordained by God is obviously a blasphemer and traitor,' he wrote.[6]

But to rail against the fact that any man should set himself up as the unquestioned authority on God's word was not to propose that God did not exist: in one of his articles in the *Dictionnaire philosophique* Voltaire suggested only that 'almost everything that goes beyond the adoration of a Supreme Being, and of submitting one's heart to his eternal orders, is superstition',[7] which suggests that he suspected that there was some sort of Prime Mover, while denying that anyone knew or could know anything about His or Its true nature.

His relationship with the civic authorities of Geneva continued to be distinctly frosty, and unfortunately his encouragement of watch-making on his own estate put him on the wrong side of the citizens themselves, who saw this as a direct attack upon their own incomes – and by foreign workers at that. Nor were they enchanted by a circular Voltaire wrote and distributed in Paris which suggested that while the Genevese were busy murdering each other, a number of honest workmen were producing watches of great quality on his own estate.

They soon had something else to think about. By the winter of 1766/7 the relationship between the strict Calvinists and those who leaned towards Voltaire's more liberal view (though few went as far as he did in criticising the influence of the Church) had gone from bad to worse, and open violence broke out in the streets. Voltaire did his best to moderate between the two factions, but it was a hopeless task (particularly for a foreigner, and especially for him). The French Ambassador, Chevalier Pierre de Buisson Beauteville also failed to reconcile the opposing parties, and the French Prime Minister, the Duc de Choiseul, sent an army to occupy the city.

Ferney suffered considerably from the food shortages which followed while Geneva was blockaded. The blockade failed, since liberal quantities of food reached the city from Savoy, but at Ferney they almost starved – they could get no meat, and what little they had was often appropriated by soldiers who also broke into the cellars and stole the wine, and devastated the gardens by cutting down trees to make their fires. De Choiseul eventually sent a pass which allowed Voltaire and some servants through the blockade to collect food, some of which he generously served to visiting French officers. The war came to an end without undue violence, but it had been an uncomfortable episode for Voltaire, during which he suffered a minor stroke.

He showed no signs of mellowing. Indeed, if anything his impatience with the fools who were attempting to govern society increased, and book after book, pamphlet after pamphlet were fired off from Ferney, printed in Paris, Amsterdam, London, Berlin – so many that the public came to believe that any book critical of the social structure of France must have been written by Voltaire. Usually it had been, whatever name appeared on the title-page. He continued to attack the Church but, just as riskily, turned his fire on the government, whose failures in social and political economy infuriated him. In *L'Homme aux quarante écus*, a book about political economy disguised as a fiction, he argued for a complete overhaul of France's system of taxation, attacking the neglect of agriculture, the profligate spending of the aristocracy, the waging of unnecessary wars. The book was quickly burned by the hangman.

The fact that he still found it necessary to publish pseud-onymously is easily understood: recently a Parisian apprentice who had accepted some books in settlement of a debt had sold them on to a bookseller. They included *L'Homme aux quarante écus* and a few other works suspected by the authorities of being blasphemous. The bookseller was branded, set in the pillory for three days, and then sent to the galleys for nine years; the apprentice was also branded and put in the pillory, but did not follow the bookseller to the galleys, for he died while his neck was still gripped by the pillory. The bookseller's widow was imprisoned for five years. No one could blame Voltaire for being cautious. He had always occasionally used pseudonyms, and now did so almost as a matter of course. Somewhat to the surprise of the public, a dead poet, Saint-Hyacinthe, brought out a new book in 1767: *Le Dîner du Comte Boulainvilliers*, in which a number of real characters discussed, over dinner, matters of life and death, among other things arguing that freethinking was superior to the Catholic religion and that the communion service was a celebration of idolatry (what could be said for eating and drinking one's god and then discharging him into a chamber pot?). Five minutes after picking the book up, most readers realised who was its real author.

Voltaire sometimes signed his more determined attacks on religion as the Archbishop of Canterbury, sometimes as the Archbishop of Paris. Other books were published under his own name, repudiating every aspect of the Christian religion. He also continued to deal with a greatly increased correspondence which went out to all quarters of Europe. Many people must have wondered whether all this could have come from the pen of one man, or whether (as Frederick had suggested years earlier) 'somewhere in France there is a select society of superior and equal geniuses who all work together and publish their writings under the name of Voltaire . . .'.[8] Even so, he convinced himself that he had some spare time, and once more turned his mind after many years to science, this time to biology, spending many hours cutting the heads off snails in order to determine whether they could regenerate (he concluded, mistakenly, that they could).

In 1768 came a distressing crisis. Marie-Louise Denis had continued to live with him, probably not for many years as his mistress, but certainly as mistress of his houses. The general view of his friends was still that she was an ignorant, unintelligent, blowsy, over-sexed termagant, but he put up with her both for his convenience and because he found it next to impossible to dismiss anyone from his household who had not seriously offended him; his capacity for tolerance and forgiveness was properly legendary. But his patience gave out during the winter of 1768, when a young man called Jean François de La Harpe came to stay at Ferney. He was personable if rather ill-bred, and had pretensions to literature which were not completely unfounded. Voltaire encouraged him to write poetry, and to everyone's surprise, the result was not bad – he even won a prize at the Académie (we may be forgiven for suspecting that Voltaire may have touched up the entry a little).

His success went to La Harpe's head, and visitors to Ferney were astonished at the rudeness he showed his host – and at the affection Voltaire continued to display towards him (he used to call him '*ma petite*', almost an amorous term). He even condescendingly 'improved' some of the lines in one of Voltaire's plays, but far from resenting his impertinence Voltaire wrote to the Comptroller General of the Treasury requesting that half his own pension should be paid to La Harpe, but that the latter should be persuaded to believe that the income came to him as a reward for his services to literature. The Comptroller quite properly thought the idea absurd, and declined to execute it.

As had been the case with Thiériot, another of those sheep to whose blackness Voltaire never reacted, La Harpe rewarded his benefactor by an act of treachery. Voltaire had written, some time earlier, a satirical pamphlet which combined an attack on Rousseau with passages highly critical of the parsimony and avariciousness of the people of Geneva, that

> *Noble cité, riche, fière et sournoise:*
> *On y calcule et jamais on n'y rit:*
> *L'art de Barême est le seul qui fleurit.*

> [Noble, rich, cunning city,
> where people calculate but never smile:
> where the only art is that of the ready reckoner.]

He had never intended to publish the verses or even circulate them privately. La Harpe sent copies of the manuscript to Geneva and Paris. With his almost insane capacity for forbearance[9] Voltaire might have forgiven him had it not emerged that Marie-Louise had given him the manuscript. La Harpe and his family – his wife and children had also enjoyed Voltaire's hospitality – were immediately dismissed, and Marie-Louise sent packing after him. Apart from her treachery, there was also the suspicion that she had been La Harpe's mistress (though by all accounts that is not saying a great deal for his taste). She made for Paris, broadcasting her innocence to anyone who would listen and at the same time carefully calculating how to worm her way back into her uncle's confidence, if not his bed. Among her doubtful charms was a keen affection for money, and Voltaire was the only rich man on whose wealth she might be able to get her hands.[10]

The break was distressing for them both, but while Marie-Louise faced the loss of financial security and a comfortable home, Voltaire suffered a strong emotional disappointment: Marie-Louise may have been what everyone but he saw her to be, but she had still lived with him for eighteen years. He was so obviously distressed that the other guests at Ferney packed up and departed, leaving him alone with his servants. But with the resilience he so often showed in the face of disaster, within a week he had plunged again into the unremitting work which filled his days. Within the next months he edited two sets of memoirs, by the Marquis de Dangeau and by the Marquise de Caylus (the latter threw considerable light on the court of Louis XIV). He also wrote a short story, *Les Lettres d'Amabed*, two plays, some poems and a number of briefer squibs which as usual had as their targets the ridiculousness (as he saw it) of Christianity and the Church. He was now seventy-five, frailer than ever, and still subject to more illnesses than most people suffered in a lifetime; but though he spoke often of his impending death, he showed no signs of resigning himself to the arms of the Church.

Among the subscribers to the collected works of Corneille, Catherine, Empress of Russia, had been for some time an admirer of Voltaire's work. After coming to the throne on 22 September 1762, she wrote a kind message to him. Always pleased to receive a letter from royalty, he wrote a sycophantic reply – and was delighted when she wrote back rebuking him for praising her before she deserved it. She immediately became for him the model monarch, a role which he had once hoped Frederick might fulfil, and their correspondence continued until his death. There seems little doubt that she had contrived the epistolary friendship hoping that the respected writer would spread the good news of her intelligence and good intentions throughout Europe – as indeed he did, though he was perfectly aware that 'people blame her for certain trifles about her husband' (she had had the lunatic, drunken Peter III poisoned and strangled). In a letter to one of her courtiers, Count Shuvalov, he suggested that it had probably been an attack of colic that had 'delivered [Peter] from the slight annoyance of losing an empire of two thousand leagues' and that he could not bring himself to condemn a 'small crime' from which considerable good might come.[11]

He knew that the letter would be shown to Catherine, as indeed it was; she immediately ordered the production of several of his plays at court, with various members of the nobility in the cast; he sent her a copy of the *Dictionnaire philosophique portatif*, and they began a regular correspondence. Catherine wanted to import some Swiss teachers to educate the children of the Russian aristocracy, and Voltaire selected a number for her – though unfortunately, the Genevan authorities refused to allow them to leave the city. He sent her instead a play which the young people could perform. He attempted to persuade her to annexe Greece, put in a puppet king, and restore the Byzantine Empire. She took to the idea, but unfortunately the Greeks were unenthusiastic.

In February 1769 Catherine did him the honour of sending Prince Fedor Alexeevich Kozlovsky to Ferney at the head of a mission to pay tribute to her still enthusiastic correspondent. The Prince handed Voltaire a gold and ivory box, the decoration of which had been finished by the Empress herself, a portrait of Catherine set in a diamond-encrusted frame, a collection of exquisitely bound books in Russian (which Voltaire was unable to read) and a fine full-length coat in black fox fur. In response to the gifts Voltaire commissioned a drawing in which (as a visitor to Ferney, who had watched the ceremony, wrote) he was 'exhibited in rather an extraordinary position, rising out of bed in an ecstasy upon the presents being presented to him. The picture was accompanied by a copy of verses in the 'Empress's praise, in the taste of the period, and of course sufficiently nauseous and fulsome.'[12]

Meanwhile, Marie-Louise continued to make her presence felt, though she remained in Paris. Unpaid bills flooded in for Voltaire to attend to, and a regular series of letters attempting either to persuade him to ask her back to Ferney or to invite him to return to Paris, where, she said, the court would welcome him. Though she much preferred Paris to the country, her greed was stronger than her love of society and in October 1769 she reappeared at the château, where (she told a friend) her uncle was 'very pleased to see her'. Be that as it may, she certainly resumed her housekeeping duties, while he continued to work (when not interrupted) for fifteen hours a day.

The Universal Man

News now came of a scheme to commission a public statue of the old man – an extraordinary idea, many people thought, to set up such a memorial to a commoner who, however distinguished, was still alive. But it went ahead, though the subject himself expressed some doubts to the sculptor, Jean-Baptiste Pigalle – of course, in verse:

> Que feriez vous d'un pauvre auteur
> Don't la taille & le cou de grue
> Et la line très-peu jouflue
> Feront rire le connaisseur . . .

> [An author – of a dwarfish stature,
> By much too mean in limb and feature;
> With long crane neck, and cheeks so thin
> They'll force from connoisseurs a grin.[13]]

He goes on:

> To please is still the sculptor's duty,
> Then carve us out some naked beauty
> Whose fair plump charms may please our eyes . . .

Pigalle, a celebrated sculptor who had executed among other work two beautiful busts of Mme de Pompadour, seemed almost to take the hint and portrayed Voltaire naked except for a cloak thrown over one shoulder and across his loins; it is an extremely lively and characteristic statue, and indeed perhaps has the best portrait head of any likeness of the philosopher. Voltaire himself was, in the end, impressed by it and grateful for the compliment. Similar tributes began to come his way: his old friend Mlle Clairon, for instance, set up a bust on a sort of altar in her house.

Pigalle's statue was seen by the musician and traveller Dr Charles Burney, who called at Ferney in 1770. He approached Ferney with some trepidation, for he had heard that 'some English lady' had recently called on Voltaire with a few companions but without any letter of introduction, and when asked what they wanted 'upon their replying that they wished only to see so extraordinary a man, he said, "Well, Gentlemen, you now see me; and did you take me to be a Wild Beast or a Monster that was fit only to be stared at, as a show?"[14]

However, Burney plucked up his courage and called. Voltaire was talking to some workmen, but came up to the visitor amiably enough, who

> could not conceive it possible for life to subsist in a form so nearly composed of mere skin and bone . . . . He complained of decrepitude, and said he supposed I was curious to form an idea of the figure of one walking after death. However, his eyes and whole countenance are still full of fire; and though so emaciated, a more lively expression cannot be imagined.[15]

They had some conversation about English writers; Voltaire regretted that there was now none living to equal Dryden, Pope or Swift.

> During this conversation, we approached the buildings he was constructing near the road to his château. These, said he, pointing to them, are the most innocent, and, perhaps, the most useful of all my works . . . .[16]

Since the theatre he had built at Ferney was now given over to the activities of silkworms, he had built another on the road between the château and Geneva, and in 1771 invited Lekain, whose reputation was now greater than ever, to appear in revivals of *Sémiramis* and *Mahomet*. The great actor's performances caused a considerable sensation, and though there was some attempt to cause trouble – a few of the more intense Calvinist critics of the theatre hired hoodlums to shout insults at the audience as they arrived and left – even some pastors attended performances. One of them, himself overcome by Lekain's genius, described Voltaire in a paroxysm of delight, sitting in the wings in one of his old velvet coats, his stockings about his ankles, taking the actor by the hands as he came off-stage.

The man for whom to write was as natural and necessary as to breathe, continued to send out pamphlet after pamphlet, article after article, book after book from his study or his bed, where he wrote during the morning, the invariable pot of coffee at his elbow. ('It's slow poison,' a friend told him. 'Must be,' he said, 'I've been drinking it for sixty-five years.')[17] Back in Paris, lacking any real accounts of him save the anecdotes of an occasional visitor, people made up stories about him. At seventy-nine, suffering from ague and gout and impotent these many years, he had, it was said, tried so desperately to seduce a young visitor that he had fainted three times. He did conduct a literary flirtation with the King's new mistress, Mme du Barry, who asked a friend to kiss him for her, on both cheeks: 'Quoi! Deux baisers sur la fin de ma vie?' he exclaimed in verse: 'What, two kisses at the end of my life? What a passport to the underworld. Two! One too many . . . I would die of pleasure at the first!'

He had always enjoyed a regular routine, and still kept to one. Work in the morning, then rising at noon, some coffee or chocolate – no food at midday – and if it was fine an outing in his coach, sometimes for as long as four hours, but always with his secretary at his side ready to take dictation. (He even dictated while dressing in the morning.[18]) If the weather was inclement, he might have a game of chess with Père Adam, whom he was inclined (as we would say) to send up, on one occasion writing to Cardinal de Bernis asking him to obtain the permission of the Pope for Adam to wear a wig when saying mass – the father had rheumatism, and needed to keep his head warm. The Cardinal, not known for his sense of humour, straight-faced sent the authorisation. Chess might be interrupted by visitors, or conversation with guests (there were always guests in that hospitable house, some staying for several months), but soon enough Voltaire would vanish to his study to work until eight, perhaps coming down for supper if he felt up to it. Even at table, a pen was always in his hand, or by it.

While he continued to work with and for his people at Ferney, he would happily have returned to Paris had it been feasible; the antagonism of the King made it impossible, and now in his eighties Voltaire became reluctantly reconciled to exile. Hope revived when Louis XV died in May of 1774; but Louis XVI disliked Voltaire even more than his predecessor, and even instigated an order that officials should do their best to confiscate all the writer's papers the moment he was dead and unable to protect them (later, apparently and not ill-advisedly feeling guilty, he rescinded it). Always ill, always dying, or so he protested, Voltaire showed no signs of actually doing so, his pen as productive as ever. He saw the first bound edition of his collected works through the press in 1775 (the year in which he also presided, beaming, over a *fête* held in his honour by the people of Ferney), and in 1776 published *La Bible enfin expliquée*, in which he set down the conclusions of a lifetime's reading of that book. In 1777, at the age of eighty-three, he started work on his last play, *Irène*.

He intended this for production at the Comédie with his old friend and colleague Lekain in the leading role. It was accepted and cast, but without Lekain, who was about to be married and did not feel he wanted the strain, at his age, of learning a new part;[19] Voltaire understood and forgave. Nevertheless considerably excited, he began to make preparations to return to Paris for the first time for twenty-seven years, for the première. Although it had been made clear to him for many years that arrest followed by prison or official exile would be the consequence of his appearance in the city, it now seemed that Louis XVI, while under no circumstances willing to receive him, would at least not insist on the arrest, on sight, of the man who after all was still France's official historian and a Gentleman of the King's Chamber. His friends had been assured that he could attend the first performance of *Irène* without danger.

On 5 February 1778 he set out with Marie-Louise Denis and his secretary of over twenty years, Jean Louis Wagnière. The people of Ferney wept, as though they believed they would never see him again. He himself said that he was making a little journey to Paris and to eternity, though he tidied his desk and his room meticulously against his return. At the entrance to the city customs officers recognised him and waved his carriage through. He alighted at the town house of the Marquis de Villette in the Rue de Beaune, where an apartment had been set in order for him. Villette was an old acquaintance, and the Marquise a delightful young woman whom Voltaire had befriended and introduced to her husband in 1776. Now both of them were delighted and honoured to be the hosts of the distinguished old man.

The Universal Man

Even he, who had a proper appreciation of his achievements and place in French literature and history, could not have been prepared for the sensation made by his reappearance in the capital. From the day after his arrival a continual stream of visitors queued for admission to his rooms – a few old friends like D'Argental, a few men almost equally famous (the composer Gluck, for instance), but also an enormous number of ordinary men and women who came to see a living legend and were determined to do so. The Académie Française sent a deputation announcing a special session to honour him.

The old man enjoyed the fuss but was desperately exhausted by it, as his physician Dr Trenching recognised; he went so far as to insert a paragraph in the *Journal de Paris* warning everyone that Voltaire was living on the capital of his strength rather than the interest, and that the way things were going those visitors who were impertinently pressing their company upon him would bear the responsibility for his death. Within a few days it began to look as though the doctor was right, for Voltaire developed inflammation of the bladder; he had to cancel a visit to the theatre, but was not allowed by his visitors to decline to see them – they filed past him, as he sat uncomfortably in an easy chair, as though past some astonishing animal at a zoo.

Among the people for whom he painfully roused himself were Mme du Barry, no longer the King's mistress (she had been banished from the court in 1774 for her enormous profligacy, after bringing about the downfall of the finance minister, Voltaire's supporter and friend the Duc de Choiseul), the British Ambassador, Viscount Storming, and perhaps more interestingly the American statesman and scientist Benjamin Franklin, who had been sent to Paris in 1776 to attempt to raise financial assistance for the States in their war against England.[20] Franklin had his fifteen-year-old grandson with him, and Voltaire stood to place his hands on the boy's head with the benison of 'God and Liberty'.

Another visitor for whom he made a special effort was the 24-year-old Tallyrand, already a priest and a delegate to the Assembly of the Clergy, a young man after Voltaire's own heart, as scornful of authority and convention as the old man had been in his day, and indeed remained. He had idolised Voltaire for years, and now came to the house in the Rue de Beaune and to the small dark room where a single ray of light from the drawn shutters fell on to the face of the old man, to find that he was still capable of enthusiasm: words 'flew from him, so rapid, so neat, yet so distinct and so clear . . . . He spoke quickly and nervously with a play of features I have never seen in any man except him . . . . His eye kindled with vivid fire, almost dazzling.' The old man laid his hand on the blond curls of the younger, who never forgot the encounter until his dying day: 'I see it now before me,' he said when he himself was old; 'the small fiery eyes staring from shrunken sockets not unlike those of a chameleon.'[21]

Voltaire, who began to feel that he was being suffocated beneath a shower of roses, dragged himself to at least some of the rehearsals of *Irène*, and flew into the father and mother of all rages when he found his text had been altered without his permission, a rage that can have done his health no good. Meanwhile, the realisation that the lifelong enemy of Christianity was ill and likely to die was meat and drink to the clerics of Paris, and the vultures began to gather to peck at the body in the hope of saving the soul. Letters and (worse) visits from priests of all shades of opinion pressed upon him. The more fanatical and foolish clerics were persuaded to leave; one, the Abbé Gautier, was at least intelligent, and on 26 February 1778 Voltaire apparently made his confession, and actually signed a document recanting his disbelief. Various witnesses made various claims as to what he had actually signed; but while there seems to be no doubt that he put his name to a number of documents which went some way to satisfying the Church, there is equally no doubt at all as to the reason why he did so: he was not throwing himself, after all those years, into the arms of the God he so despised. What he was concerned about was the fate of his body after his death; he had always had a morbid fear of his corpse being treated like that of his poor friend Adrienne Lecouvreur – thrown on to a rubbish dump.

He was now clearly failing. There was blood in his urine, and he had begun to spit blood (it was one of the reasons he gave the Abbé Gautier for not taking Communion; it would be anathema, he suggested, to risk mixing his blood with that of Christ).

On 30 March he struggled downstairs and into his handsome

carriage with the sky-blue upholstery, and was driven to the Académie. The courtyard of the Louvre was crowded with cheering onlookers – wherever he went, somehow the people seemed to know, and to gather to see and applaud him. A few clergymen pointedly stayed away from the special session during which Voltaire took the President's chair and listened to tributes from D'Alembert and others. Then he was carried off to the Comédie Française, where a special performance of *Irène* was to be given. When he walked into the theatre, in a suit of rusty black in the style of the 1750s, the audience rose to him. He took his place in the box usually occupied by the Gentlemen of the Privy Chamber and sat between Marie-Louise Denis and Mme de Villette. Suddenly the company's leading actor, Brizard, appeared behind him and placed a laurel crown on his head. The cheering redoubled. Voltaire was heard to murmur 'Do you want to kill me with glory?' The evening might have been even more glorious had the King permitted the Queen, Marie Antoinette, to attend; she had wished it, but he had vetoed the suggestion.

There were undeniably elements of farce about the occasion. Voltaire removed the laurel crown and placed it on the head of Mme de Villette. The audience roared its disapproval, and the Prince de Beauvau rushed in from a neighbouring box, seized it, and returned it to the head for which it had been intended, where it perched uneasily on top of the voluminous old-fashioned wig the philosopher had worn since the days when it had been the height of fashion.

No one watched the play or heard a line of it above the continual clamour. Every time Voltaire made a move the cheers broke out again and redoubled in energy. There were cries of 'Hail to the universal man!' The play was, to be truthful, a failure – the unkind said that the wonder of the last act was that anyone could contrive to stay awake through it. There was no such boredom, however, on this particular evening. The curtain fell at the end of the play, then after a pause rose again to display Mlle Clairon's bust of the philosopher, centre-stage, with the actors grouped around it. One of them stepped forward to wind garlands of flowers around it. More flowers were thrown upon the stage.

By now Voltaire had taken refuge in the shadows at the back of his box – but was led forward to take another bow, tears streaming down his face. The actress Françoise Vestris stepped forward to recite a verse in his honour. She was forced to recite it again and again, until members of the audience had memorised and could chant it with her. Another actress stepped forward and kissed the bust; the entire cast followed suit.

The slight farce *Nanine*, which Voltaire had written years earlier, might have been an anti-climax had anyone listened to it; the audience was far more often facing the box in which the hero of the evening sat than paying attention to the stage. When, finally, the performance ended and Voltaire was escorted from the theatre, it was the turn of the hundreds who had been waiting outside. They wanted to uncouple the horses and pull his carriage back to the Rue de Beaune, but he would not allow it. However, he did allow the coachman to drive at a walking pace through the streets, so that everyone could see him. Back at his apartment, he broke down in tears, then collapsed.

For a while he appeared to recover and even bought a house in Paris, contemplating, it seemed, a permanent return. He was never averse either to fame or to applause, and thoroughly enjoyed the fact that the entire city, except possibly the King, wanted to pay homage. April went by and he was still able to get around – to attend, for instance, the Freemason's lodge of Neuf-Soeurs, to which he was admitted as a brother. He paid a visit to the former Suzanne de Livry, the actress he had encouraged so many years ago. She was now Mme la Marquise de La Tour du Pin-Gouvernet; they scarcely recognised each other – but in her rooms he saw his own portrait, as a fine young man, which had been painted for her sixty years earlier by Nicolas de Largillière.

In May, his health began seriously to deteriorate. He was now in continual pain from his bladder and kidneys, and an excessive dose of pain-killing opium had a fatal effect on his constitution. Dr Trenching was out of his depth, but consulted no other physician. Gradually, the news leaked out that Voltaire was dying. A black swarm of priests again began to gather, and this time no one cared to keep them out.

When one asked him if he recognised the divinity of Christ, he replied impatiently 'Christ? Christ? – Let me die in peace!' and waved the man away. In great pain, he nevertheless retained his sense of humour; it is said that, asked to renounce the Devil, he replied that it was a little late to be making new enemies. Even if it is an apocryphal story, it is highly characteristic; nor is there reason to suppose that he did not, as several people reported, say that he hoped to die laughing. The manner of his death was, however, no laughing matter. When he asked Trenching if there was no means of relieving him of his agony, the good doctor replied 'There's nothing I can do, monsieur. You'll just have to die.'

The descriptions by various witnesses of his last days are distressing in the extreme. Nothing was done by Mme Denis or anyone else to keep idle visitors at bay – his secretary, Wagnière, later said that his bedroom seemed to be full of drunken peasants. Occasionally, in a lucid moment, the dying man would summon enough strength to reach for something at his bedside and throw it across the room in fury at the continual disturbance.

On 30 May Trenching brought two colleagues to see him. As they laid their hands on his forehead, he opened his eyes and said 'Let me die.' They left him. At eleven o'clock he gave one loud cry, and his bright eyes closed for ever.

Envoi

For days after Voltaire's death crowds continued to collect outside the house in the Rue de Beaune, calling for him to come out on the balcony. But he was not at home.

All his attempts to placate the Church had been in vain. It would be quite improper to approve any kind of religious funeral, the priests claimed; the body must be thrown on to some convenient piece of unconsecrated ground, and left to rot. Voltaire's nephews, the Abbé Mignot and M. d'Hornoy, appealed to the Chief of Police, the Archbishop of Paris, without result. Two members of the Paris *parlement* attempted to plead Voltaire's greatness – surely he should be given a proper funeral? They were told that if they pressed their appeal they would be forced to resign. Louis XVI, when they turned to him, simply said that the priests must be allowed to deal with the matter.

The two nephews reached a brave conclusion: they must spirit the body out of the city before the Church could confiscate it. After an autopsy which embalmed the body (a local doctor, M. Mithouart, made off with the brain, while M. de Villette claimed the heart, which he placed in a gold-plated box), Voltaire was clothed in one of his dressing-gowns and propped up in his coach. A footman sat beside him to keep him upright, and the coach started for the decayed Abbey of Seillières, near Troyes, of which the Abbé Mignot was abbot. The entourage passed through the customs barrier without incident and the Abbey was successfully reached. Flagstones were removed from the church floor near the choir and a coffin was made of rough planks (Mme Denis had been asked to commission a lead coffin, but replied that that would be very expensive, and what was the point?). At five in the morning of 1 June the Office for the Dead was sung by the monks of the Abbey, followed by five masses. A rough stone was placed on the grave, inscribed 'A 1778 V'.

As soon as the Archbishop of Paris heard of the burial he and the Bishop of Troyes, in whose diocese the Abbey lay, demanded the exhumation of the body; the prior bravely did nothing, and rather than make a fuss the matter was allowed to drop – for a time – though the Archbishop refused permission for the Académie Française to have the customary mass said for one of its members. However once again he was not successful in denying some recognition to Voltaire; in November the Lodge of Neuf-Soeurs held a mass attended by Marie-Louise Denis, Mme de Villette and Benjamin Franklin. Frederick also had a mass said in Berlin Cathedral. M. de Villette sent the dead man's heart back to Ferney, where it was placed in Voltaire's study, with the motto 'His heart is here, his spirit is everywhere'.

When, in 1790, the Abbey of Sellières was about to be demolished, the now revolutionary Marquis Charles de La Villette made a speech urging that Voltaire's remains should be given honourable reburial. By now, the Revolution was in its first phase and the Constituent Assembly sent a message to Troyes asserting that the philosopher's body was the property of the State and that 'the glorious Revolution has been the fruit of his works'. The body, now thirteen years old, was lifted from the grave, crowned with oak leaves, and carried to nearby Romilly-sur-Seine, where the National Guardsmen fired a volley over it and it was transferred to a new coffin. In the interim various parts of it went missing – one foot, several bones of the other foot, and two teeth.

On 11 July 1791, the day on which Louis XVI was arrested at Varennes during his attempted flight, and returned to Paris, a procession brought Voltaire's body to the Panthéon. The route was almost as crowded for him in death as it had been in life. At every small town the rough waggon on which the coffin lay beneath a blue cloth paused while the mayor made a speech and the guard fired a salute. It was taken first to the ruins of the Bastille, where Voltaire had twice been imprisoned. There it was lifted from the farm cart and spent the night defended by National Guardsmen and girls dressed in classical white robes.

Next morning it was placed on a huge chariot, literally as high as a house, which had been designed by a committee headed by the artist Jacques-Louis David. Its bronze wheels held a porphyry sarcophagus on which Voltaire's body lay, a broken lyre at his side, the figure of Eternity standing behind him in the act of placing a crown of stars on his head. Figures representing Genius stood at each corner, their torches reversed. On the base of the chariot were inscribed the words: 'O gods, give us death rather than slavery!', a quotation from his play *Brutus*, which had been quoted at the revolutionary club, the Cordeliers, when the oath for tyrannicide was taken.

Four white horses, the tricolour draped over their flanks, drew the chariot through the streets, followed by men in Roman dress carrying editions of Voltaire's works and actors representing scenes from his life and plays. A model of the Bastille made from stones taken from the prison's ruins preceded a tableau showing the family of Jean Calas.

From the gates of the city the augmented procession wound its way to the house in which Voltaire had died, where a choir sang memorial music and Citoyenne Villette emerged, dressed all in white, and crowned the body with laurels, embracing it and bedewing it with (according to a reporter) 'the delicious tears of sensibility'.

The procession came to a halt outside the Comédie Française, where stood a bust of Voltaire bearing the inscription 'At the age of seventeen he wrote *Œdipe*'. At the Odéon, which the procession did not reach until seven in the evening, was another inscription – 'At the age of eighty-four he wrote *Irène*'. There the chorus of the Opéra sang a special hymn with words by the poet André Chénier set to music by François-Joseph Gossec. Outside the Théâtre-Français the aria from Handel's *Samson* was sung in which men were urged to 'Awake, break your chains, ascend to your past greatness' – at which the heavens opened and pelting rain soaked the choristers' thin white dresses; they fled, and the catafalque stood deserted in the downpour. After a while the rain eased and the coffin proceeded, albeit with rather less ceremony, to the Panthéon, where late in the evening it was finally laid in the crypt.

It was a great symbolic moment for the Revolution. Even if it is not true, as was rumoured, that Louis XVI had watched the procession pass from behind the curtains of his window at the Pont-Royal, the press made the most of the contrast between the disgraced monarch and the apotheosis of the great humanitarian. While he would no doubt have been flattered by the *fête de Voltaire*, one suspects that he would not entirely have approved of the arrest of the King, and would most certainly have been appalled at the often unjust blood-letting of the Terror which was to follow, and in which Émilie's son and grandson were to perish. During all that ensued, he lay at peace in his grave.

But not for ever. In 1814, when the Bourbons had been restored in the person of Louis XVIII, a group of reactionary zealots decided that it was improper for the skeleton of an unbeliever to lie in what had once been a church. Quietly, at night, they sneaked into the Panthéon, broke open the coffin, removed the bones and threw them on to a rubbish dump on waste land at Bercy. Voltaire's fear of sharing the fate of Adrienne Lecouvreur was realised. The fact was not known until fifty years later, when a journalist who knew the story revealed it. On the Emperor's orders the coffin was opened, and was indeed found to be empty. By then, the waste land had been cleared and there was no prospect of finding any remains.

What did remain, of course, was Voltaire's work – some fifteen million words, as it has been calculated, together with twenty thousand letters written to seventeen hundred correspondents.[1] These days, perhaps because the Age of Reason seems largely to have been replaced by the Age of Unreason, he is less read than perhaps at any time since his death – most people only know the pithier of his aphorisms, most suitable for a time when the sound-bite has largely replaced considered argument. But the force of his arguments remains, and those who make war for specious reasons, or cling to superstition for their emotional comfort, do so increasingly against the grain of the march of reason upon which the first steps, in modern times, were taken by the Universal Man.

Voltaire Quoted

It is doubtful whether there is a single dictionary of quotations or anthology of epigrams or aphorisms that does not contain several quotations from Voltaire, some carefully attributed, some unattributable but bearing the unmistakeable fingerprint of the author. The following is a selection of well- and less well-known examples which do not appear in the text of this book. Some are omitted: for instance 'The best is the enemy of the good,' which though often ascribed to Voltaire is in fact an old Italian proverb; 'I disapprove of what you say, but I will defend to the death your right to say it', which are the words of S.G. Tallentyre; and 'All's for the best in the best of all possible worlds' because while it is believed by many to represent Voltaire's view, put into the mouth of the philosopher Pangloss in *Candide* it represents the very antithesis.

All styles [in literature] are good except the tiresome kind.

(Preface to *L'enfant prodigue*, 1736)

Liberty was born in England from the quarrels of tyrants.

(*Lettres philosophiques*, 1734)

In philosophy, we must distrust the things we understand too easily, as well as the things we don't understand.

(*Lettres philosophiques*, 1734)

The most amazing and effective inventions are not those which do most honour to human genius.

(*Lettres philosophiques*, 1734)

The superfluous – now there's a very necessary thing!

(*Le Mondain*, 1736)

Governments need both shepherds and butchers.

(*Notebooks*, 1735–50)

God is not on the side of the big battalions, but of the best shots.
(*Notebooks*, 1735–50)

If the first law of friendship is that it has to be cultivated, the second law is to be indulgent when the first law has been neglected.
(*Letter*, 1740)

Never having been able to succeed in the world, he took his revenge by speaking ill of it. (*Zadig*, 1747)

Fear follows crime, and is its punishment. (*Sémiramis*, 1748)

If God created us in his own image we have more than reciprocated.
(Quoted in *Le Sottisier*, 18C)

The world is a vast temple dedicated to Discord. (*Letter*, 1752)

This agglomeration which was called and which still calls itself the Holy Roman Empire was neither holy, nor Roman, nor an empire.
(*Essai sur l'histoire générale*, 1756)

Work keeps away those three great evils: boredom, vice and poverty.
(*Candide*, 1759)

Whatever you do, stamp out abuses, and love those who love you.
(*Letter*, 1762)

Men will always be mad, and those who think they can cure them are the maddest of all. (*Letter*, 1762)

Nothing would be more tiresome than eating and drinking if God had not made them a pleasure as well as a necessity.
(*Dialogues philosophiques*)

The secret of the arts is to correct nature. (*Epîtres*)

Men use thought only to justify their injustices, and speech only to conceal their thoughts. (*Dialogues*, 1763)

Self-love resembles the instrument by which we perpetuate the species. It is necessary, it is dear to us, it gives us pleasure, and it has to be concealed. (*Dictionnaire philosophique*, 1764)

The gloomy Englishman, even in love, always wants to reason. We are more reasonable in France.
(*Les Oreiginaux, Entrée des Diverses Nations*)

Antiquity is full of eulogies of another more remote antiquity.
(*Dictionnaire philosophique*, 1764)

If there were only two men in the world, how would they get on? They would help one another, harm one another, flatter one another, slander one another, fight one another, make it up; they could neither live together nor do without one another.

(*Dictionnaire philosophique*, 1764)

Nature has made us frivolous to console us for our miseries.

(*Dictionnaire philosophique*, 1764)

It is amusing that a virtue is made of the vice of chastity; and it's a pretty odd sort of chastity, at that, which leads men straight into the sin of Onan, and girls to the waning of their colour.

(Letter, 1766)

I am not like the lady at the court of Versailles who said: 'What a dreadful pity that the bother at the tower of Babel should have got language all mixed up; but for it, everyone would always have spoken French.'

(Letter, 1767)

I have never made but one prayer to God, a very short one: 'O Lord, make my enemies ridiculous.' And God granted it.

(Letter to Damilaville, 1767)

One always speaks badly when one has nothing to say.

(*Commentary on Corneille*)

Indeed, history is nothing more than a tableau of crimes and misfortunes.

(*L'Ingénu*, 1767)

The man who leaves money to charity in his will is only giving away what no longer belongs to him.

(Letter, 1769)

There has never been a perfect government, because men have passions, and if they did not have passions, there would be no need for government.

(*Politique et législation*, 1770)

Faith consists in believing what reason does not believe . . . it is not enough that a thing may be possible for it to be believed.

(*Questions sur l'Encyclopédie*, 1772)

We owe respect to the living; to the dead we owe only truth.

(*Lettre sur Oedipe*, 1785)

Notes

Introduction

1. See descriptions of the execution of Robert François Damiens for the attempted assassination of Louis XV in 1757; he was tortured with red-hot pincers, then melted oil and resin were poured into his wounds before he was torn limb from limb by four horses.

Chapter One

1. Voltaire, *Letters on England*, tr. Leonard Tancock (London, 1980), p. 124.
2. Not to be confused with the much more famous Jean-Jacques Rousseau, who was born two years after Voltaire's meeting with his namesake.
3. Theodore Besterman (ed.), *Collected Letters of Voltaire* (Geneva, 1950); letter 3044 (1 April 1746).
4. A French *parlement* was not like, for instance, the British Parliament, but a court of law. There were several – in Paris, Toulouse, Dijon and elsewhere.
5. Louis Moland (ed.), *Works of Voltaire* (Paris, 1877) vol. xiv, p. 76.
6. He did not become a regular attender at Temple meetings until about seven years later.
7. Paul Hazard, *European Thought in the Eighteenth Century* (New Haven, 1954), p. 129.
8. Voltaire, *Letters on England*, tr. Tancock, p. 39.
9. These memoirs were written by Voltaire in 1759, in the first person, and were first published in English in 1777. They are republished in the original translation, as a postscript to Besterman's *Voltaire* (London, 1969).
10. *Ibid., Memoirs*, see note 9, p. 546.

Chapter Two

1. N. Torrey, *The Spirit of Voltaire* (New York, 1938), p. 21.

2. T. Besterman, *Voltaire* (London, 1969), p. 54.

3. The original Giton is a catamite in the novel *Satyricon* by the first-century novelist Petronius.

4. A *lettre de cachet* was a letter signed by the king and countersigned by a secretary of state, used to authorise someone's imprisonment. The police, or more rarely a private individual with influence, could obtain a *lettre*, commanding the recipient to obey the orders therein without delay, and giving no explanation. This was followed by imprisonment, without appeal and for an unspecified period, in a State fortress, particularly the Bastille.

5. She made an effect by a simple, very natural style of acting, new to the French stage.

6. *Pucelle*, III, xxiv–ix.

7. Henri Martin, *Histoire de France* (Paris, 1916), quoted in Durant, *The Age of Voltaire* (New York, 1965) at p. 21.

8. *Memoirs* in Besterman, *Voltaire*, p. 546.

9. Letter to the Marquise de Mimeure, quoted in G. Desnoiresterres, *Voltaire et la société française au dix-huitième siècle* (Paris, 1871).

10. Georg Brandes, *Voltaire* (New York, 1930) at p. 97 of Vol. I.

11. Besterman, *Voltaire*, pp. 69–70.

12. James Parton, *Life of Voltaire* (Boston, 1882), p. 115.

13. *Épître des vous et de tu* (c. 1730).

Chapter Three

1. This was the failure of the Mississippi Company, part of an ingenious plan by the Scottish financier John Law to rescue France from virtual bankruptcy. Shares in a company to exploit the Mississippi basin, then controlled by France, caught the imagination of the public, and 200,000 shares were sold at 500 livres per share. The enterprise failed, and shares fell from 12,000 livres to 2,000 amid speculation that the Regent had made 3 billion francs from the venture, most of it spent on his mistresses. When the speculation was proved, the shares fell to 200 livres, and the Regent was forced to take action.

2. *Select Letters of Voltaire*, ed. and tr. Theodore Besterman (London, 1963), p. 17.

3. George Sherburn (ed.), *The Correspondence of Alexander Pope* (Oxford, 1956); letter of 20 April 1724.

4. Besterman, *Select Letters*, pp. 19–20.

5. Charles Duclos was the author who years later was to succeed Voltaire as official historiographer of France.

Notes

6. Denis Diderot, 'On Women' in *Dialogues* (New York, 1927).
7. John Hearsey, *Voltaire* (London, 1976) at p. 54.
8. Jean Orieux, *Voltaire*, tr Barbara Bray and Helen R. Lane (New York, 1979) at p. 72.
9. Voltaire, *Works*, XVIa, 157.
10. Voltaire, *Memoirs* in T. Besterman, *Voltaire* (London, 1969), p. 550.
11. Besterman, *Voltaire*, p. 23. The reference to Maurepas is somewhat equivocal, since everyone knew that he was an enthusiastic homosexual.
12. *Ibid.*, p. 24.
13. '*Monsieur de Voltaire, Monsieur Arouet – comment vous applez-vous?*'
14. Hearsey, *Voltaire*, p. 61.

Chapter Four

1. Jean Orieux, *Voltaire*, tr. Barbara Bray and Helen R. Lane (London, 1979), at p. 82.
2. *Select Letters of Voltaire*, ed. and tr. T. Besterman (London, 1963), p. 25.
3. Also spelt Falkner, or Fawkner.
4. John Hearsey, *Voltaire* (London, 1976), p. 69.
5. N.L. Torrey, *Voltaire and the English Deists* (New Haven, 1930), p. 149.
6. J.J. Hearnshaw (ed.), *Social and Political Ideas of Some English Thinkers of the Augustan Age* (New York, 1950), p. 240.
7. John Hervey, Baron Ickworth, *Memoirs of the Court of George II*, ed. R. Sedgwick (London, 1931) in his introduction to Mandeville's *Fable of the Bees*.
8. T. Besterman, *Voltaire* (London, 1969), p. 114. Voltaire's English was never entirely free from error, but was perfectly comprehensible and often inventive and witty.
9. Joseph Spence, *Anecdotes*, ed. J.M. Osborne (London, 1966); no. 1033.
10. Colley Cibber recorded an occasion on which 'when a malignant beau rose in the pit to hiss her, she made him instantly hide his head and vanish, by a pausing look, and her utterance of the words "poor creature!"' (quoted in W. Clark Russell, *Representative Actors* (London, n.d.) at p. 59.
11. Voltaire, *Letters on England*, tr. Leonard Tancock (London, 1980), pp. 92–6.
12. The most interesting discussion of Voltaire's views on Shakespeare occupies the whole of Chapter XI of Besterman's *Voltaire*.
13. *Letters on England*, p. 107.
14. *Ibid.*, pp. 99–100.
15. *Ibid.*, p. 107.

16. *Ibid.*, p. 108.
17. Rabelais.
18. *Letters on England*, p. 108.
19. *Ibid.*, p. 23.
20. *Ibid.*, p. 24.
21. *Ibid.*, pp. 24–5.
22. *Ibid.*, pp. 40–1.
23. *Ibid.*, p. 41.
24. He quite enjoyed English beer; though the dregs at the bottom of the glass and the froth at the top were unpalatable, the liquid in the middle was very pleasant.
25. 'Cuts' – illustrations.
26. *Letters on England*, p. 37.

Chapter Five

1. One of the best and most intelligent considerations of the *Henriade* can be found at pp. 149–52 of Richard Aldington's excellent short book *Voltaire* (London, 1925).
2. *Select Letters of Voltaire*, ed. and tr. T. Besterman (London, 1963), p. 31.
3. Voltaire, *Oeuvres* [Works] (Paris, 1900) Vol. XXIX, letter 108.
4. T. Besterman, *Voltaire* (London, 1969), p. 160.
5. *Ibid.*, p. 123.
6. *La Mort de mlle Lecouvreur.*
7. In the notes to *Don Juan*, Byron remarks that 'Voltaire has been termed a "shallow fellow" by some of the same school who called Dryden's *Ode* "a drunken song"; a *school* (as it is called, I presume, from their education being still incomplete) the whole of whose filthy trash of Epics, Excursions, &c, &c, &c, is not worth the two words in *Zaire*, "Vous pleurez?" . . .'.
8. *Representative Actors*, ed. W. Clark Russell (London, n.d.), p. 439.
9. Voltaire, *Works*, Vol. XXIX, letter 133.
10. *Pucelle*, I, 244–5.
11. *Ibid.*, II, 51–2.

Chapter Six

1. Jean Orieux, *Voltaire*, tr. Barbara Bray and Helen R. Lane (London, 1979), p. 103.
2. Nancy Mitford, *Voltaire in Love* (London, 1957), pp. 17–18.

Notes

3. L.J. Moorman, 'Tuberculosis and Genius: Voltaire', *Annals of Medical History*, New Series, Vol. III (New York, 1931).
4. Voltaire, *Lettres philosophiques*, letter VIII.
5. John Hearsey, *Voltaire* (London, 1976), p. 100.
6. Gustave Lanson, *Voltaire* (Paris, 1906), p. 52.
7. The essay on Pascal was added to the book in 1734.
8. *Select Letters of Voltaire*, ed. and tr. T. Besterman (London, 1963), p. 40.
9. *Ibid.*, p. 41.
10. T. Brandes, *Voltaire* (New York, 1930), Vol. I, p. 104.
11. Orieux, *Voltaire*, p. 111.
12. There was a plan for Boucher to execute five paintings of scenes from the *Henriade*, which alas seem never to have been completed.
13. The rococo gallery and theatre still exist.
14. Richard Aldington, *Voltaire* (London, 1925), p. 54.
15. *Ibid.*, pp. 119–20.
16. T. Besterman, *Voltaire* (London, 1969).
17. *Elements de la philosophie de Newton*, banned at first in France, came out in 1738, and as a result Voltaire was elected a Fellow of the Royal Society and of the Royal Society of Edinburgh, honours which meant much to him.

Chapter Seven

1. The Prince, with his passion for all things French, always signed himself thus; we will, however, continue to refer to him as Frederick.
2. *Select Letters of Voltaire*, ed. and tr. T. Besterman (New York, 1963), p. 48.
3. He did so in 1740.
4. This might seem a matter for laughter until one realises that it could have very serious consequences for the unfortunate author.
5. *Select Letters of Voltaire*, p. 49.
6. E.M. Forster wrote a wonderful essay on this episode, which is reprinted in his collection *Abinger Harvest*.
7. She lived for a time as a guest of other generous hosts, kept a lodging house with an Irish lover, then astonishingly published in 1747 a sensationally popular novel, *Lettres d'une peruvienne* followed by an equally successful play, *Cenie*. She became a well-known literary hostess and died leaving debts of 47,000 livres.
8. Nancy Mitford, *Voltaire in Love* (London, 1957), p. 140.
9. Voltaire, *La Defence de mon oncle* (1767).
10. Letter of December 1745 in T. Besterman, *Voltaire* (London, 1969), p. 165.

11. The production was at Lille because Voltaire had gone there to meet Mme Denis, who was living there with her husband.
12. In fact the play is an attack on fanaticism in any religion (its alternative title was *La Fanatisme*), although it could scarcely be presented today without incurring severe danger of a *fatwa*.
13. Jean Orieux, *Voltaire*, tr. Barbara Bray and Helen R. Lane (London, 1979), p. 159.
14. Letter of 14 November 1743, quoted in Besterman, *Voltaire*, p. 272.
15. Letter of 1 December 1740, quoted in *ibid.*, p. 258.

Chapter Eight

1. Albert Sorel, *Montesquieu* (Chicago, 1888), p. 165.
2. It must be said that Voltaire's application to the Académie was not without equivocation: he stressed the fact that he was a true Catholic, insisted that many pages of his works were 'sanctified by religion', and actually went so far as to deny authorship of the *Lettres philosophiques*. The King, however, was entirely in agreement with the Bishop of Mirepois when he suggested that it would be ridiculous that Fleury's place should be filled by the greatest infidel in Europe.
3. Jean Orieux, *Voltaire*, tr. Barbara Bray and Helen R. Lane (London, 1979), p. 160.
4. *Select Letters of Voltaire*, ed. and tr. T. Besterman (New York, 1963), p. 84.
5. Frederick's compositions included a number of concertos and sonatas for the flute, which he had been taught to play by Johann Joachim Quantz (1697–1773), his court composer and teacher, whose work for the flute influenced his own. Frederick also wrote a number of arias for the operas of his *Kapellmeister*, C.H. Graun, and several libretti, including that for Graun's *Montezuma* (1755).
6. Nancy Mitford neatly said that it was 'as though the seven sages of Greece were in a brothel.'
7. Orieux, *Voltaire*, p. 163.
8. T. Besterman, *Voltaire* (London, 1969), p. 86.
9. Thomas Brandes, *Voltaire* (New York, 1920), I, p. 405.
10. The King's favour may also have been the result of a violently patriotic poem in which Voltaire celebrated the French defeat of Cumberland at the battle of Fontenoy, which was printed by the royal press and became widely popular.
11. Besterman, *Voltaire*, p. 90.
12. John Hearsey, *Voltaire* (London, 1976), p. 174.

Notes

13. Orieux, *Voltaire*, p. 181.
14. Letter of 10 May 1746, quoted in Besterman, *Voltaire*, p. 279.
15. Ben Ray Redman, *The Portable Voltaire*, tr. H.I. Woolf (New York, 1949), p. 337.
16. The situation is described by Longchamps; quoted in James Parton, *Life of Voltaire* (New York, 1981), I, p. 554.
17. Nancy Mitford, *Voltaire in Love* (London, 1957), p. 266.
18. 'Oh, my friend, you have killed her for me. Whatever gave you the idea of getting her with child?'
19. Orieux, *Voltaire*, p. 213.
20. The child did not long survive her.
21. Besterman, *Voltaire*, p. 183.
22. Mme du Châtelet, *Reflections sur le bonheur*.

Chapter Nine

1. Voltaire, *Works*, XXIa, 213.
2. Carlyle in his *History of Friedrich II of Prussia* (New York, 1901), Vol. XIV, v–vi.
3. James Parton, *Life of Voltaire* (Boston, 1882), I, 610.
4. W. and A. Durant, *The Age of Voltaire* (New York, 1965) at pp. 462–3.
5. Job 31: 35.
6. *Response d'un academicien de Berlin à un academicien de Paris*.
7. Harold Nicholson, *The Age of Reason* (London, 1960), p. 111.
8. T. Besterman, *Voltaire* (London, 1969), p. 572.
9. Durant and Durant, *Age of Voltaire*, p. 463.
10. Incidentally, the original printing enshrines Voltaire's attempt to reform French spelling, abolishing capital letters and spelling a number of words as they were pronounced: '*français*' instead of '*françois*'. However, as with Bernard Shaw's attempt to reform English spelling two centuries later, nothing much came of it.

Chapter Ten

1. *Mémoires* in T. Besterman, *Voltaire* (London, 1969), p. 572.
2. He completed *Annales de l'empire* after much work on the archives of Gotha, but it was not one of his more successful books.
3. Jean Orieux, *Voltaire*, tr. Barbara Bray and Helen R. Lane (London, 1979), p. 276.
4. Longchamps had remained in Paris, where Mme Denis accused him of

stealing some of Voltaire's manuscripts; the matter was confused and unresolved, but the man left Voltaire's service.

5. Marie-Louise's sister had joined the household.

6. Letter of 9 August 1756, in T. Besterman, *Voltaire*, p. 349.

7. John Hearsey, *Voltaire* (London, 1976), p. 209.

8. Voltaire, *Memoires*, p. 573.

9. Voltaire, *Lettres d'Alsace à sa nièce Mme Denis* (Paris, 1935), p.136: letter, 14 December 1753.

10. In the article on Quakers in the *Philosophical Dictionary*.

11. L.G. Crocker, *Embattled Philosopher* (Michigan, 1854), p. 5.

12. Hearsey, *Voltaire*, pp. 217–18.

13. In 1766 the Grand Conseil revoked the law which prohibited theatrical performances in Geneva.

14. His *Pensées philosophiques*.

15. On Sects, from *The Philosophical Dictionary*, ed. H.I. Woolf (New York, 1924).

16. On papal decrees, *ibid*.

17. On Laws, *ibid*.

18. On Nakedness, *ibid*.

19. Herbert Fisher, *History of Europe* (London, 1935), p. 274.

Chapter Eleven

1. P. Smith, *History of Modern Culture* (New York, 1930), Vol. II, p. 540.

2. Letter of March 1744, quoted in T. Besterman, *Voltaire* (London, 1969), p. 353.

3. Tobias Smollett the novelist (1721–71), author of *Roderick Random*, *Peregrine Pickle*, *Humphrey Clinker* and other works.

4. Voltaire, *The Lisbon Earthquake*, tr. Tobias Smollett, in *The Portable Voltaire* p. 560, ll.7–27.

5. *Portable Voltaire*, pp. 558–9.

6. Jean-Jacques Rousseau, *Confessions*, tr. J.M. Cohen (London, 1953), p. 401.

7. *Essai sur l'histoire générale* . . ., VXVII, M. xiii.177.

8. 'Coinnerie', he called it, which can be translated as 'balderdash'.

9. Voltaire, *Candide*, tr. John Butt (London, 1947), p. 20.

10. *Ibid*., p. 25.

11. *Ibid*., pp. 29–30.

12. *Ibid*., p. 144.

13. W.F. Bottiglia, *Voltaire's* Candide (Geneva, 1959), p. 249.

14. Besterman, *Voltaire*, p. 390.

Notes

15. Jean Orieux, *Voltaire,* tr. Barbara Bray and Helen R. Lane (London, 1979), p. 314.
16. Besterman, *Voltaire,* p. 395.
17. Theodore Besterman in his *Voltaire.*
18. Notes to *Don Juan* in Byron, *Poetical Works* (Oxford, 1945), p. 913.

Chapter Twelve

1. John Calvin, *Institutes of the Christian Religion,* tr. anon. (London, 1928), Vol. I, p. 360.
2. Probably the strappado, or suspending of the accused person by the arms, twisted behind their backs, then hoisted off their feet and allowed to fall with a jerk which often dislocated their limbs.
3. La Vaysse's father, well known for religious tolerance, and therefore no doubt disliked, was also accused, though de Beaudrige did not succeed in making the accusation stick.
4. For a short while, de Beaudrige was indeed congratulated; later, however, an excuse was found to dismiss him from office. He eventually went mad, and died after suffering perpetual visions of Hell.
5. For the complete text, see James Parton, *Life of Voltaire* (Boston, 1882), Vol. II, p. 356.
6. Voltaire would certainly today be called a master of spin.
7. Jean Orieux, *Voltaire,* tr. Barbara Bray and Helen R. Lane (London, 1979), p. 356.
8. Voltaire, *A Treatise on Tolerance,* tr. Brian Masters (London, 1994), p. 144.
9. In his autobiographical third-person memoir, Voltaire declares that 'The whole of the [Calas] family have been warmly attached to M. de Voltaire ever since, who thinks himself honoured by continuing their friend.' He kept a picture of the family always by him; it was on the wall of his bedroom when he died.
10. Gustave Desnoiresterres, *Voltaire et la société française au dix-huitième siècle* (Paris, 1871), Vol. VII, p. 469.
11. Parton, *Life of Voltaire,* Vol. II, p. 397.
12. Desnoiresterres, *Voltaire et la société française . . .,* Vol. VII, p. 493.
13. Letter of Frederick the Great, 7 August 1766.

Chapter Thirteen

1. His old friend and ally Mme de Pompadour was, however, not among them; she died, probably from cancer, in the spring.

2. *Treatise on Tolerance*, tr. Brian Masters (London, 1994), pp. 26–7.
3. *Ibid.*, p. 71.
4. *Ibid.*, p. 38.
5. John Morley, in Voltaire, *Works* (New York, 1927), p. 164.
6. Thomas Pennant, *Tour on the Continent 1765*, ed. G.R. De Beer (London, 1948), pp. 76–6.
7. *Ibid.*
8. Edward Gibbon's work in French, *Essai sur l'etude de la littérature*, was published in 1761 and in an English translation in 1764.
9. Letter to Dorothea Gibbon, 6 August 1763, quoted in T. Besterman, *Voltaire* (London, 1969), pp. 431–2.
10. James Boswell, *Boswell on the Grand Tour* (London, 1953), p. 273.
11. The letter is dated 26 December 1764.
12. Boswell, *Boswell on the Grand Tour*, pp. 285–6.
13. *Ibid.*, pp. 292–3.
14. *Ibid.*, p. 334.
15. Jean Orieux, *Voltaire*, tr. Barbara Bray and Helen R. Lane (London, 1979), p. 334.
16. *Ibid.*
17. Besterman, *Voltaire*, p. 420.
18. With this dowry she was able to marry a young dragoon, Pierre Dupuits; the wedding was in the church at Ferney, and the couple settled in as part of the establishment at the château.
19. Jean-Jacques Rousseau, *Lettres ecrites de la montagne*.
20. Orieux, *Voltaire*, pp. 383–4.

Chapter Fourteen

1. Claire Joseph Hippolyte Leyris de Latude, whose first triumph had been as Electra in Voltaire's *Oreste*. She had a notable partnership with her fellow actor Henri Louis Cain, called Lekain.
2. *Questions sur les miracles*.
3. *Le Philosophe ignorant*.
4. *Commentaire sur le livre des délits et des peines*.
5. The words he used were 'Écrasez l'infâme!' – literally, 'Smash the infamy!', but the words do not have the same resonance in English.
6. Voltaire, *Philosophie de l'histoire*, Chapter LIII.
7. Article on 'superstition' in the *Dictionnaire*.
8. Letter, Frederick to Voltaire, 9 September 1739.
9. It even extended to La Harpe, for Voltaire almost immediately made

enquiries as to his circumstances, and promised to come to his rescue should he need financial help.

10. She eventually inherited half his capital and the estate at Ferney, and sold Voltaire's great library and manuscripts for a small fortune to Catherine the Great.

11. Jean Orieux, *Voltaire*, tr. Barbara Bray and Helen R. Lane (London, 1979), pp. 386–7.

12. Theodore Besterman, *Voltaire* (London, 1969), p. 493.

13. Voltaire, *Autobiography*; reproduced in Besterman, *Voltaire*, p. 591.

14. Charles Burney, *Music, Men and Manners in France and Italy, 1770*, ed. H. Edmond Poole (London, 1969), p. 30.

15. *Ibid*.

16. *Ibid*.

17. Tristram Issen, *Recollections of Voltaire* (Bristol, 1904), p. 37.

18. See p. 5 of plates.

19. Lekain died, in fact, before the first night of the play or his marriage – some said, from the exertions of his courtship.

20. His impassioned argument was to result, in September 1778, in the signing of a treaty of alliance, and the provision by France of money and munitions.

21. Simon Schama, *Citizens* (London, 1989), pp. 23–4.

Envoi

1. The estimation is by Theodore Besterman, in his *Voltaire* (London, 1969).

Bibliography

A full bibliography of a writer so profuse and prolix as Voltaire has so far not been available. Now, with the use of computers, the situation is better, but still far from ideal. Translations into English, available and out of print, have yet to be completely codified. The reader will find various translations by various authors published by various publishers, in and out of print, and the situation seems to change almost daily.

The University of Sheffield's *Voltaire électronique* is invaluable. It is based on the Oxford Edition of the Voltaire Foundation's *Oeuvres complètes de Voltaire*, and is the first complete critical edition to be undertaken. Each text is edited by one or more specialists. Texts yet to be published by Oxford are reproduced from elsewhere (for instance, from the last complete edition of Voltaire's works, published between 1877 and 1885). Application to access the texts should be made to libweb@sheffield.ac.uk

The author's major works in editions most readily accessible (but not necessarily in print) are probably:

Selected Works, ed. Joseph McCabe [London 1911]
Select Letters of Voltaire, tr. and ed. Theodore Besterman [London 1963]
Letters on England, tr. Leonard Tancock from *Lettres sur les Anglais* [London 1980]
Lettres d'amour de Voltaire à sa nièce Mme Denis [Paris 1938]
Notebooks, ed. Theodore Besterman [Geneva 1950]
The Romances of Voltaire, ed. Manuel Komroff [New York 1936]
Mélanges [a selection of most of Voltaire's most important essays and pamphlets, Paris 1961]
Age of Louis XIV [Glasgow 1771]
History of Charles XII [London 1937]
Lettres d'Alcase à sa Nièce [Paris 1938]
Romans [Paris, n.d.]
Dictionnaire philosophique [Paris 1936; English selection tr. H.I. Woolf, New York 1924]
Letters of Voltaire and Frederick the Great, tr. Richard Aldington [London 1927]

Bibliography

Candide [innumerable versions; recommended: Theodore Besterman, London 1966]

Notebooks ed. T. Besterman [Geneva 1952]

Voltaire and Frederick the Great: Letters, tr. Richard Aldington [New York 1927]

LETTERS

In *Les Œuvres Complètes* (ed. Theodore Besterman, Giles Barber, Geneva, 1953–75) 54 volumes of Volatire's letters are so far available. Also, see Besterman, below. And see Theodore Besterman and Andrew Brown (eds), *Concordance to the Correspondence of Voltaire* (Geneva 1977).

BIOGRAPHIES AND CRITICAL WORKS

Aldington, Richard, *Voltaire* [London 1925]

Aldridge, A. Owen, *Voltaire and the Century of Light* [London 1975]

Andrews, Wayne, *Voltaire* [New York 1981]

Apgar, Garry, *L'Art singulier de Jean Huber: Voir Voltaire* [Paris 1995]

Ausubel, Nathan, *Superman: the Life of Frederick the Great* [New York 1931]

Ballentyne, Archibald, *Voltaire's Visit to England* [London 1893]

Barr, Mary Margaret H., *Century of Voltaire: a bibliography* [New York 1972]

Beaune, H., *Voltaire au collège* [Paris 1867]

Becker, Karl, *The Heavenly City of the Eighteenth-Century Philosophers* [New Haven 1951]

Besterman, Theodore, *Studies on Voltaire and the Eighteenth Century* [Geneva 1955]

——*Select Letters of Voltaire* [New York 1963]

——*Voltaire* [London 1969]

Bien, David D., *The Calas Affair* [(London 1979]

Brailsford, H.N., *Voltaire* [London 1968]

Brandes, Thomas, *Voltaire* [2 vols, New York 1930]

Brooks, Richard A., *Voltaire and Leibniz* [London 1964]

Brumfitt; J.H., *Voltaire, Historian* [London 1985]

Carlyle, Thomas, *Frederick the Great* [London, 1855]

——*Voltaire* [London 1856]

Caussy, Fernand, *Voltaire seigneur de village* [Paris 1912]

Chaponnière, Paul, *Voltaire chez les Calvinistes* [Paris 1936]

Clogenson, Jean, *Lettre à M. le rédacteur du Nouvelliste de Rouen, sur la naissance de Voltaire* [Rouen 1860]

Voltaire

Collins, J. Churton, *Voltaire, Montesquieu and Rousseau in England* [London 1886]

De Beer, Sir Gavin and J.J. Rousseau (eds.), 'Voltaire's British Visitors', *Studies on Voltaire and the Eighteenth Century*, Vol. XLIX (1967)

Deschanel, E., *Théâtre de Voltaire* [Paris 1886]

Desnoiresterres, G., *Voltaire et la société française au dix-huitième siècle* [Paris 1867–76]

Edwards, H. Sutherland, *Idols of the French Stage* [London 1889]

Edwards, Samuel, *The Divine Mistress* [New York 1970]

Ercole, Lucienne, *Gay Court Life: France in the Eighteenth Century* [New York 1932]

Faguet, Émile, *Dix-huitième siècle: Études littéraires* [Paris n.d.]

——*Literary History of France* [New York 1907]

Fahmy, Jean Mohsen, *Voltaire et Paris* [Paris 1981]

Fellowes, Otis E., and Torrey, Norman L. (eds.), *The Age of Enlightenment* [New York 1942]

Fisher, Herbert, *History of Europe* [London 1935]

Fletcher, Dennuis: *Voltaire: Lettres philosophiques* [London 1986]

Florida, R.E., *Voltaire and the Socinians* [New York 1974]

Forster, E.M., *Ferney in Two Cheers for Democracy* [London 1951]

Frederick II, 'the Great', *Mémoirs* [Paris 1866]

Funck-Brentano, Frantz, *L'Ancien Régime* [Paris 1926]

Gaberel, J., *Voltaire et les Genevois* [Paris 1857]

Garget, Graham, *Voltaire and Protestantism* [London 1980]

Gay, Peter, *Voltaire's Politics* [London 1988]

Gibbon, Edward, *Memoirs of My Life*, ed. A. Bonnard [London 1966]

Goncourt, Edmund and Goncourt, Jules, *The Women of the Eighteenth Century* [New York 1927]

Gooch, G.P., *Catherine the Great and Other Studies* [New York 1954]

Guizot, François, *History of France* [London 1872]

Gunny, Ahmad, *Voltaire and English Literature* [London 1979]

Havens, George, *The Age of Ideas* [New York 1955]

Hazard, Paul, *European Thought in the Eighteenth Century* [New Haven 1954]

Hearnshaw, F.J. (ed.), *Social and Political Ideas of Some Great French Thinkers of the Augustan Age* [New York 1950]

Hearsey, John E.N., *Voltaire* [London 1976]

Hendel, Charles W., *Citizen of Geneva: selections from the letters of Jean-Jacques Rousseau* [Oxford 1937]

Henry, Patrick, *Voltaire and Camus* [London 1975]

Heuvel, Jacques van den, *Voltaire dans ses contes* [Paris 1982]

Horowitz, I.L., *Claude Helvétius* [New York 1954]

Issen, Tristram, *Recollections of Voltaire* [Bristol 1904]

Jaurés, Jean, *Histoire socialiste de la Révolution française* [Paris 1922]

Bibliography

Jusserand, J.A., *English Essays from a French Pen* [London 1895]

Kavanagh, Julia, *Women in France during the Eighteenth Century* [New York 1893]

Köhler, Karl, *A History of Costume* [New York 1928]

Labat, Eugene, *Hôtel de la Presidence* [Paris 1844]

La Bruyère and Vauvenargues, *Selections* [New York 1903]

Lacrois, Paul, *The Eighteenth Century in France* [London n.d.]

La Fontainerie, F. de, *French Liberalism and Education in the Eighteenth Century* [New York 1932]

Lanson, Gustave, *Voltaire* [Paris 1906]

LeClerc, Paul O., *Voltaire and Crébillon Père: History of an Enmity* [London 1973]

Lichtenberger, André, *Le Socialisme et la Révolution française* [Paris 1899]

Lounsbury, T.R., *Shakespeare and Voltaire* [London n.d.]

Lovejoy, Arthur, *Essays in the History of Ideas* [Baltimore 1948]

Macaulay, Thomas Babington, *Critical, Historical and Miscellaneous Essays and Poems* [London 1886]

McCabe, Joseph, *Candid History of the Jesuits* [New York 1913]

Martin, Kingsley, *The Rise of French Liberal Thought* [London 1956]

Mason, Haydn, *Voltaire* [London 1981]

Maurois, André, *Voltaire* (Paris, 1931)

——*The Living Thoughts of Voltaire* [London 1939]

Mervaux, Christiane, *Voltaire et Frédéric II: une dramaturgie des lumières, 1736–1778* [Paris 1985]

Meyer, Henry, *Voltaire on War and Peace* [London 1976]

Mitford, Nancy, *Voltaire in Love* [London 1957]

——*Madame de Pompadour* [London 1953]

Montagu, Lady Mary Wortley, *Letters and Works* [London 1893]

Montesquieu, Charles de Secondat, Baron de, *Grandeur et décadence des Romains* [Paris 1924]

Morley, John, *Voltaire* [London 1872]

Mowat, R.B., *The Age of Reason* [Boston 1934]

Nablow, Ralph Arthur, *A Study of Voltaire's Lighter Verse* [New York 1974]

Naves, Raymond, *Voltaire et l'Encyclopédie* [Paris 1938]

Nicolson, Harold, *The Age of Reason* [London 1960]

Noyes, Alfred, *Voltaire* [London 1936]

Oechsli, Wilhelm, *History of Switzerland* [Cambridge 1922]

Orieux, Jean, *Voltaire*, tr. Barbara Bray and Helen R. Lane [London 1979]

Palmer, R.R., *Catholics and Unbelievers in Eighteenth-Century France* [Princeton 1939]

Parton, James, *Life of Voltaire* [New York 1881]

Pennant, Thomas, *Tour on the Continent*, ed. G.R. de Beer [London 1948]

Pierron, A., *Voltaire et ses maîtres* [Paris 1866]

Voltaire

Pomeau, René, *La Religion de Voltaire* [Paris 1820]

Pope, Alexander, *The Correspondence*, ed. George Sherburn [Oxford 1956]

——*Collected Poems* [London 1978]

Rendwick, John, *Marmontel, Voltaire and the Bélisaire Affair* [London 1974]

Richter, Peyton and Ricardo, Ilona, *Voltaire* [New York 1980]

Ridgway, R.S., *Voltaire and Sensibility* [London 1973]

Robertson, J.M., *Short History of Freethought* [London 1914]

——*Voltaire* [London 1922]

Rousseau, Jean-Jacques, *Confessions* [London 1954]

Russell, Bertrand, *History of Western Philosophy* [London 1946]

Russell, W. Clark (ed.), *Representative Actors: a collection of criticism, anecdotes, personal descriptions, etc., etc., referring to many celebrated British actors from the sixteenth to the present century* [London n.d.]

Schwarzbach, Bertram Eugene, *Voltaire's Old Testament Criticism* [New York 1971]

Spence, Joseph, *Anecdotes*, ed. J.M. Osborne [London 1966]

Stern, Jean, *Voltaire et sa nièce Madame Denis* [Paris 1957]

Strachey, Lytton, *Books and Characters* [London 1922]

Stryienski, Casimir, *The Eighteenth Century* [London 1916]

Styles McLeod, Catherine, 'Historic Houses: Voltaire at Ferney', *Architectural Digest*, March 1990, pp. 180–4, 244

Tallentyre, S.G., *Voltaire* [London 1903]

Texte, Joseph, *Jean-Jacques Rousseau* [New York 1926]

Topazio, Virgil W., *Voltaire: A critical study of his major works* [London 1967]

Torrey, Norman L. *Voltaire and the English Deists* [New Haven 1930]

——*The Spirit of Voltaire* [New York 1938]

Trapnell, William H., eds Mason, Haydn, *Christ and his Associates in Voltairian Polemic: an assault on the Trinity and the Two Natures* [New York 1982]

——*Voltaire and the Eucharist* [Oxford 1981]

Voltaire and the English (various contributors) [London 1979]

Vrooman, Jack Rochford, *Voltaire's Theatre* [London 1970]

Vulliamy, C., *Voltaire* [London 1930]

Wade, Ira O., *Voltaire and Madame du Châtelet* [Princeton 1941]

——*Studies in Voltaire* [Princeton, 1947]

Walpole, Horace, *Letters*, ed. Peter Cunningham [London 1880]

Wilberger, Carolyn H., *Voltaire's Russia: Window on the East* [New York 1976]

Willens, Lilian, *Voltaire's Comic Theatre* [New York 1975]

The Institut et Musée Voltaire in Geneva and the Voltaire foundation at the Taylor Institute in Oxford regularly publish additions to their series of 'Studies on Voltaire and the Eighteenth Century', with new works appearing every year.

Index

Index

Index

Index